Dying Empir

By the 1970s the global hegemony established by an American Empire in the post-World War II period faced increasing resistance abroad and contradictions at home. Contextualizing that hegemony, resistance, and contradictions is the focus of *Dying Empire*.

Presenting a wide-ranging synthesis of approaches, the book attempts to shed light on the construction of and challenges to the military, economic, and cultural imperial projects of the United States in the late twentieth and early twenty-first centuries. Opposing US imperialism and global domination, Francis Shor combines academic and activist perspectives to analyze the crises endemic to empire and to propose a vision for the realization of another more socially just world. The text incorporates the most recent critical discussions of US imperialism and globalization from above and below to illuminate the practices and possibilities for global resistance.

Offering insights into the political and cultural convulsions of recent decades whilst raising profound and compelling questions, this book will be of interest to activists, students, and scholars of American political culture, US foreign policy, globalization, imperialism, international relations, and social movements.

Francis Shor is a Professor of History at Wayne State University, USA.

Rethinking Globalizations
Edited by Barry K. Gills,
University of Newcastle, UK

This series is designed to break new ground in the literature on globalization and its academic and popular understanding. Rather than perpetuating or simply reacting to the economic understanding of globalization, this series seeks to capture the term and broaden its meaning to encompass a wide range of issues and disciplines and convey a sense of alternative possibilities for the future.

Dying Empire

U.S. imperialism and global resistance

Francis Shor

Routledge
Taylor & Francis Group

LONDON AND NEW YORK

First published 2010
by Routledge
2 Park Square, Milton Park, Abingdon, Oxon OX14 4RN

Simultaneously published in the USA and Canada
by Routledge
270 Madison Avenue, New York, NY 10016

Routledge is an imprint of the Taylor & Francis Group, an informa business

© 2010 Francis Shor

Typeset in Times New Roman by
Taylor and Francis
Printed and bound in Great Britain by
TJ International, Padstow

British Library Cataloguing in Publication Data
A catalogue record for this book is available from the British Library

Library of Congress Cataloging in Publication Data
A catalog record for this book has been requested

ISBN 10: 0-415-77822-0 (hbk)
ISBN 10: 0-415-77823-9 (pbk)
ISBN 10: 0-203-86535-9 (ebk)

ISBN 13: 978-0-415-77822-0 (hbk)
ISBN 13: 978-0-415-77823-7 (pbk)
ISBN 13: 978-0-203-86535-4 (ebk)

Contents

Acknowledgments

The germination of this book, like a flowering bulb, has taken time and required nurturing. The earliest preparation and planting, I suppose, came with the political commentaries I felt compelled to write as the Bush Administration went to war in Afghanistan and Iraq. Fortunately, the web offered a variety of sites to post these commentaries. Responses from around the world from people too numerous to mention demonstrated the keen desire to utilize this technology for alternative means of expression and solidarity. With the encouragement of Joel Kuszai and Factory School Press, many of these electronic postings became the basis for a 2005 publication entitled *Bush-League Spectacles: Empire, Politics, and Culture in Bushwhacked America*.

However, as an historian, I felt compelled to look beyond the policies of the Bush Administration and to seek explanations for the broader context and persistence of U. S. imperialism. In addition, I wanted to account for specific types of global resistance and the emergent aspirations for "another world." Thus, I began to plow numerous fields, some of which were new to me, in order to integrate recent scholarship on U. S. imperialism with various perspectives on globalization from above and below. The result of this synthesis, I trust, is critically grounded in that scholarship without being overwhelmed by it, achieving, in the process, a desired accessibility for a wide audience.

There are many people to thank for the variety of nurturing they have provided to me and this book, albeit often in an indirect manner. A 2006 summer seminar on "Globalization," led by Jackie Smith, a dedicated academic and activist, opened up the whole field to me. Over the last few years, colleagues and comrades in the Global Studies Association, especially Jerry Harris, have also helped to expand my understanding of and concern with all of the implications of imperialism and globalization. Members of the Utopian Studies Association in the United States and Europe have shared their insights on numerous related topics. Two international colleagues, Verity Burgmann from the University of Melbourne and Marcel van der Linden from the Institute for Social History in Amsterdam, have enlightened me with their global perspectives.

Through a variety of formal and informal seminars, meetings, and discussions, colleagues at Wayne State University have also nurtured my work in this general area. These colleagues include the following from the former Interdisciplinary Studies Program (ISP): Ron Aronson, the late Eric Bockstael, David Bowen, André Furtado, Gloria House, Julie Klein, Bill Lynch, Daphne Ntiri, and Marsha Richmond. In addition, the adult working students in the former ISP were instrumental in challenging me to articulate and make accessible my ideas about imperialism and globalization in a senior seminar. Other colleagues from Wayne State and especially my new department, History, have aided immensely in the exploration of related issues. Among the most helpful have been Tom Abowd, Jorge Chinea, José Cuello, David Fasenfest, Liz Faue, Heidi Gottfried, Marc Krugman, Janine Lanza, Guerin Montilus, Marilyn Rashid, Aaron Retish, Brad Roth, Nicole Trujillo-Pagan, and Monica White. I especially want to thank my History colleague and fellow-traveler, Alex Day, for the close readings he did of over half of the manuscript. I actually took account of some of his suggestions even though he should not be tagged with what finally emerged. In addition, the History department secretary, Terri Patton, helped with some of the aspects of manuscript production.

Outside WSU and in the greater Detroit area, there are many who have helped nurture this project in so many different ways. First and foremost, I want to acknowledge the careful reading of a portion of the manuscript that my neighbor and friend David Palmer did. He, too, like Alex, should not be held accountable for the final text. As a participant and sometimes speaker in programs sponsored by Peace Action of Michigan, Michigan Coalition for Human Rights, and Huntington Woods Peace and Citizenship Project, I gained both the clarity and empathy that made my writing for this book more compelling. My long-time friends and anarchist provocateurs, Ralph Franklin, David Watson, and, especially, Peter Werbe (my genial traveling companion to the Caracas World Social Forum) have had an enormous impact on my thinking, even as I have stubbornly clung to my own idiosyncratic readings of local, national, and global events. Also, Ralph managed to solve some tricky formatting problems for which I owe him my thanks.

Of course, this book would have never seen the light of day without the encouragement and support from Barry Gills, editor of the Routledge "Rethinking Globalizations" Series. He has been responsive in so many different ways to the twists and turns in bringing this project to publication. The two anonymous readers who recommended giving me an advance contract for the book must be acknowledged. It is impossible to convey what a comfort it was to have a publisher already committed to the book. My editor at Routledge, Heidi Bagtazo, and her assistant, Lucy Dunne, have been incredibly generous with their time, especially in light of the blizzard of questions with which I pestered Heidi in particular. Thanks also to Harriet Frramminghan, Rosemary Morlin, Ann King and Abi Bennett Humphries.

Finally, my deepest gratitude goes to my immediate intimate others, from my Dad and Uncle Ed to my daughters, Molly, Miriam, and Emma, to the Grand Nurturer, my wife, Barbara Logan, who has the patience of Job. That patience and the computer skills I lack came into valuable play in the formatting of the manuscript. In addition, Barb's capacity to listen to my constant rants about all of the items that went into this book, both large and small, proves that love is a potent force, even in the face of daily dour pessimistic rants.

Hopefully, the blossoming of this book is part of the flowering of that other world which is needed now more than ever. To all those working in their own fields for a more equitable and sustainable world, I dedicate this book.

The author acknowledges permission to incorporate his article on Habitat for Humanity in New Orleans ("Hammerin' on Heaven's Door"), which appeared in the Winter 2008 edition of the journal, *New Politics* <www. newpol.org>, as part of Chapter 3 of this book.

The author acknowledges permission from Peter Lang Publishers in Oxford to incorporate material from his chapter, "A Better (or, Battered) World is Possible: Utopian/Dystopian Dialectics in the American Century," in Liz Russell, ed. *Trans/Forming Utopia*. Portions of Chapter 1 on the American Century and World Social Forum and Chapter 8 on the WSF appeared in an earlier form in the aforementioned chapter.

The author acknowledges permission of Susan Bergholz Literary services. New York, NY and Lamy, NM to include material from *Upside Down: A Primer for the Looking-Glass World*. copyright ©1998 by Eduardo Galeano; translation, copyright ©2000 by Mark Fried. Published by Metropolitan Books, Henry Holt & co.

"Notes on the House of Bondage" by James Baldwin reprinted with per-mission from November 1, 1980 issue of *The Nation* magazine.

Thanks also go to the James Baldwin Estate for permission to reprint excerpts from "The Fire Next Time".

One can speak ... of the fall of an empire at the moment when, though all of the paraphernalia of power remain intact and visible and seem to function, neither the citizen-subject within the gates nor the indescribable hordes outside it believe in the morality or the reality of the kingdom anymore – when no one, any longer, anywhere, aspires to the empire's standards.

James Baldwin, "Notes on the House of Bondage"

Introduction
The world turned over

> If the world is upside down the way it is now, wouldn't we have to turn it over to get it to stand up straight?
>
> Eduardo Galeano

All empires die, but not in the exact same way. Certainly, as analyzed by world systems scholars, there are similar patterns that determine the rise and fall of empires. Moreover, there are generic characteristics that define empires, even though these characteristics are constantly subjected to historical circumstances and contradictions. Central to the operation of any empire is the compulsion to establish a matrix of control, whether formal or informal, through several overlapping domains, i.e. socio-economic, geo-political, and ideological/cultural, which, in turn, help to create the hegemony empires need to legitimatize their rule. To realize control in one or all of these domains, empires utilize imperial domination through direct state and military mechanisms or through more indirect economic and cultural links. In the older forms of imperialism, direct territorial and/or political control was imposed through colonial domination. Although there were certainly manifestations of internal and external colonial domination by U. S. imperialism in the nineteenth and early twentieth centuries, for the most part, and particularly after World War II, U. S. imperial policies relied less on direct territorial and/or political control than on a range of indirect strategies, some of which, however, resulted in direct military intervention.[1]

The drive to impose control and domination, whether indirect or direct, invariably engenders resistance on an individual and/or collective level. Such resistance necessarily alters the shape of imperial geo-political strategy. That dialectical play of forces, furthermore, complicates the range of imperial options and forms of resistance. Moreover, there are inevitable consequences for the institutions and ideology of the mother country as a result of the enactment of imperialism at home and abroad. *Dying Empire: U. S. Imperialism and Global Resistance* will scrutinize the specific historical and socio-cultural peculiarities of an American empire in its death throes and the myriad forms of global resistance to the dying empire.

Although the death of the United States Empire may be greatly exaggerated, the historical exploration of how an empire emerged and what its material and ideological impact has been on its own citizens as well as people around the globe demands detailed analysis. Beyond the particulars rendered by that analysis, history, as an interpretive enterprise, contains its own purposeful cunning. To paraphrase and reverse Picasso's notorious comment on art, history is a truth (albeit, provisional and selective) that shows us the lie. The lie at the root of the historical investigation in *Dying Empire* is that the United States, especially since the end of World War II, has operated abroad with heartfelt charity and wise leadership. That lie, repeated over and over, with bipartisan faith among the ruling elite and with substantial support from a blinkered citizenry, requires forthright and extensive examination. Certainly, as noted by the historian Gabriel Kolko, "the conviction that the United States has a universal calling and the economic and military power to fulfill it is a notion with deep historical roots." Probing those roots and their repercussions will be the essential task of this book. The book also shares another critical perspective with Kolko: "That other nations have in the past also believed they were predestined for imperialist missions only confirms that the United States is not the only imprudent country in the world, but it has been much slower than others to learn from its errors and adjust to reality."[2] Hopefully, *Dying Empire* will be the kind of educational experience that allows its readers to comprehend the errors of the past and participate in the rectification of those errors in the present and future.

My own education about the imperialist mission of the United States owes much to my first direct encounter with the tragic repercussions of U. S. imperial policy in Central America. This resulted in generating an emotional resonance to my rather academic and remote sense of the deleterious nature of that policy. In October of 1984, I traveled to Nicaragua as part of a small Michigan delegation for Witness for Peace, an organization that had been founded the year before with the intention of bringing U. S. citizens to that embattled county.[3] Our dual role was to observe the dynamics of political, social, and economic changes in Nicaragua and to intervene non-violently, where and when possible, against the increasingly lethal U. S.-sponsored Contra War. In that dual capacity, we interviewed a variety of participants in the Sandinista government, in the opposition political parties and press, and in the U. S. embassy in Managua. We also visited the Nicaraguan *campo*, or countryside, where we engaged in such activities as a day of work on a coffee plantation and numerous solidarity meetings with peasant cooperatives and inhabitants of border villages that had come under attack by the Contras.

Obviously, as a member of Witness for Peace, the expression of solidarity with certain groups of Nicaraguans meant that we would be actively involved in the polarized politics of that country and ours. Without endorsing the policies of the Sandinista government, we, nonetheless, were unalterably opposed to our own government's illegal proxy intervention in Nicaragua. There were some among us who naively embraced whole-heartedly all of the manifestations of revolutionary change in Nicaragua, as charged by hardened war correspondent Chris Hedges. But what motivated all of us then, and what inspires me now in the recollections that follow, was a fundamental commitment to expressing solidarity with those who were seeking another and better world for themselves and their families.[4] In order to express that solidarity, one must achieve, in the words of human rights scholar, Carol Gould, "an empathic understanding of the common needs and interests of others and a standing with them in view of this."[5] The instances where such solidarity may have occurred in this trip provide certain common threads that will run throughout the text and an essential emotional and empirical grounding for understanding the perspectives articulated herein – hence, the need to delve further into what transpired as a way to begin to explore the issues that inform this book.

Even before we arrived in Nicaragua, a few of us had an unsettling, but revelatory, experience on our flight from Detroit to Miami. The co-pilot on this first leg of our trip verbally accosted those of us sitting nearest to the pilot's cabin of the plane. He had apparently found out that we were a group of *Nortamericanos* going to Nicaragua. Assuming that we were partisans of the Sandinistas, he proceeded to tell us that, as a Cuban-American and former participant in the Bay of Pigs debacle, he viewed all those "communists" in Nicaragua as forever tainted. In exceedingly vitriolic language, he made clear that the only thing to do with them was outright extermination. The degree and depth of anger he displayed was a reminder that, for some, the Manichean divisions of the Cold War were not merely intellectual parlor games. In effect, we were about to enter a zone of conflict in which ideological and emotional investments were already preformed.

I certainly had preformed opinions, not only about the situation in Nicaragua, but the on-going U. S. role throughout the world. As a veteran anti-war activist from the Vietnam Era, I believed that my country and its citizens often supported interventions in the affairs of other countries that impeded, if not destroyed, the possibility of autonomous social change, let alone revolutionary development. Yet, if that support by the public wavered over time, it was also the case that citizens of the U. S. were either in the dark about what was happening in their name globally or they were bombarded by media images and political constructions that kept them witless and passive supporters of U. S. imperial policies. Even during certain moments when the media glare actually revealed those victimized by imperial interventions, it proved difficult for the average American to see beyond the other as victim as opposed to a historical agent with sovereign rights. Thus, any country attempting to realize its sovereign rights outside the U. S. sphere of influence, especially seen through the ideological filters of the Cold War, seemed doomed to be cast as aligned with the "enemy" camp.

Given the propaganda spread by the Reagan Administration and often absorbed unalloyed by the mainstream media, entering Nicaragua in 1984 on the eve of its election already meant encountering significant discrepancies between what was being reported in the United States and the not-so-surreptitious machinations of the Reagan Administration.[6] Those discrepancies were felt by everyone in our Witness for Peace delegation in the most profound way. In fact, as indicated by another Witness for Peace participant, "anyone who comes on a delegation and sees what U. S. policies are doing here in Nicaragua can't go back without questioning everything we were ever taught by our own country. The experience challenged us not just about Nicaragua, but about everything we are as North Americans."[7] While the shock of recognition concerning U. S. policies was shattering, more compelling were the actual engagements with everyday Nicaraguans who were trying to build a new and better life for themselves, often with the aid of the government.

Of our encounters, one, in particular, stands out as example of attempting to build that better world in the midst of the Contra War, a war sponsored by the U. S. government and waged primarily against the civilian population and the Nicaraguan infrastructure erected by the Sandinista government. We visited a small cooperative that had grown out of a Christian Base Community where the inhabitants were not only motivated by liberation theology but also, as a consequence of the government's literacy program, had undertaken numerous opportunities of managing their own economic and political affairs. What was so striking then, later when I returned to the United States through Miami airport with its ostentatious glut of consumer goods, and now as I reflect on how we in the United States can truly stand in solidarity with the rest of the world, was how the members of that community interpreted their transformation and progress. While there were certainly important material advances, the primary one being land ownership, the key seemed to be an intellectual and spiritual change that marked their profound sense of historical agency. In other words, what had opened up for them as self-determining actors in creating new communities was something that even those of us who were standing in solidarity with them could only dimly comprehend.

It is that lack of comprehension of how others live in the world and the impediments they face as a consequence of U. S. imperialism that informs the underlying imperative for this book. It offers a challenge to U. S. citizens to reflect on their imperial past, present, and future. In addition, it raises questions about the possibilities for establishing real community at home while also becoming global citizens of another kind of world, one without imperial domination and, indeed, even empire itself. What follows is, in many respects, a further elaboration of what the still relevant revisionist American historian, William Appleman Williams, wrote in the concluding paragraph of the "Preface" to his essential book-length essay, *Empire as a Way of Life*:

> This essay is ... a blunt attempt to help us understand and accept our past as an imperial people who must now 'order' ourselves rather than policing and saving the world ... (W)e must leave that imperial incubator if we are to become citizens of the real world. Our future is here and now, a community to be created among ourselves so that we can be citizens – not imperial overlords – of the world.[8]

With the underlying thematic thread to stop being imperial overlords and to become citizens of the world, *Dying Empire* is divided into three parts. Part I, "Imperial constructions and deconstructions," deals with the what Williams has called the imperial incubator and efforts to deconstruct it at the global and local levels. Part II, "Whose globalization?," traces the continuing military and economic efforts by the United States to maintain global dominance and the impact that has and is having on questions of equity and justice. It also considers the degree to which the American version of imperial capitalism informs the economic and cultural ordering of the globe. Part III, "Other publics, other worlds," looks at the emergent global networks of resistance and their visions and practices for another and better world. All three parts of the book aim to foster a dialogue not only among citizens in the U. S. but also between the United States and the rest of the world, the latter conversation having been especially complicated by the bellicose and unlawful policies of the Bush Junior Administration during his two terms in office. Given what cultural analysts Ziauddin Sardar and Merryl Wyn Davies regard as the "antipathy" towards the United States, their posing of the following question is clearly linked to the concerns herein:

> If America cannot reflect upon itself, its history, its uses and abuses of power and wealth at home and abroad, the consequences of its lifestyle and abundance, the relations between quality of life and values, the relation between ideals and practical application of those ideals to all of its people, then what chance has the rest of the world of engaging America in reasoned discussion?[9]

Chapter 1, "Imperial burdens: constructing and contesting U. S. empire," is a concise overview of both the long history of U. S. imperialism, especially its racial and gender orientations, the emergence of the ideological construction, the "American Century," and those ideological challenges to the recent neo-conservative re-articulation of the "New American Century." Paying special attention to the claims that a U. S. empire is naturally a force for good in the world underscores the insight of cultural critic, Edward Said, that "this latest empire astonishingly affirms its sacrosanct altruism and well-meaning innocence."[10] Whether as a willing or reluctant sheriff, the United States seems compelled to confront all those wrongdoers in the world and bring American-style "law and order" to bear. Thus, whoever challenges the self-appointed sheriff's role, whether the "effete" French or the "savage" Chávez, must be demonized and demeaned by the U. S. government and its supporting media.

If the construction of a U. S. empire abroad has engendered catastrophic consequences, the hollowing out of civic life at home, especially because of the squandering of resources for an imperial and military-industrial complex, occupies the focus of Chapter 2, "Fortress America *redux*: breaking down imperial and civic enclosures." As posed by William Appleman Williams and other critics of the impact of empire on the erosion of a healthy and sustainable community in the United States, can the citizens of this country recognize and re-order the links between perpetuating empire abroad and the lack of an authentic and just society at home? Are we capable of confronting the fear and paranoia that have been entrenched in our political culture as a result of the domestic and foreign campaigns undertaken by U. S. ruling circles from the red scare to the war on terror?

Chapter 3, "Afflicted solidarities: contradictions in local and global citizen movements," offers a critical examination of how U. S. citizens attempt to enact solidarity in the context of an imperial culture. Confronting the local and global repercussions of U. S. imperialism from the rebuilding of housing in New Orleans to a variety of anti-sweatshop campaigns, the chapter tries to probe how ethical and political responsibility is manifested in ways that reflect a variety of solidarities which run the gamut from afflicted to altruistic, but stop short of a more rewarding mutual solidarity. Drawing a connection between what Naomi Klein calls "Disaster apartheid"[11] and my own involvement with a housing project in New Orleans, the first part of this chapter tries to sort out the limitations of even well-intentioned efforts to make housing available to disadvantaged U. S. citizens. The second part explores how consumers in the United States attempt to influence changes in global sweatshops. In both instances, the contradicted and afflicted active expressions of solidarity will be investigated.

While Chapter 4, "U. S. military imperialism and the pursuit of global dominance," begins Part II, "Whose globalization?," it also continues some of the threads in Chapter 1 dealing with the on-going legitimation crisis both nationally and globally for U. S. hegemony. This chapter tries to sort through recent military and geopolitical strategies by different U. S. Administrations to remain the pre-eminent power in the world, especially dating from the critical moment in the 1970s when U. S. hegemony appeared to be on an inevitable decline to the most recent efforts by neo-Conservatives to re-assert U. S. hege-mony and imperial dominance. In navigating the convergences between mili-tary and geopolitical imperial policies, this chapter will further probe the "rhetoric about the national burden of being the 'indispensable nation,' or what the Council of Foreign Relations calls the world's 'reluctant sheriff.' "[12] In the process, the chapter will explore the U. S.'s overt and covert support of repressive or friendly governments and investigate the repercussions and contradictions of military imperialism for U. S. global dominance and hegemony.

Beyond the overt or covert support of repressive governments is the spon-sorship by the United States and U. S.-based transnational corporations of economic global policies that create what European human rights scholar, Susan George, calls "induced inequities."[13] Chapter 5, "U. S. economic imperialism and global inequities," analyzes those inequities that emerged as a direct consequence of the crisis of profitability and increasing financialization of capital in the 1970s with its class strategy of neoliberal privatization and deregulation. The encouragement and adoption of structural adjustment pro-grams will be examined, especially in perpetrating and perpetuating policies against the global poor and those now deeply entrenched in what Mike Davis has labeled the "planet of slums."[14] Also, particular struggles which developed around the world against the policies of U. S. controlled international capital and transnational corporations will be highlighted as a way of recognizing the variety of global resistances against these induced inequities.

The last chapter in Part II, Chapter 6, "U. S. cultural imperialism and global dissonance," attempts to clarify the degree to which the spread of specific American values and habits is an extension of U. S. cultural patterns or part of the larger project of modern consumer capitalism. Contrasting models of ana-lysis will be critically investigated in order to address what kind of overlap, if any, there is between cultural imperialism and globalization. Special attention will be paid to dissident and dissonant voices (from José Bové to Bob Marley) which have complicated and contested the made-in-America global stamp.

Part III, "Other publics, other worlds," begins with an investigation of the emergence of what some call global civil society and the sort of transnational networks that have participated in the globalization of resistance. Chapter 7, "Transnational counterpublics and the globalization of resistance," looks at how groups coalesced around opposition to U. S. and neoliberal policies. It also considers the role of new information and communication technologies in advancing and enhancing global resistance. The final chapter, Chapter 8, "Is another world possible?," looks to the visionary and utopian options found in both fiction and fact to consider what the radical alternatives are to U. S. imperialism and how they reflect a grassroots democratic effort to establish globalization from below. Special emphasis is placed on the actual agents of social change whether in the form of the heroine of Marge Piercy's novel, *Woman on the Edge of Time*, the poor in the liberation theology of Gustavo Gutiérrez or the global multitudes from the Zapatistas to the participants in the World Social Forum. It should not be surprising that what connects the exemplary historical agency of those "base communities" that I observed and which flourished in the 1980s in Nicaragua to these contemporary historical agents will provide some symmetry to the larger issue of global resistance.

The conclusion of the book, "It's the end of the world as we know it," will explore the harsh and potentially transformative circumstances facing the United States and the world from the recent economic meltdown to the demise of U. S. global dominance. Beyond identifying recurrent themes and threads and analyzing what constitutes new challenges and new opportunities, the conclusion of *Dying Empire* will provide further grounding for the title of the book, as well as considering the tasks confronting citizens of this country and its new president, Barack Obama. Ultimately, that confrontation will be not only a theoretical one, but a very practical matter for all of the inhabi-tants of our imperiled planet. In effect, transforming the United States from its imperial posture as overlord to one of equal footing in the world is essen-tial if we are to achieve a more equitable and sustainable world, a world, as indicated by the quotation from Uruguayan writer, Eduardo Galeano, that must, itself, be turned over.[15]

Part I
Imperial constructions and deconstructions

1 Imperial burdens: constructing and contesting the U. S. empire

> Throughout the seventeenth, eighteenth and nineteenth centuries, this continent teemed with manifold projects and magnificent purposes. Above them all and weaving them all together into the most exciting flag of all the world and of all history was the triumphal purpose of freedom. ... It is in this spirit that all of us are called, each to his own measure of capacity, and each in the widest horizon of his vision, to create the first great American century.
>
> Henry Luce

> Where there is imperialism, all you find is exploitation and the pillaging of natural resources. With no imperialism there is development, justice, and there is freedom.
>
> Evo Morales

Surveying the post-Cold War geopolitical landscape, neoconservative political scientist, Ernest W. Lefever, acknowledged that the U. S. had an imperial burden to fulfill. However, according to Lefever, that "burden does not involve conquest or vainglory, but a commitment to work for greater peace and freedom in a conflicted world; anything less would be unworthy of a second American Century."[1] For Lefever and his fellow ideologues, fighting a culture war against so-called revisionist historians, the obliteration or obfuscation of the imperial past is essential to project U. S. geopolitical power for securing "greater peace and freedom in a conflicted world." But the history of how the U. S. expanded that empire of freedom is replete with anything but peace and hardly absent of conquest and vainglory. In fact, imperial wars and interventions have been integral to the establishment and expansion of the United States and its emergence after World War II as the pre-eminent superpower in the world.

To understand the imperial threads woven throughout the past and the ways in which the United States established its global hegemony is to confront how empire has been embedded in the rise and decline of that hegemony. Part of the process of revealing the patterns of empire is to underscore the degree to which race and gender have intersected with class as integral factors in the construction of empire. In his glowing review of *The Savage Wars of Peace: Small Wars and the Rise of American Power* by Max Boot, the *Wall Street Journal*'s resident macho imperialist, Thomas Donnelly, one of the key architects of the *Project for a New American Century*, the ur-text for the Bush Doctrine of empire-building, conveniently obfuscates the racial and gender dimensions of past savage wars. Donnelly brazenly transcodes Kipling's iconic imperialist reference to the "white man's burden" into the "free man's burden" in order to sanitize the savagery perpetuated by U. S. imperialism.[2] Nevertheless, Donnelly's construction of the "free man's burden" affords an obvious opening to explore, in conjunction with other constituent elements, the racial and gender dimensions of U. S. empire-building.

Of course, the consistency, complexity, and contradictions of those racial and gender dimensions have been susceptible to changing ideological and cultural constructions which, in turn, have been subject to economic, social, and political conditions. On the other hand, a constant thread of "empire as a way of life" could be traced to how the "routine lust for land, markets, or security became justifications for noble rhetoric about prosperity, liberty, and security."[3] Such rhetoric provided the ideological cover for the genocidal displacement of Native Americans throughout the eighteenth and nineteenth centuries and the foreign interventions in Latin America, Asia, and the Middle East in the nineteenth, twentieth, and twenty-first centuries. What follow are brief, and by no means complete or unproblematic, highlights of the racial and gender coding of the imperial ideology underlying U. S. empire-building from its national inception to the present day.[4] In particular, this overview of imperial constructions is intended not only to underscore the deep roots of empire as a way of life but also to provide insights into the persistence of certain ideological threads in the more recent constructions of U. S. imperialism, especially those under the discursive designation of the American Century. Finally, the chapter will conclude with a brief overview of specific political formations that contest the perpetuation of U. S. imperialism and hegemony.

At the root of the rhetoric of "free men" deployed in the struggle against the British Empire by colonial Americans was the ideology of possessive individualism. That possessive individualism necessarily implied the dispossession of others' land, rights, and way of life. As William Appleman Williams contends, "Locke said it as well as anyone and more honestly than most: empire as a way of life involves taking wealth and freedom away from others to provide for your own welfare, pleasure, and power."[5] In effect, the ideology of possessive individualism inscribed the idea of freedom and the "free man" inside the instrumentality of capital and what David Harvey calls "accumulation by dispossession."[6] Although constrained by property rights and exchange values, the free man was obsessed with self-ownership and its multiple and paradoxical meanings, even when such self-ownership was based on the appropriation of the lands and liberty of others. Thus, the formation of an American empire had at its core an ideological commitment to a particular set of constructions about "free men."

Most prominent among the paradoxical meanings of "free men" were the universalist pretensions and its white supremacist and patriarchal formulations.

In particular, given the subjugation of Africans through disciplinary regimes that obliterated their freedom, liberty, and self-ownership, the ideology of republicanism concerning "natural rights" in a society committed to slavery was obviously an artificial and violent construction. According to Barbara Jean Fields, "racial ideology supplied the means of explaining slavery to people whose terrain was a republic founded on radical doctrines of liberty and natural rights."[7] Yet, the very same racial ideology was interpenetrated by patriarchal presumptions that infantilized not only Africans, but American Indians. Perceived as unruly and backward children, neither blacks nor American Indians were entitled to the exercise of liberty and certainly not to the possession of land and liberty. Thus, in the early stages of empire-building, a racialized and patriarchal form of internal colonialism developed in tandem with the emergence of free men in the American republic.

The empire-building incorporated into Jeffersonian and Jacksonian democracy relied upon racial and gender constructions that restricted the definitions of free men while expanding the territory such free men were "entitled" to claim and administer. Jefferson's commitment to the ideology of self-ownership extended only to whites who could control their savage instincts. In turn, Jefferson's civilizing mission to turn Indians into willing supporters of possessive individualism by converting them to yeoman farmers guaranteed the actual dispossession of massive amounts of tribal territory. Appropriating the symbol of the "Great White Father," both Jefferson and Jackson expanded the imperial reach of the United States. Jackson's indebtedness to slavery, according to Michael Paul Rogin, helped him "define the paternal state in whose name he removed Indians. Marrying paternalism to liberal egalitarian assumptions, he provided a structure for American expansion. But that slave model of paternalism, appropriate enough to Indian removal, contained force and violence at its core."[8]

Viewing the westward expansion fostered by the policies of Jefferson and Jackson, the French political observer, Alexis de Tocqueville, writing in the 1830s, revealed insights into the ideological dynamics of white approval of the dispossession of Indian lands:

> The world belongs to us (white Americans), they tell themselves every day: the Indian race is destined for final destruction which one cannot prevent and which is not desirable to delay. Heaven has not made them to become civilized; it is necessary that they die. ... In time I will have their lands and will be innocent of their death. Satisfied with his reasoning, the American goes to church where he hears the minister of the gospel repeat every day that all men are brothers, and that the Eternal Being who has made them all in like image, has given them all the duty to help one another.[9]

Tocqueville's implicit indictment of such reasoning carries with it the further understanding of how such expansion in the creation of a white republic was disconnected from the actual victimization of those who stood in the way.

Untroubled by the inevitable march of progress and, seemingly, blessed in the efforts to extend that progress westward, the white patriarchal racial order blissfully undertook its divine mission.

On the other hand, some of those proponents of a slave republic were often wary of expansionist efforts in the nineteenth century. In particular, the debates surrounding annexation efforts during the Mexican War underscored the complexities of deploying racial arguments. While slave apologist Senator John Calhoun of South Carolina favored annexing Texas, he feared absorbing Mexico with its "mixed blood" population. For Calhoun, the Union should be preserved for "the Caucasian race."[10] Abolitionists, such as Frederick Douglas, who opposed both the Mexican War and a slave republic that excluded those of African descent from citizenship, would condemn the war as "disgraceful, cruel and iniquitous ... Mexico seems a doomed victim to Anglo-Saxon cupidity and love of dominion."[11] Hence, expansion and empire in the early republic raised questions and contradictions that would define and confound the very meanings of freedom.

While slavery would be contested by abolitionists who attacked its violation of the universalist implications of self-ownership, some of those same abolitionists were involved in articulating a racial construction of Anglo-Saxonism that endorsed empire-building as "manifest destiny." As noted by Richard Slotkin, the abolitionist Theodore Parker "declared that expansion was inevitable as a consequence of racial gifts and that it would bring a regime of Anglo-Saxon dominance." Slotkin further contends that the

> use of "Anglo-Saxon" rather than "White" signaled the emergence of a crucial distinction in the language of American racialism, a need to differentiate not only Whites from Blacks and Indians but to distinguish between different classes of Whites – for example, to mark a difference between Anglo-Americans and the Irish or German immigrants or the Mexicans in Texas and the Far West that would entitle Anglo-Americans to subordinate or subjugate them.[12]

In effect, racial constructions were integral to the incorporation and subordination of others into the empire of free men.

However, for proponents of U. S. "manifest destiny", conquest of new territories did not mean subordination or subjugation; it meant liberation from tyranny, as well as the enactment of "martial manhood" and "manifest domesticity," gendered representations of aggressive expansionism.[13] In the original formulation of Manifest Destiny by John L. O'Sullivan, he points to the "defense of humanity, of the oppressed of all nations, of the rights of conscience, the rights of personal enfranchisement," even as a slaveholding Texas republic where O'Sullivan resides prepares to become the launching pad for the Mexican War.[14] But that war would be waged, as other wars, in the name of rescuing unfree racial others.

The Spanish-American War became another site of "rescue" for the oppressed of Cuba and the Philippines at the beginning of the twentieth century as the U. S. joined the imperial race for global empire. While racial constructions and masculinist presumptions in Cuba and the Philippines quickly led to exclusionary control in Cuba and brutal counterinsurgency in the Philippines, one of the outspoken advocates for U. S. imperial expansion, Theodore Roosevelt, still touted the virtues of empire building for "free men." According to Roosevelt,

> the timid man, the lazy man, the man who distrusts his country, the over-civilized man, who has lost the great fighting, masterful virtues, the ignorant man, and the man of dull mind, whose soul is incapable of feeling the mighty lift that thrills "stern men with empires in their brains" – all these, of course, shrink from seeing the nation undertake its new duties; shrink from seeing us build a navy and army adequate to our needs; shrink from seeing us do our share of the world's work, by bringing order out of chaos in the great, fair tropic islands from which the valor of our soldiers and sailors has driven the Spanish flag.[15]

On the other hand, resistance to the annexation of Cuba and the Philippines, in particular, was often expressed in racial terms. The inhabitants of the Philippines were seen as a "savage" and "alien" race, unfit for incorporation into an Anglo-Saxon culture. While debates over the fate of the Philippines were invariably focused on protecting white civilization in the continental United States, that very civilization was undergoing rapid transformation away from a bastion of Anglo-Saxon privilege. Hence, fears of the immigrant hordes and absorbing foreign peoples at home and abroad led many to reject empire-building in the Philippines. Anti-imperialists from capital and labor, e.g. Andrew Carnegie and Samuel Gompers, decried the erosion of homogeneity and inclusion of "semi-barbaric laborers."[16]

Because of racial and other complications about imperialist interventions, empire-building in the twentieth century reformulated its objectives "through the more abstract geography of the world market rather than through direct political control of territory."[17] On the other hand, in developing his 1903 corollary to the Monroe Doctrine, Roosevelt continued to display masculinist discourse in calling for U. S. intervention as "an international police power" against "chronic wrongdoing, or an impotence which results in the general loosening of the ties of civilized society."[18] Other racial and masculinist constructions were transcoded into abstract references about "making the world safe for democracy." As noted by Chalmers Johnson,

> (Woodrow) Wilson ... provided an idealistic grounding for American imperialism, what in our time would become a "global mission" to "democratize" the world. More than any other figure, he provided the intellectual foundations for an interventionist foreign policy, expressed in humanitarian and democratic rhetoric. Wilson remains the godfather of those contemporary ideologists who justify American imperial power in exporting democracy.[19]

For Wilson and the other outspoken advocates of an imperial brotherhood in the twentieth century, the civilizing mission of the United States requires real men to take up the cudgel of war-making, albeit in the case of those imperial presidents in the late twentieth and early twenty-first century, minus the overt white supremacist ideology that informed the geopolitical orientation of Roosevelt and Wilson.[20] Yet, the racial and masculinist dimensions of U. S. imperialism still persist. As argued by Zillah Eisenstein, "U. S. empire-building Americanizes the globe in its particularly racialized and masculinist form."[21] Given the present focus on the Middle East,

> the degraded popular image of Arabs and Islam and official policies towards visitors and immigrants from Arab countries are all too indicative of the rising tide of racism in the U. S. that may do untold future damage both internally and internationally.[22]

In calling for pre-emptive strikes and what the 2000 version of the *Project for a New American Century* called "full spectrum dominance," the Bush Administration has magnified the masculinism endemic to empire-building. Eschewing any international constraints, Bush's drive for a renewed American empire incorporates past economic, geopolitical, and ideological positions into an aggressive posturing to make the world over in the image of a self-righteous hegemon. The March 2005 publication of the Bush National Defense Strategy makes clear these imperial geopolitical and gendered postures by maintaining the right to invade countries that "do not exercise their sovereignty responsibly" and to counter "those who employ as a strategy of the weak, using international fora (and) judicial processes." The appearance of what might be construed as the "wimp factor" in the reference to the "strategy of the weak" was certainly evident in George H. W. Bush's Administration's motivation for the first Gulf War. (A more extensive discussion of the Gulf War will be part of Chapter 4.) In this iteration, however, the wimp factor becomes a scurrilous attack on those committed to international law and treaties, something the Bush Administration has violated whenever and wherever possible. In pursuing its unilateralist agenda, the Bush Administration has raised the possibility of the end of what has been called the "American Century."

Although the emergence of the United States as a global hegemon had roots in national and international conditions prior to World War II, that war provided the U. S. with the historical opportunity to establish its global hegemony.[23] U. S. global hegemony was not only a consequence of economic, political, and military domination, but also a reflection of the diffusion of cultural and ideological orientations that advanced U. S. moral and intellectual leadership. Among the ideological orientations that attempted to foist U. S. hegemony on the rest of the world was the articulation of the "American Century." On the eve of the United States's entrance into World War II, Henry Luce, editor and owner of *Time-Life* magazines, proclaimed the American Century in the pages of *Life*. Incorporating long-standing beliefs in the United

States as a redeemer nation compelled to engage in messianic missions in the world, Luce assumed that the United States was the true inheritor of the best that civilization offered. It naturally followed that the inevitable global dominance of the U. S. would be marked by the superlative qualities of American democracy and culture. Luce boldly declared that the U. S. must

> accept wholeheartedly our duty and our opportunity as the most powerful and vital nation in the world and in consequence to exert upon the world the full impact of our influence, for such purposes as we see fit and by such means as we see fit.[24]

Thus, Luce's vision of the American Century was predicated on the belief that the U. S. had both the natural right and ordained responsibility to wield political and military power as a guarantor of progress and prosperity throughout the world. Accordingly, "U. S. global dominance was presented as the natural result of historical progress, implicitly the pinnacle of European civilization, rather than the competitive outcome of political-economic power."[25] For Luce and the proponents of an American Century with its exceptionalist trajectory, the United States "was exempted from the ordinary forces of history that trapped everyone else 'in history.'"[26] Moreover, the U. S. could and did present itself as the embodiment of the future, a future necessarily defined by the idealized political, economic, and cultural experiences of the United States. Nonetheless, "America's idealized view of the human future," note the authors of *Why Do People Hate America?*,

> permits a perverse, dangerous and often brutally destructive disconnection between ends and means. To define the idea of America as *the* future is an arrogant denial of the freedom of others, and of the potential of the present to create alternative futures in the complex image of the whole world and all its peoples.[27]

In effect, contesting this version of the American Century and its recent iteration has been part of an antagonistic political discourse, according to Immanuel Wallerstein, "ever since the United States became the world-system's hegemonic power after 1945. It is a reaction to those with great power and to the arrogance that seems almost inevitably to become natural to those who hold such power."[28] What I intend to explore in the rest of this chapter is how advocates of the American Century and New American Century have framed their ideological perspectives and how those ideological perspectives and imperial practices of U. S. hegemony have been challenged by contradictions unleashed by U. S. global hegemony and by counter-hegemonic articulations that can be identified as falling under the following broad categories: first, the "European Model"; second, the post-colonial; and third, the post-modern. By no means do these previous categories of contestation exhaust counter-hegemonic articulations. In fact, one could also delineate counter-hegemonic articulations along the lines suggested by anthropologist Bruce Knauft: "self-determination, including political self-determination via democracy, national, subnational, and transnational opposition via terrorism or insurgency, and alternative forms of capitalism."[29] While various components of Knauft's categories will be explored in this chapter, especially national resistance and insurgencies, and throughout Part II, for now I want to turn to the construction of a U. S. hegemony represented by the ideological and institutional formation of the American Century and its deconstruction in the U. S. wars in Southeast Asia and Iraq.

Convinced that they were beyond the reproach of history and owners of the future, postwar U. S. policymakers and their ideological advocates sought to establish U. S. pre-eminence in the world by overt and covert means. Among the overt designs were developing numerous international and multilateral organizations, such as the United Nations, the North Atlantic Treaty Organization, the World Bank, and the International Monetary Fund. The covert means focused primarily on the role of a newly created Central Intelligence Agency to foster favorable governments around the world and to underwrite cultural enterprises during the Cold War. Although U. S. interventions and "regime change" had predated the operationalizing of the American Century, those foreign adventures increased during the Cold War through a kind of "stealth imperialism" and became even more frequent, open, and brazen after the fall of the Berlin Wall.[30]

The proponents of a muscular intervention in the world found inspiration in the resonant words of President John Kennedy "to bear any burden" and "pay any price" for spreading freedom. However, that muscular intervention came to a crashing halt in the Vietnam War, causing a crisis in what had been the "triumphalism" embedded in the American Century.[31] Instead of saving Vietnam for the "free world," the U. S. undertook a vicious campaign of death and destruction whose ideological resonances and imperial realities still persist in the Iraq War. The following concise comparison of those imperial realities underscores how U. S. muscular intervention with its "American way of war" was about "the killing and punishing of the civilian population."[32] In turn, the resistance unleashed against such U. S. imperial interventions suggests the limitations of the political-military strategies pursued by the champions of the American and New American Century and the concomitant de-legitimizing of U. S. moral and intellectual leadership.[33]

From the air and on the ground, the punitive expeditions launched by U. S. imperialism have devastated whole countries and their populations, from Vietnam to Iraq. While most studies of the war in Southeast Asia acknowledge that four times the tonnage of bombs was dropped on Vietnam, Cambodia, and Laos than that used by the U. S. in all theaters of operation during World War II, only a few books have analyzed the full extent of such bombing. Not only were thousands of villages in Vietnam destroyed, but massive civilian deaths, numbering close to 3 million, resulted in large part from such indiscriminate bombing. Integral to the bombing strategy was the use of weapons that violated international law, such as napalm and anti-personnel fragmentation bombs. As a result of establishing free-fire zones where any-thing and everything could be attacked, including hospitals, U. S. military operations led to the deliberate murder of mostly civilians.[34]

While Donald Rumsfeld and the Pentagon touted the "clean" weapons used in Iraq, the fact is that aerial cluster bombs and free-fire were part of the military operations in the first years of the war. Villages throughout Iraq, from Hilla to Fallujah, suffered air assaults that took a heavy civilian toll. Occasionally, criticism of the type of ordnance used in Iraq found its way into the mainstream U. S. press, especially when left-over cluster bomblets looking like yellow food packages blew up in children's hands or depleted uranium weapons were inadvertently dropped on British soldiers. However, questions in the corporate media about the immorality of "shock and awe" bombing strategy were often buried deeper than any of the cluster bomblets.[35]

In Vietnam, a primary ground war tactic was the "search and destroy" mission with its over-inflated body counts. As Christian Appy has forcefully demonstrated, such tactics were guaranteed to produce atrocities.[36] Any cri-tical personal account of the war in Vietnam from the perspective of U. S. grunts fighting the war, such as Ron Kovic's *Born on the Fourth of July*, reveals how those atrocities took their toll on civilians and U. S. soldiers like Kovic.[37] Of course, certain high-profile atrocities, such as My Lai (and Haditha in Iraq) achieved prominent media coverage (nearly a year after the incident, however). Nonetheless, My Lai was seen either as an aberration and, therefore, not part of murderous campaigns such as Operation Phoenix or a result of a few bad apples, like a Lt. William Calley, who received minor punishment for his command of the massacre of hundreds of women and children. When "65% of Americans claimed not to be upset by the massacre," it suggested that the solipsism imbibed by the violence-prone citizens of the American Century prevented apprehending the destruction carried out in their name.[38]

Of course, the racism that led the U. S. military to see every "gook" as VC in Vietnam also reappeared in Iraq. According to one British commander in Iraq, American troops often saw Iraqis as "untermenschen – the Nazi expression for sub-humans." Although embedded U. S. reporters rarely pro-vided an insight into this racist mentality, Mark Franchetti of the *London Times* quoted one U. S. soldier as asserting that "Iraqis are sick people and we are the chemotherapy."[39] And with chemotherapy if the sick person dies it was only to help cure the person. This reminds one of the infamous pro-nouncement by a U. S. military officer on the destruction of a Vietnamese village during the war in that ravaged country: "We had to destroy the village in order to save it."

With the defeat of the U. S. in Vietnam and other American political and economic setbacks throughout the 1970s, it seemed as if the American Century was on the wane. (Covert and overt efforts to reconstitute U. S. hege-mony and reinforce imperial dominance from the 1970s until the present day will be presented in Chapter 4.) However, the ideologues of the Reagan

Administration loudly proclaimed their intention to restore American pre-eminence in the world, making the U. S. once again the "shining city on the hill." With the collapse of the Soviet Union (for which the Reaganites took sole credit), these ideologues confronted a dual challenge for their muscular foreign policy: first, how to sustain and expand the military-industrial complex that was the core of U. S. dominance, and second, how to convince the American public to support military interventions for strategic purposes. Out of this challenge grew the neoconservative iteration for U. S. dominance called the Project for the New American Century (PNAC).[40]

Formulated in 1997, the PNAC defined its mission in a rhetorical question reminiscent of Luce's discourse: "Does the United States have the resolve to shape a new century favorable to American principles and interests?"[41] Among the signatories to this statement of principles were Dick Cheney, Lewis Libby, Donald Rumsfeld, and Paul Wolfowitz, all of whom would become key members of George W. Bush's Administration. Translating the PNAC 2000 statement for "full spectrum dominance" into the Bush Doctrine of unilateral pre-emptive war, the 2002 National Security Strategy document decreed its messianic mission:

> The United States will use this moment of opportunity to extend the benefits of freedom across the globe. ... We will actively work to bring the hope of democracy, development, free markets, and free trade to every corner of the world.

As noted by Ira Chernus, the 2002 NSS statement "turns the story of a globalized American dream, with all its mythic overtones, into official United States policy."[42]

Translating PNAC rhetoric into policy, the Bush regime launched wars in Afghanistan and Iraq that have called into question whether the U. S. should or could be a unilateral actor on the global stage. Even previous promoters of muscular intervention, such as Zbigniew Brzezinski, and neoconservative ideology, such as Francis Fukuyama, have raised doubts about the viability of Bush's version of the American Century.[43] Nevertheless, there are neoconservative ideologues who continue to express confidence in a revised American Century, even as critics now openly discuss the end of the American Century. While noting some of the flaws of the Bush Doctrine, Robert Kagan in *Of Paradise and Power* underscores the deeply rooted belief of U. S. power as the prime mover for progress in the world. Calling the U. S. "a behemoth with a conscience," Kagan contends that "American power, even employed under a double standard, may be the best means of advancing human progress – and perhaps the only means."[44] In contradistinction, Immanuel Wallerstein sees the United States as now lacking the power to effectuate U. S. dominance. "The real question," Wallerstein contends, "is not whether U. S. hegemony is waning, but whether the United States can devise a way to descend gracefully, with minimum damage to the world and itself."[45] Other critics see this "new imperialism" of the U. S. under the Bush Administration as a failing strategy in the "endgame of globalization."[46] These critics contend that the American Century and PNAC projects are doomed to failure not because of a lack of resolve by segments of the ruling elite in the United States, but because American power has reached its apex and is in the critical phase of imperial overreach.

Raising questions and concerns about imperial overreach against the backdrop of the optimism and operationalizing of the American Century invariably highlights the degree to which the Pax Americana was and is a "benevolent" form of imperialism. One can find those policymakers in liberal and neoconservative administrations, from Madeline Albright to Condoleezza Rice, who still regard the United States as the indispensable nation and believe in its universalizing mission. As noted by one critic, "the neoconservative and liberal internationalist stories are merely two different routes to the same conclusion – a conclusion that is actually the premise of all the stories that dominate mainstream American life: There will always be monsters to destroy."[47] The ideological division among these policymakers is often over whether the U. S. should act unilaterally to effectuate the changes it wants in the world. Academic supporters of a U. S. imperial mission, such as Robert Kagan, argue that the success of such a mission depends on shouldering the economic and political burdens, irrespective of internal and external criticisms and contradictions. Opponents of such an imperial mission note its "hubris" and "sorrows" are so rampant and debilitating that to continue an imperial course would be a delusion and disaster.[48] Certain European critics of U. S. global hegemony, such as Emmanuel Todd, contend that

> the United States is pretending to remain the world's indispensable superpower by attacking insignificant adversaries. But this America – a militaristic, agitated, uncertain, anxious country projecting its own disorder around the globe – is hardly the indispensable nation it claims to be and is certainly not what the rest of the world really needs now.[49]

European adversaries, such as Todd, regard Europe as a potential counter to the reckless policies promoted by U. S. proponents of the New American Century. Certainly, the opposition of France and Germany to the Bush intervention in Iraq was reflective of the critical assessment of the doctrine of pre-emption and its rationales. Beyond that momentary dissent, other advocates of European counters to U. S. hegemony define a more inclusive and on-going contestation. One of the most articulate and active European voices is Susan George who asserts that if

> Europe doesn't actively and consciously play the role of counterweight to the United States, politically, economically, socially and ecologically, then everything that matters will soon be decided and overseen by an iron-fisted hegemonic American leadership with velvet gloves optional.[50]

In delineating the "European Versus the American Model," George invokes the social democratic policies that have provided a degree of security unmatched in the United States.[51] According to George, the European "model, at its best, rests on solidarity, inclusion and a sense of obligation to those who can't work and to the less fortunate both at home and abroad."[52] While, obviously, idealizing the sweep and persistence of that social democratic model, George posits Europe as the primary contending power to the United States. In rather stark terms, she asserts that "Europe's choice is either to accept subservience to the Empire or to move forward in constructing a model which attracts the support of others and gradually isolates the U. S."[53] Given the recent victory in George's France of the right-wing, immigrant-bashing, and American-leaning Nicolas Sarkozy as President, perhaps the "European model" is too tenuous and still riddled with its own imperial and racial specters. Yet, even Sarkozy has discovered his own independent voice in the search for finding a more distinctive European alternative to U. S. political and, especially, economic leadership.

On the other hand, the growing international sense of the demise of the American Empire and the neo-liberal "Washington Consensus" (to be discussed in greater detail in Chapter 5) found in George and other critics may point to on-going contestation.[54] However, instead of seeing Europe as the focal point for that contestation of the New American Century, the real challenges are now emanating from Latin America, specifically from Hugo Chávez of Venezuela and Evo Morales of Bolivia. Chávez and, even more so, Morales represent a kind of post-colonial opposition that plays off the indigenous and populist national struggles to achieve degrees of independence from Yankee and colonial control.

In the immediate aftermath of his election in December 2005 as the first indigenous president of Bolivia, Evo Morales acknowledged the "great revolt by those who have been oppressed for more than 500 years." He went on to claim that the "uprising of the Bolivian people has been not only about gas and hydrocarbons, but an intersection of many issues: discrimination, marginalization, and most importantly, the failure of neoliberalism." Concluding his remarks, Morales asserted that "if we want to defend humanity we must change system, and this means overthrowing U. S. imperialism."[55] A little over a month later in Caracas Venezuela, President Hugo Chávez addressed delegates to the 2006 World Social Forum. In the midst of a two-and-a-half-hour speech, Chávez denounced George W. Bush as "the world's biggest terrorist." He condemned U. S. imperialism as "the most perverse empire in history: it talks about freedom while invading and destroying other nations." Chávez's conclusion to this denunciation was a bold declaration: "This century we will bury the U. S. empire."[56]

While Chávez and Morales critique the imperial political project of the United States, with its legacy of interventions in Latin America, they are caught in certain contradictions in their attempts to navigate the political economy of transnational capital and the internal class contradictions of their respective countries and region.[57] According to sociologist James Petras,

Chávez and Morales are merely modernizing and updating petrol-nation state relations to present world standards; in a sense they are normalizing regulatory relations in the face of exceptional or windfall profits, resulting from corrupt agreements with complicit state executive officials.[58]

On the other hand, there are more sympathetic readings of Chávez's direct challenge to the Washington Consensus that see such a challenge as "a point of reference throughout the hemisphere."[59]

I want to explore in a very brief manner the articulation of and contradictions of this post-colonial contestation in the policies of Morales and Chávez. While some critics see Morales working toward a "de-colonization of the State," others see him as reliant on extracting greater tax revenues from multinational corporations who still have control over the natural gas resources in Bolivia.[60] Yet, there is no denying that Morales was swept to an unprecedented electoral victory on the back of massive social movements of indigenous Bolivians against the commodification of water rights (more on this in Chapter 5), for land reform, and nationalization of resources. In the extra-ordinary indigenous ceremony at an ancient Inca site before his official swearing-in, Morales promised the indigenous crowd that "with the strength of the people, we will put an end to the colonial state and the neoliberal model." At a special session at the Caracas World Social Forum in 2006, two Bolivian indigenous leaders assessed the Morales victory. While both of these Bolivian activists from different social movements agreed that Morales would oppose neoliberalism and de-colonize the state, they articulated different political alternatives. One saw socialism as the only alternative while the other spoke of being different from the traditional left in the embrace of a communal struggle for primordial rights. Even as both agreed that nationalization of oil and gas reserves was imperative and representative of the aspirations of the Bolivian people, how Bolivia proceeds under Morales, beyond his national populist agenda, is still an open matter.

In Venezuela, Chávez has talked about socialism of the twenty-first century, one that would move beyond the visions and practices of the past. Sharply critical of U. S. imperialism and the Bush regime, the Chávez government remains a leading supplier of oil to the United States at the same time that it engages in efforts to stymie U. S. hegemony in international fora. While Chávez has, in turn, used the revenues from Venezuelan oil to fund social programs for the poor in his country, such as health clinics, subsidized food stores, and literacy campaigns, and in other countries, especially in the Caribbean and even in the U. S. where the Venezuelan subsidiary, Citgo, is providing home heating oil to poor residents in New York City and Boston, he has only recently begun to take back some control and revenue from those transnational corporations. In addition, the Venezuelan government is in the process of working with some of those same companies to exploit coal reserves in the northwest region of Venezuela at the expense of land claims and environmental security of the indigenous groups that inhabit that region.[61]

As Chávez and Morales seek to realize those post-colonial practices that contest the New American Century, a postmodern version of challenging U. S. global dominance owes its origins to the political struggles emerging from the Zapatista experience in Mexico. The Zapatistas emerged almost at the very moment that the North American Free Trade Agreement (NAFTA) took effect. Challenging the imposition of U. S. economic imperialism, along with the continuing neglect by the Mexican government of issues surrounding indigenous communities in Mexico, the Zapastitas offered another moment and vision of counter-hegemony. Reflecting on the Zapatista movement, Roger Burbach highlights the post-modern moment of this struggle. "The opposition," contends Burbach,

> is postmodern in the sense that it has no clear rationale or logic to its activities while it instinctively recognizes that it cannot be effective by working through a 'modern' political party, or by taking state power. It functions from below as an almost permanent rebellion, placing continuous demands on all the powers that be.[62]

In effect, the Zapatistas are exploring non-state networks that are part of subnational insurgencies in Latin America and new transnational attempts to realize another world. (The Zapatistas and other transnational movements will be further examined in Chapters 7 and 8.)

The Zapatistas were certainly a primary force in bringing about the development of the World Social Forum (WSF), launched in 2001 in Porto Alegre, Brazil. With an impetus from the Brazilian social movements and confrontations with the World Trade Organization begun in Seattle in 1999, the WSF soon became a key site for a postmodern contestation of the New American Century and the Washington Consensus. Moreover, the WSF, according to one of its intellectual luminaries, Boaventura de Sousa Santos, "created a global consciousness for the different movements" that embodied a form of plural counter-hegemonic globalization.[63] As a global space for the articulation of emancipatory grassroots democracy, the WSF also offered a countervailing vision of "one no and many yeses" that clearly challenged U. S. political-military and political-economic global hegemony.[64]

For the time being, however, Latin America has become a site of challenging certain hegemonic models in a profound, if not revolutionary, way. Contradicting the arrogant and imperial perspective of Henry Kissinger that "nothing important can come from the South," the new experiments spawned by social movements throughout the continent, from workers' self-management in Argentina to indigenous movements to protect water and land in Bolivia and Brazil, there is hope for, at least, a fairer world in that region. But the long-range issue of countering and even eroding hegemony, especially from the North, is still a critically open-ended matter, one that was given inspiring consideration throughout the 2006 World Social Forum in Caracas.[65] (Chapter 8 will have a more extensive description and analysis of this particular WSF and the whole concept of the WSF as a possible incubator for another world.)

As a way of concluding where this world-historical struggle against U. S. hegemony is heading, I want to consider a few final points. Although Michael Hardt and Antonio Negri have proposed an interesting paradigm about the dispersal of deterritorialized power and the growth of the counter-hegemonic "multitude" under postmodern globalization, they overlook the persistence of reterritorialization, especially by the premier rogue state: the United States.[66] In fact, according to one study of the political strategy of "American militarism and endless war": "We are at a point where U. S. global ambitions supersede all hope for shared norms, laws, customs, and treaties. The deadly cycle of militarism and terrorism, involving perpetual war waged from the White House and Pentagon, can only exacerbate this predicament."[67] One confirmation of this dystopian future can be found in the projections of a former U. S. intelligence officer:

> We are entering a new American century, in which we will become still wealthier, culturally more lethal, and increasingly powerful. We will excite hatreds without precedent. ... The de facto role of the U. S. armed forces will be to keep the world safe for our economy and open to our cultural assault. To those ends, we will do a fair amount of killing.[68]

To stop that cycle of killing and endless war requires not only the defeat of specific U. S. political-military policies, but also the recognition that, according to Samir Amin, the "hegemonist strategy of the United States ... seeks nothing less than to establish Washington's military control over the entire planet."[69] It has always been a function of those advocates of the American and New American Century to provide a universalist and idealistic gloss to U. S. hegemony and its political-military strategy. However, as argued by Immanuel Wallerstein, an

> America that continues to relate to the world by a unilateral assertion that it represents civilization ... cannot live in peace with the world, and therefore will not live in peace with itself. ... Can the land of liberty and privilege, even amidst its decline, learn to be a land that treats everyone everywhere as equals?[70]

In effect, can we recognize that the true burden of freedom is freeing ourselves from the debilitating constructions embedded in "empire as a way of life" and getting beyond the imperial U. S.? Can we admit, along with Michael Mann, that our "democratic values are flagrantly contradicted by an imperialism which is strong on military offense, but weak on the ability to bring order, peace, and democracy afterwards"?[71] Can we not finally acknowledge that death and destruction more often have been the legacy of the geopolitical project of the American Century than spreading freedom and democracy?

For all of the rhetoric about extending the American Century, a little reflection and critical self-awareness would suggest that such extension is neither possible nor warranted given the past record and present conditions. Perhaps, as a way of conclusion, one can take seriously the recommendations of one of the key interpreters of American power and war in the twentieth century, Gabriel Kolko:

> Everyone – Americans and those people who are the objects of their efforts – would be far better off if the U. S. did nothing, closed its bases overseas and withdrew its fleet everywhere, and allowed the rest of the world to find its own way without American weapons and troops. ... [T]o continue as it has over the past half century is to admit it has the vainglorious and irrational ambition to run the world.[72]

Moreover, as discussed in the next chapter, the attempt to run the world has also resulted in ruining not only a democratic ethos and community at home but also eroding the possibilities for a fair and equitable sharing of resources and social goods. In effect, as much as the United States has projected an empire abroad, the repercussions of empire-building at home have resulted in a collapsing fortress as well as a dissolving fortitude for an imperial way of life.

2 Fortress America *redux*

Breaking down imperial and civic enclosures

We are controlled here by our confusion, far more than we know, and the American dream has therefore become something much more resembling a nightmare, on the private, domestic, and international levels. Privately, we cannot stand our lives and dare not examine them; domestically, we take no responsibility for (and no pride in) what goes on in our country; and internationally, for millions of people, we are an unmitigated disaster.

James Baldwin

The modern state, we would argue, has come to need weak citizenship. It depends more and more on maintaining an impoverished and hygenized public realm, in which only the ghosts of an older, more idiosyncratic civil society live on.

Retort

At the end of the twentieth century political journalist William Greider cast a critical eye on the institutions that constituted "Fortress America," especially those represented by the military-industrial complex. According to Greider, "the U. S. military-industrial complex, as we have known it, is in the process of devouring itself, literally and tangibly. The awesome interlocking structure of armed forces, industrial interests, and political alliances that has sprawled across American public life and purpose for two generations cannot endure for long, not in its familiar shape and size."[1] Yet, at the beginning of the twenty-first century, a reconfigured "Fortress America" has not only revived and expanded the military-industrial complex, but also added additional layers to the construction of fear and paranoia endemic in an imperial culture. This chapter attempts to shed light on the interconnections of foreign and domestic policies as they simultaneously bolster and batter down the physical and psychological enclosures of Fortress America.

On April 12, 2007 a truck bomb destroyed the Sarrafiya Bridge in Baghdad, killing innocent civilians and severing the city into two equally desperate halves. That same day in the so-called "Green Zone," an area of Baghdad surrounded by walls and myriad check points and monitors, a suicide bomber detonated an explosive device in the cafeteria of the Iraqi Parliament

Building. Once more, there were several deaths and scores injured. In the fifth year of the Iraq War, the delusions perpetrated by the Bush Administration and their supporters in Congress and the media were torn asunder by such brazen acts of violence.

Meanwhile, the Pentagon's "surge" was meeting with intense resistance in Baghdad, even in the face of aggressive counter-insurgency tactics. According to Robert Fisk's April 2007 report in *The Independent*, that counter-insurgency was premised on a strategy of establishing "gated communities" throughout the city. Walling off neighborhoods and setting-up extensive pass systems, the U. S. and Iraqi military began a process that combined forms of ethnic cleansing with massive sweeps and myriad arrests. In effect, the civilian population, not shunted into already overcrowded prisons, were themselves incarcerated in these "gated communities."[2]

Although more troops and National Guard were rushed off to Iraq, the imperial designs of the Bush Administration lay in ruins. Those ruins became evident, not just in the broken bridges and wrecked walls of Baghdad, but also in the domestic failures fostered by the arrogance and incompetence of policymakers in Washington, DC, especially the colossal ineptitude of the federal government before and after the devastation of Hurricane Katrina. Katrina did such damage in New Orleans and other coastal cities, in part, because of inadequate levees and outmoded bridges. "When Hurricane Katrina exploded," opined Helene Moglen and Sheila Namir,

> it revealed the inside – the guts – of Bush's war on terrorism. It provided a lens through which we could see that war's complex social under-pinnings, the greed that propels it, the political hypocrisy that veils it, and the gross incompetence that has shaped it in virtually all of its aspects.[3]

Hurricane Katrina also afforded a cautionary note about the implosions of civic violence in the United States. There were a number of incidents of ethnic/racial animosity accompanying Katrina that should give U. S. citizens pause in their denunciation of sectarian violence in Iraq. In the midst of the battering of New Orleans by Katrina, hundreds of residents of the city fled the floodwaters by trying to cross the Crescent City Connection Bridge into the suburb of Gretna. However, they were viciously repulsed by Gretna police who fired warning shots in the direction of the fleeing crowd. The Gretna police chief justified this action by asserting that "if we had opened the bridge, our city would have looked like New Orleans does now, looted, burned, and pillaged."[4]

Gretna is only one example of the U. S. version of "gated communities" that seek to keep out the dark hordes festering in the projections of paranoid white supremacists. Those paranoid projections are also evident in the nativist response to other dark hordes, i.e. brown illegal immigrants transgressing the southwestern borders of the United States. A particularly telling strategy promoted by the nativist forces is a plan to build an enormous wall along the

U. S./Mexican border. Somehow, this desire to wall off *El Norte* is a further example of an imploding imperial system. That system creates the global economic and social dislocations which drive migrants to seek refuge in a land which has become even more inhospitable to the stranger.

As the poet Robert Frost once wrote, "something there is that doesn't like a wall." This remains true whether along the U. S./Mexican border or in Baghdad's "Green Zone." For that matter, the insularity of gated communities, from Baghdad to San Diego, is an admission that reality is too difficult to confront. Such gated communities, both here and abroad, may offer seeming protection from those very forces created by those blinded by their own delusions. In fact, the repression and insularity represented by gated communities only wall off what promises to fester and explode.

On another level, gated communities reflect imperial and civic enclosures. As historian William Appleman Williams notes, empire "substitutes paranoid togetherness for community."[5] In effect, the paranoid togetherness enacted by gated communities "mirrors a foreign policy that seeks to control the world but … increases terror and instability instead."[6] Such communities are, also, a further representation of segregated suburbanization based on fear. Situating the gated community in the "militarization of the city," urban anthropologist, Setha Low, observes how this socially controlled fortress "contributes to a geography of social relations that produces fear and anxiety simply by locating a person's home and place identity in a secured enclave, gated, guarded, and locked."[7] In this manner the civic isolation and irresponsibility fostered by a class and race mediated defensive space seems to be another kind of "blowback" from the U. S. imperial agenda.

While the U. S. imperial efforts in Iraq and Afghanistan have fallen far short of the neoconservative projections of instant "democracy" and "progress," the domestic agenda achieved certain goals. Attempting to drive government domestic spending on social programs into the ground, the neoconservative geopolitical grab for global dominance, oil resources, and military bases has propelled military spending to exorbitant levels. Some estimates of the total amount of federal dollars allocated to imperial projects and so-called "homeland security" for 2008 amount to 1 trillion dollars.[8] The building of bridges, walls, and gated communities within this fracturing paradigm are really last ditch efforts to protect an imperial racket that has lost its capacity to deliver the goods, except to those corporate and mercenary scavenger companies like Halliburton and Blackwater.

One irony of these imperial enclosures is that the actual physical infrastructure in the United States, with the exception of the aforementioned targeted building projects, is in massive disrepair. In the concluding commentary of a September 2003 report issued by the American Society of Civil Engineers, it was noted that the "condition of our nation's roads, bridges, drinking water systems and other public works have shown little improvement since they were graded an overall D+ in 2001, with some areas sliding towards a failing grade."[9] In effect, continued expenditures on military and imperial projects abroad deplete the economic resources for necessary reconstruction efforts, let alone for the construction of an equitable and sustainable society at home. As argued by David Harvey, only by downgrading or denying "its imperialist trajectory" could the U. S. redirect "capital flows into the production and renewal of physical and social infrastructures."[10]

To downgrade or deny its imperialist trajectory, the citizens of the U. S. must fully comprehend the insidious effects of imperialism at home and abroad. Perhaps the current economic crisis (explored in more depth in Chapter 5 and the Conclusion) will provide a wake-up call to citizens about all of the costs of empire. On the other hand, as Barbara Kingsolver observes:

> The writing has been on the wall for some years now, but we are a nation illiterate in the language of the wall. The writing just gets bigger. Something *will* eventually bring down the charming, infuriating naïveté of Americans that allows us our blithe consumption and cheerful ignorance of the secret ugliness that bring us whatever we want.[11]

Beyond this necessary critical consciousness concerning imperialism and all its ramifications, there needs to be a collective political will to conceive of and realize an alternative America. "America is unlikely to play a different role in the world," maintains Gar Alperovitz, "until it is a different America – until it finds ways once again to realize values of equality, liberty, democracy, and, one day perhaps even of community in our own land."[12]

Yet, the difficulty in realizing a different America must contend with the political and psychological fallout from imperialism. As noted incisively by Mansour Farhang,

> it seems to be in the nature of imperialism to fear everything that is not subject to its influence. This fear, which has always been present in the imperialist countries, has a functional value for the state. Without continuing insecurity and fear in the public, imperialism as a form of government cannot be maintained and rationalized.[13]

In effect, the institutionalization of such insecurity and fear was integral to the establishment of the national security state. With roots in legislation dating back to the origin of the nation that branded internal threats as the work of foreign agents, the prosecution of two world wars in the twentieth century created even more fertile ground for the national security state. More central to the modern national security state was the National Security Act of 1947 and its obsession with criminalizing dissent through loyalty oaths and a host of other federal mechanisms that roused the suspicion and fear of U. S. citizens as part of the Cold War.[14]

Perhaps no Cold War document better reflects the paranoia endemic in the national security state than National Security Council (NSC) Document No. 68. Although focused on responding to the Soviet Union and the world-wide communist threat, as a consequence of the explosion of a Soviet nuclear bomb in 1949 and the victory of the Chinese Communist Party in the same year, NSC-68 also urged renewed efforts for internal security. In many respects this Cold War document is the godfather of the emergence of Homeland Security with its relentless erosion of constitutional rights and its institutionalization of fear through a color-coded scale of alerts.[15] From the passage of the USA Patriot Act with its chilling impact on civil liberties to the FBI's recent reorganization that facilitates spying on the public without any court orders or even evidence of wrong-doing, one confronts a pernicious and pervasive extension of the national security state. In reviewing the nearly sixty-year legacy of the national security state, former soldier and foreign policy critic, Andrew Bacevich, poses the following poignant question and response:

> When considering the national security state as it has evolved and grown over the past six decades, what exactly has been the value added? And if the answer is none – if, indeed, the return on the investment has been essentially negative – then perhaps the time has come to consider dismantling an apparatus that demonstrably serves no useful purpose.[16]

On the other hand, beyond the expansion of the bureaucratic business of state repression, the national security state, as an ideological apparatus, has served a particularly essential service of binding the population to the imperial state. As asserted by Indian writer and activist, Arundhati Roy, "Ordinary people in the United States have been manipulated into imagining they are a people under siege ..., a people bonded to the state not by social services, or public health care or employment guarantees, but by fear."[17] In effect, refusing to expand the funding of social services that nurture social and psychological well-being, the federal government has spent trillions of dollars to project its imperial power abroad and to shore up its imperial legitimacy at home. Through the proliferation of ideological and institutional arrangements, we languish in a culture of imperial enclosures that engender fear and paranoia.

Breaking down any and all imperial enclosures requires the recognition that such enclosures are both physical and psychological. Everywhere that U. S. imperialism will try to build its remaining walls will undoubtedly be scaled by growing bands of insurgents, migrants, and miscreants. Identifying with those who seek to tear down such walls, let us recall the lyrics of a song by Los Lobos, that driving rock band from East LA: "Some day that wall will tumble and fall/And the sun will shine that day." For that day to come, however, acts of intervention, from analyzing the impediments of imperial enclosures to breaking through those impediments, must be undertaken. As stated eloquently by Rebecca Solnit, "Blind hope faces a blank wall waiting for a door in it to open. ... The great liberation movements hacked doorways into walls."[18]

In order to excavate and explode the mental landscapes created by imperial enclosures, we will need to confront and transcend the blinkered intelligence, impeded wills, and hectored hearts that are integral to the imperial and civic enclosures that surround us in the United States. These enclosures are generated by ideological mechanisms, media constructions, and daily social practices that are deeply embedded in the political culture of an imperial U. S. From uncritical patriotism, induced by ruling elites and ritualized by the corporate media, to cultural provincialism, U. S. citizens are ensconced in an imperial matrix that distorts reality and nurtures "aggressive militarism" and "escalating authoritarianism."[19] "As the militarization of American society proceeds," contends Carl Boggs, "the confluence of the domestic war economy and global Empire generates popular attitudes inconsistent with a vibrant, democratic public sphere: fear hatred, jingoism, racism, and aggression. We have arrived at a bizarre mixture of imperial arrogance and collective paranoia, violent impulses and a retreat from the norms of civic engagement and obligation that patriotic energies furnish only falsely and ephemerally."[20]

Recognizing how falsely and ephemerally patriotism attempts to assuage the assaults of militarism and imperialism, a number of feminist dissenters have promoted "matriotism" as a key component of critical opposition. Among the more prominent proponents of matriotism was Cindy Sheehan, the anti-war advocate who became a lightning rod for opponents of the Iraq War after her son, Casey, was killed in Iraq. Writing in January 2006, Sheehan argued that a "true Matriot would never drop an atomic bomb or bombs filled with white phosphorous, carpet bomb cities, and villages, or control drones from thousands of miles away to kill innocent men, women and children." Beyond this critique of war-making, Sheehan urged those among her readers who would join other matriots "to stand up and say: 'No, I am not giving my child to the fake patriotism of the war machine which chews up my flesh and blood to spit out obscene profits.'"[21]

While flag-waving patriotism may provide ideological cover for the mendacity of ruling elites and compensatory status for the powerless, it also reinforces the self-enclosures of imperialism. The desperate need to display the flag, from the phalanxes of those that now accompany the public appearances of U. S. presidents to the periodic fluttering outside the homes of average citizens, provides a symbolic ritual for imperial legitimacy. In effect, the

> more uncritical the kind of patriotism that rules popular imagination and public discourse, the more alone, insulated, special and different the American ethos makes people feel. The more it holds up a distorting mirror to itself and the rest of the world, the more incomprehensible the rest of the world becomes, full of inarticulate, hostile elements.[22]

That distorting mirror is not only part of the imperial narrative that represents the United States as the repository of good in the world, but is also a function of the role of corporate media's presentation of the world.

Through the use of framing and filtering devices, U. S. corporate media, especially television, manage to narrow and exclude critical perspectives, leading to significant misperceptions. In fact, according to a University of Massachusetts study of television viewers during Operation Desert Storm in 1991: "The more TV people watched, the less they knew. ... Despite months of coverage, most people do not know basic facts about the political situation in the Middle East, or about the recent history of U. S. policy towards Iraq."[23] Added to media distortions, misrepresentations, and complicity, the Bush Administration's deliberate policy of disinformation in the lead-up to the Iraq War in 2003 further eroded the public's critical understanding of the situation in the Middle East and Iraq. Erroneously insisting on ties between Saddam Hussein and al Qaeda and the presence of weapons of mass destruction in Iraq, the Bush Administration and complicit corporate media helped to frame the invasion and occupation of Iraq.[24] Such misperceptions persisted into 2006 when a Harris Poll found that 64 percent still believed that Hussein had strong links to al Qaeda and 50 percent were convinced that Iraq had weapons of mass destruction when the U. S. invaded.[25]

The kind of disinformation spread by politicians and pundits and reinforced by the media follows from our national and imperial myths which, in turn, both literally and figuratively separate us from the rest of the world. While not a new phenomenon, such imperial self-enclosure does seem even more striking in the globalized and interconnected world we now inhabit. "As the American media has acquired a global reach," argue cultural critics Ziauddin Sardar and Merryl Wyn Davies, "it has simultaneously, and paradoxically, become even more parochial and banal."[26] According to Sardar and Davies, the media reinforce what they call "knowledgeable ignorance" by acting as "the gatekeeper of what is relevant and necessary to know about Third World civilizations."[27] Often, most evident in those media images are ones of random violence or poverty and disease unrelated to U. S. policies. However, it is not just those countries caught up in conflict, whether initiated by the United States or endemic to a particular region, that suffer from media frames that diminish or denigrate the reality of others' lives. "As a function of American narcissism," notes another critic, "American media tend to problematize all countries except the United States. ... The absence of self-reflexivity or a sense of humor and irony in viewing America's place in the world seems to be part of the collective habitus."[28]

Even when U. S. citizens are aware of some vague relationship between their government and conditions elsewhere, there remains a kind of phenomenological disconnection, inherent in life in an imperial culture, which impedes understanding of the causal connections. Commenting on the violations perpetrated against peasants in Central America by U. S. sponsored militaries and para-militaries and the resultant gross violations of human rights, Christian Smith observes:

> Most Americans probably were, in fact, concerned about these problems. But for most U. S. citizens, these injustices and atrocities remained

essentially abstract and remote, detached from the immediate affairs that shaped their lives. It is not that most Americans were necessarily callous. They simply lacked the cultural and social positioning that would have infused these violations with a sense of personal immediacy and urgency.[29]

The lack of a cultural and social positioning is evident in the way some U. S. citizens continue to see the world through the same blinkered filters that inform the dynamics of knowledgeable ignorance. A good example of the misperception of the U. S. role in the world is how the vast majority of U. S. citizens continue to overestimate the largesse of their government's foreign aid. Although most citizens believe the U. S. gives close to 10 percent of its GDP for foreign aid, the U. S. actually gives closer to 0.1 percent. Moreover, much of that aid is military material sent to Israel, Egypt, and Saudi Arabia.[30] A fictional example, albeit representative, of such knowledgable ignorance or imperial arrogance while abroad is the evangelical Baptist father in Barbara Kingsolver's 1998 novel, *The Poisonwood Bible*. Nathan Price stubbornly insists that every last bit of U. S. culture and horticulture can be easily transplanted in the Congo in the midst of the Cold War. With such imperial blinders and blinkered intelligence he manages to endanger his whole family, resulting in the death of one child and his own demise.

If imperial blinders and blinkered intelligence continue to plague the U. S. and its citizens both here and abroad, those who strive to break down the imperial and civic enclosures confront a labyrinth that often leads to dead-ends. More significantly, even the most implacable foes of the imperial enclosures face mental cul-de-sacs from misguided optimism to bitter cynicism to impeded wills. Perhaps as a consequence of blinkered intelligence, many anti-war and anti-militarist advocates assume that the absence of shooting wars represents a transformation of the system. In fact, as argued by the Retort collective,

> unless the anti-war movement comes to recognize the full dynamics of U. S. militarism – to understand that peace, under current arrangements, is no more than war by other means – then massive mobilizations at the approach of full-dress military campaigns must inevitably be followed by demoralization and bewilderment.[31]

Certainly, it is true that the massive mobilizations in February 2003 led to demoralization when the Bush Administration demonstrated its utter contempt for international opinion and law by its war on and occupation of Iraq. (There will be more on those 2003 demonstrations in Chapter 7.) Nonetheless, the anti-war movement slowly regained urgency and popularity as the Bush Administration's war machine proved incapable of establishing its imperial "peace" in Iraq. Reinvigorated demonstrations, before and after the 2006 elections, sought to leverage widespread public antagonism to the Iraq

War into pressuring the Congress to enact specific legislation for cutting off funds and bringing home the troops by a speedy withdrawal. Elected to the majority in 2006, the Democrats refused to end the war, leading to further disillusionment. One heartfelt response came from Cindy Sheehan who announced on Memorial Day 2007 her retirement from the anti-war movement. A similar perspective emerged from another grieving parent, Andrew Bacevich, who also happened to be an academic critic of the Iraq War. In his denunciation of Beltway politics, Bacevich provided even more insight into on-going blinkered intelligence and the insidious effect of impeded will:

> Money maintains the Republican/Democratic duopoly of trivialized politics. It confines the debate over U. S. policy to well-hewn channels. It preserves intact the clichés of 1933–45 about isolationism, appeasement and the nation's call to 'global leadership.' It inhibits any serious accounting of exactly how much our misadventure in Iraq is costing. It ignores completely the question of who actually pays. It negates democracy, rendering free speech little more than a means of recording dissent.[32]

From another perspective, the accumulation of dictatorial powers of a revised imperial presidency and expansion of the military-industrial complex has further hamstrung even the timid protestations of Congress. Indeed, imagining that the electoral arena holds the key to reversing the war machine is one of the major illusions of a variety of political factions which constitute the anti-war movement. Being reduced to a lobbying mechanism for legislative relief from an imperial presidency and permanent war has marginalized what passes for an anti-war movement. Hence, irrespective of how large demonstrations may grow in Washington, DC, they occupy only symbolic space with a narrow political focus and imagination.

The incapacity to confront how deeply embedded the war machine is in the political culture of the United States further compounds the misguided efforts of the anti-war movement to pursue the legislative and electoral route. As the Pentagon's tentacles have spread beyond the military-industrial complex to the manipulation of media images, militarism has injected its values even deeper into the veins of the society of the spectacle. An obvious vehicle for socializing young boys in particular into militarist values is the video game. As consultants to video games, retired military personnel transferred their obsession with "shock and awe" technology to advance the agenda of the virtual performance of permanent war. In November 2002 the Pentagon released for free the video game, "America's Army." As an explicit recruitment tool for the Pentagon, the video game had a separate webpage of links with local recruiters. Another video game, "Splinter Cell," touted its mission to neutralize the terrorist threat with ads that read like a Cheney-Rumsfeld wet-dream: "I alone have the fifth freedom: the right to spy, steal, destroy, and assassinate to insure that American freedoms are protected."[33]

On the other hand, this virtual bombardment of militarism could not bolster recruitment efforts in the face of the debilitating wars in Iraq and Afghanistan. Military recruiters fell short of their goal in April 2005 by 42 percent, even with the bonuses and other promised benefits, although economic hard times now are adding to an up-tick in recruitment. While efforts to combat military recruitment in the schools are an important arena for countering the influence of the war machine, the more insidious conditioning continues apace. Moreover, trying to create communities of resistance in an era of highly privatized space and hyper-consumerism is, if not impossible, assuredly very difficult. In effect, the very possibility of developing and sustaining an anti-war *movement* is open to question. Yet, without confronting both the cultural representations of the permanent war machine and its daily material production and cultural reproduction, any anti-war movement may be reduced to a mere shadow of actual resistance.

At a certain level, that shadow resistance and even its evanescent existence may be a reflection of how pervasive and insidious imperial enclosures have become. One could even suggest that those imperial enclosures are almost equivalent to the kind of all-encompassing technological enclosure epitomized in the 1999 film, *The Matrix*. According to the character, Morpheus, the leader of a band of human resisters who have escaped the matrix and are seeking to protect their tenuous freedom, the matrix "is everywhere. It is all around us. ... It is the world that has been pulled over your eyes to blind you from the truth ... a prison that you cannot smell, or taste, or touch." It is not inconsequential that these words are uttered by a black man played by Lawrence Fishburne. His ability to identify the imprisonment represented by the matrix recalls the penetrating insights of the African-American writer, James Baldwin: "We know, in the case of the person, that whoever cannot tell himself the truth about his past is trapped in it, is immobilized in the prison of his undiscovered self. This is also true of nations."[34]

While Morpheus and other characters in *The Matrix* wrestle with the physical and metaphysical implications of the matrix, our own attention, following Baldwin's, must necessarily look at the historical conditions that have made the contemporary imperial enclosures that much more ubiquitous and difficult to transcend. When one compares the anti-war movement that emerged in the 1960s with the pale imitation today, one not only recognizes the lack of real organizing and movement-building, but also the transformed historical conditions. The insurgencies that marked the 1960s attack on the war machine from anti-draft activities to military mutinies to factory uprisings to blockading supply trains were part of a collective revolt against the state's colonization of the body and the mind. Alternative institutions flourished in college towns, on the outskirts of military bases, and within communities of color and young people in general. Where are those forces or sectors in the U. S. willing to reject in the most radical way the military neo-liberalism that has become the hallmark of the latest incarnation of the American imperial project?

Has our intelligence become so impoverished, our wills so impeded, and our social conditions so debased that we have neither the mental nor material capacities even to disrupt the warmachine, let alone dismantle it? Given the argument that any oppositional movement in the U. S. is itself an "afflicted power" as a consequence of "weak citizenship" and the ubiquitous effects of advanced pacification and spectatorship, perhaps the only hope for dismantling the war machine is its own self-destruction through imperial overreach.[35] Yet, even though the political dynamics at work internationally may erode the U. S. imperial agenda, the domestic challenging of the political elite may be hampered by the nature of imperial and civic enclosures. According to Carl Boggs, "imperial stability (at home) will more likely be reinforced by postmodern conditions involving widespread depoliticization, mass apathy, and privatized retreat."[36]

A number of social critics contend that such depoliticization, apathy, and retreat are not only a consequence of historical conditions but also an instrument of on-going elite control. Philosopher Cornel West avows that as the "commitment to truth, integrity, and principle gives way to mendacity, manipulation, and misinformation" there arises what he calls "political nihilism." The "hallmark of political nihilism," according to West, is the appeal to "fear and greed."[37] Such fear mongering leads to what one political scientist calls the "Battered Citizen Syndrome," a syndrome which, in turn, produces further depoliticization.[38] Is it any wonder that even the most active of citizens, say such as a Cindy Sheehan, would seek refuge from political engagement in private family life?

On the other hand, in Sheehan's case this is not a retreat into an imperial or civic enclosure. "I will never give up trying to help people in the world who are harmed by the empire of the good old U. S. of A," Sheehan wrote in her "resignation" letter, "but I am finished working in, or outside this system. The system forcefully resists being helped and eats up the people who try to help it. I am getting out before it totally consumes me or any more people that I love."[39] In effect, Sheehan implicitly recognizes that imperial and civic enclosures engender what I call the "hectored heart," a condition whereby the inclination towards selflessness, altruism, and love is confined and constrained.[40] Moreover, in maintaining her empathy with those victimized by U. S. imperial policies, Sheehan manifests a capacity to transcend the ethical impediments embedded in imperial mental enclosures.

Those imperial mental enclosures often work to deter most U. S. citizens from expressing empathy towards those brutalized by U. S. imperial policies. "When the pain is caused by our government," asserts Robert Jensen, "we are channeled away from ... empathy. The way we are educated and entertained keeps us from knowing about or understanding the pain of others in other parts of the world."[41] The philosopher Wendy Farley analyzes this "obliviousness to another's personhood" as part of the "illusions" or ideologies that inform both individuals and their communities.[42] Noting that the "reality of other persons is effectively concealed by a dense cloud of lies, misleading images, and intonations of moral grandeur," Farley designates "eros," or the empathy of the heart, as a "nondominating proximity (that) permits an understanding of others to emerge that would otherwise be impossible."[43] Finally, from a psychoanalytic perspective, empathy "necessitates recognition of being in the place of the other, imagining one's way into the space and place of the other. This is a profound encounter of both interiority and exteriority."[44]

Obviously, in order to express empathy one must not only transcend imperial and civic enclosures but also recognize the insidiousness of blinkered intelligence and hectored hearts. Beyond the nihilism in the political arena, the socio-economic conditions that operate in the United States make it exceedingly difficult to go beyond the imperial and civic enclosures. In particular, such enclosures, from gated communities to tax shelters, have been erected to reward the privileged and to humiliate and make outcasts of the rest, especially exposing the class, gender, and racial fault lines of social divisions in the United States. Teetering on the edge of financial ruin or marginalization induces a fear that can lead to a gated community of the heart. With average household credit card debt around $9,000 and mortgage debt rising to 7.5 trillion in 2004, is it any wonder that the typical citizen is consumed by a lingering economic dread?[45]

Perhaps the fascination with popular entertainment dealing with the intimacies of crime families, such as *The Godfather* and *The Sopranos,* has as much to do with a suppressed desire to use any means necessary to protect the family as with the recognition that families often operate as masculinist protection rackets, mimicking in the process the security states that encase them.[46] From another perspective, *The Sopranos* offers a further example, albeit more critical, of the social Darwinist message in contemporary U. S. popular culture where survival of the fittest means only the most ruthless will survive. Commenting on the popularity of "reality" television series that foreground the social Darwinist message, such as *Survivor,* sociologist Zygmunt Bauman concludes: "in a game of survival, trust, compassion and mercy ... are suicidal. If you are not tougher and less scrupulous than all the others, you will be done in by them, with or without remorse."[47]

The hectoring within family life also mirrors the cultural drive to be "winners" in the larger society, even though those families just managing to hold it together are constantly reminded that they are "losers." Thus, the cultural pathologies replicated in the American family reflect and refract imperial and civic enclosures. Nonetheless, frazzled parents imagine that even more concentration on their privatized existence can save their own children from the depredations of daily life. In her incisive study of "motherhood in the age of anxiety," Judith Warner contends

> that what our obsessive looking-inward hides is a kind of despair. A lack of faith that change can come to the outside world. ... Our outlook is

something very much akin to what cognitive behavioralists call 'learned helplessness' – the kind of instinctive giving-up in the face of difficulty that people do when they've come to think they have no real power.[48]

This cultivated sense of "learned helplessness" further undermines our capacity to imagine ourselves as social agents of change and leads to a sense of fatalism and hopelessness about transcending those often invisible boundaries of imperial and civic enclosures. As an antidote to the hectored heart, hope, which Vaclav Havel called "an orientation of the heart," needs to be nurtured.[49] The poet-essayist and farmer-environmentalist, Wendell Berry, writes that

> hope is one of our duties. A part of our obligation to our own being and to our descendants is to study our life and our condition, searching always for the authentic underpinnings of hope. And if we look, those underpinnings can still be found.[50]

Perhaps the most profound underpinning for hope in our historical and cultural context is what Cornel West calls "tragicomic hope." Such hope grew out of the amazing resilience embedded in the African-American experience, "rooted in a love of freedom." "Rooted in a love of freedom," tragicomic hope is

> a sad yet sweet indictment of abusive power and blind greed run amok. It is a melancholic yet melioristic stance toward America's denial of its terrors and horrors heaped on others. It yields a courage to hope for betterment against the odds without a sense of revenge or resentment.[51]

What more appropriate hope to overcome imperial and civic enclosures! If we are to realize a better or other world beyond us, then we need that tragicomic hope, rooted in a love of freedom.

One of those loving freedom whom Cornel West cites as exemplars of tragicomic hope is James Baldwin. Still one of the most profound discussions of the contradictions of achieving freedom in the United States is Baldwin's *The Fire Next Time*. Written in the midst of the modern civil rights movement with its critical challenge to white supremacy, Baldwin also ruminates on the national myths that sustain not only white supremacy but also an illusory sense of innocence among the white citizenry of the country. Faulting white America for its inability to understand the tragic reality of its past and, indeed, "the fact that life is tragic," Baldwin goes on to maintain:

> Perhaps the whole root of our trouble, the human trouble, is that we will sacrifice all the beauty of our lives, will imprison ourselves in totems, taboos, crosses, blood sacrifices, steeples, mosques, races, armies, flags, nations in order to deny the fact of death, which is the only fact we have.

If seems to me that one ought to rejoice in the *fact* of death – ought to decide, indeed, to *earn* one's death by confronting with passion the conundrum of life.[52]

Another African-American literary figure touted by West as both prophetic and a necessary guide to comprehending tragicomic hope is Toni Morrison. In particular, Morrison's ruminations on Melville's *Moby Dick* and the figure of Ahab become the site for locating our own imperial incapacities. Cornel West sees Toni Morrison's insights into Melville's Ahab as a revelation of the legacies concerning the illusions about invulnerability and imperial denials, whether of death or destruction. Pondering Morrison's reflections on Melville's Ahab and the tortured racial dynamics of the past, West comments: "In Morrison's vision, it is fear and insecurity that drive the dogmatisms and nihilisms of imperial elites like Ahab, and love and hope that bind democratic communities in response to the offenses of imperial power and might."[53]

If we are to overcome the dogmatisms and nihilisms of imperial elites and to construct a grounded love and hope, we need to break down those imperial and civic enclosures that perpetuate the dogmatisms of the past and impede any hope for another and better world. The change that we seek, "change not on the surface but in the depths – change in the sense of renewal," according to the eloquent perspective of James Baldwin, "becomes impossible if one supposes things to be constant that are not."[54] Enclosures that have been erected over time and space may seem impervious to change, but they can be physically and psychologically dismantled if we confront our blinkered intelligence, impeded wills, and hectored hearts. For us to do that will require what West identified as a critical component of the tragicomic outlook – a courage to hope for betterment against the odds without a sense of revenge or resentment.

Given the difficulties inherent in overcoming the enclosures of an imperial culture, we also need to be reminded of the fact that fundamental transformations do not happen quickly. Indeed, during the arduous and lengthy struggle for civil rights in twentieth-century America, the hard work of overcoming racial oppression in the economic, political, and personal spheres required many sacrifices while encountering numerous setbacks. An example of those minor setbacks came in the form of the acquittal by an Oxford, Mississippi federal jury in December 1963 of five defendants responsible for jailhouse beatings of civil rights activists. One of those activists, Lawrence Guyot, denounced the fraudulent verdict. Ella Baker, the inspiring godmother of numerous civil rights organizations, counseled Guyot to "look beyond this foolishness. Don't let it stop you."[55]

Looking beyond the foolishness of an imperial culture will require, as it did to some degree in the black freedom struggle, the laborious and mundane tasks of building solidarity across various constituencies, countries, and continents and constructing authentic communities of resistance and change. The patience and long-term commitments necessary for such efforts may seem overwhelming, especially when confronting the fear and paranoia of an imperial culture and the immobilization it fosters. Yet, we cannot eschew social involvement without risking the further alienation inherent in privatized existence. Although afflicted with the dross and duress of imperial and civic enclosures and in the face of weak citizenship, there is still evidence that citizens in the United States want to connect with each other and those elsewhere struggling to realize a life free of injustice and oppression. For, "if we remain silent in the face of cruelty, injustice, and oppression," argues Paul Rogat Loeb, "we sacrifice part of our soul. In this sense, we keep on acting because by doing so we affirm our humanity – the core of who we are and what we hold in common with others."[56] To find those common connections at the local and global level is at the root of efforts by citizen movements examined in the next chapter.

3 Afflicted solidarities
Contradictions in local and global citizen movements

Solidarity is the awareness of a common humanity and global citizenship and the voluntary acceptance of the responsibilities which go with it. It is the conscious commitment to redress inequalities both within and between countries. It is based on recognition that in an interdependent world, poverty or oppression anywhere is a threat to prosperity and stability everywhere.

World Commission on the Social Dimensions of Globalization

Solidarity with the poor is the only path that can lead our nation back to a vision of community than can effectively challenge and eliminate violence and exploitation. It invites us to embrace an ethics of compassion and sharing that will renew a spirit of loving kindness and communion that can sustain and enable us to live in harmony with the whole world.

bell hooks

Situated in an imperial culture that attempts to wall off its citizens in a variety of physical and psychological gated communities, people still yearn for social connections. Attempting to make those connections through social involvement activates forms of solidarity on local, national, and transnational levels. Yet, even in those acts of local and global solidarity, it is difficult to escape the contradictions embedded in our national incubator of imperialism. The afflictions that accompany U. S. imperial dominance abroad, i.e. the arrogance of power, the missionary zeal of self-righteousness, the falsely confident over-reach, are often replicated in the well-intentioned solidarity efforts of citizen movements at home. This chapter will consider the contradictions in local and global citizen movements, taking into account both the afflicted solidarities that infect lives in a dying empire and the variety of other solidarities that attempt to transcend and even transform that empire.

Before examining specific volunteer citizen movements from Habitat for Humanity sponsored housing construction in New Orleans to the anti-sweatshop campaigns originating in the United States, I want to explore briefly the relationship between the kind of ethical and political responsibility that motivates these citizen movements. Finding common humanity in the face of so many historical and social barriers is not easy given the proliferation of imperial impediments as noted in the previous chapter. Yet, starting with a sense of empathy and ethics and developing into an awareness of social and economic connection, solidarity can find expression from the local to global. While ethical responsibility can be immobilized by guilt and restricted by charity, it may rise to a sense that the parameters of power and privilege can be transcended by forms of solidarity and political responsibility.[1]

Enacting political responsibility in the confines of an imperial culture can lead one to a dizzying array of citizen campaigns. Beyond the slogan of "thinking globally and acting locally" lies the larger issue of how the local and global are interpenetrated by conditions and contradictions that challenge even the most committed of political activists. The desire to confront the most egregious acts of omission and commission by imperial policies is laudable even when acknowledging the limitations of that confrontation. In reviewing my own engagement with Habitat for Humanity in New Orleans and numerous campaigns of the anti-sweatshop movement, I intend to reveal not only the dynamics and difficulties of such citizen movements but also to discuss the contradictions and afflictions of local/global solidarities.

It was out of a sense of ethical/political responsibility that I traveled to a Hurricane Katrina devastated New Orleans in the summer of 2007 to volunteer to build much needed housing. In the trailer for an imaginary YouTube video diary of my first work day as a volunteer for Habitat for Humanity at Musician's Village in the Upper Ninth Ward of New Orleans, here are the fleeting images that would stand out: waiting on the street behind a trash truck in my cousin's car while a neighborhood African-American woman passed out bottles of water to the black man and woman collecting the rubbish; being inundated by white Baptist church volunteers at the worksite, including a young woman named Buffy from Mississippi who, to my untrained Yankee ears, sounded like a brassier version of Sissy Spacek's Loretta Lynn; standing on a ladder in the blazing sun and withering humidity with buckets of my sweat mixed with the paint I was applying to the siding of the shot-gun-style house that our Habitat work crew was completing; sharing lunch with a group of teachers from a Minneapolis suburb while a contingent of Baptists conducted a Bible-reading session; walking back to my cousin's house after a shortened work day in mid-afternoon and witnessing two burly black cops rousting three teenage African-Americans who were just twenty yards in front of me.

So, there you have it: kindness; duty; charity; piety; and police harassment; mixing the sacred and profane, the ordinary and extraordinary, in the liminal space of one mile and limited time of one six-hour slice of June 11, 2007, my first day as a Habitat volunteer in New Orleans. What is also evident from my experiences that day and the nature of the Habitat rebuilding effort are the roles of race, class, gender, and religion. The inescapable reality of my whiteness in a majority black neighborhood, my middle-class status in a low-income area, indeed my foreign presence, was a reminder that I was, as were most of the other Habitat volunteers, little more than a philanthropic visitor. Whatever the good intentions, there were social, political, and economic problems that I could hardly address in a fundamental way. To some extent, then, the Habitat experience could be seen as a template for both the possibilities and the impediments for not only rebuilding New Orleans but also for harnessing the imagination and will to build another world.

In both the rebuilding of New Orleans and building of another world there is a fundamental spiritual component, an integral element of ethical responsibility. However, the degree to which that spirituality is nurtured or constrained by religious dogma is important to discern. Habitat, in particular, is rooted in a specific Christian religiosity. For example, there is an intimate connection between Habitat's mission to supply affordable housing to low-income people while offering service opportunities for its volunteers, reflected in what is called the "theology of the hammer." For the founder of Habitat, Millard Fuller, the hammer is viewed "as an instrument to manifest God's love."[2] This faith-based orientation has managed to attract a wide variety of religious, corporate, and individual support. Founded by Fuller in 1976 in Americus, Georgia, Habitat for Humanity has grown to a billion-dollar operation, constructing over 200,000 houses in ten countries. Certainly, Habitat's high profile as a volunteer organization has been aided by the involvement of former President, Jimmy Carter. Also, the catastrophes of Hurricane Katrina and Asian tsunamis have raised public awareness about the pressing need for housing.

In New Orleans, church affiliation with Habitat recently reached a high watermark, so to speak, with the announcement in 2007 of a five-year initiative called the "Baptist Crossroads Project." Mobilizing both human and financial resources, Baptist churches in New Orleans and around the South, already evident during my time at Musician's Village, have pledged to build 60 houses over the next five years. The pastor of the First Baptist Church in New Orleans, who initiated the "Crossroads Project" called it "a response to the challenge of Jesus Christ to love our neighbors as ourselves." Beyond the religious commitment, he added that the Crossroads Project will "address substandard housing and poverty in our community by helping hard-working people move from renting into home ownership."[3]

While both Habitat and the Crossroads Project manifest certain qualities of a social gospel, there are also evident elements of "middle-class paternalism" and individualistic spirituality that, from the perspective of sociologist Ananta Kumar Giri, emphasize "individual salvation and self-realization rather than integral transformation of self and society."[4] On the other hand, another study of Habitat asserts that it "is unreasonable to expect Habitat to become the kind of neighborhood-based housing development entity promoted by housing advocates for the poor."[5] Nevertheless, Giri contends that in Habitat "the discourse of conscience is articulated more clearly than the discourse of rights."[6] While Habitat "has tapped a vein of compassion that is not often visible in a society that glorifies self-interest and materialism," it "does little to empower low income communities to deal collectively with their housing problems."[7] Furthermore, "the house that Habitat erects is not only an altar of God's love but also a panopticon of middle class values and control."[8]

Habitat's selection process for families to qualify for a twenty-year no interest $75,000 mortgage is very rigorous, eliminating almost nine out of ten applicants who fail to demonstrate credit-worthiness. Of course, for many low-income families and people of color the economic system has built-in mechanisms that discriminate against any asset accumulation, let alone financial solvency.[9] Musicians, in particular, have encountered difficulties in sustaining or even generating fiscal responsibility. It is not surprising, therefore, that the applications of some New Orleans musicians for Habitat housing in Musicians Village have been denied. Trying to counter the criticisms, Habitat has undertaken a program to help musicians deal with the credit ratings and creditors.

The inspiration for Musician's Village came from New Orleans musicians, Harry Connick, Jr. and Branford Marsalis. Shortly after their December 2005 announcement of the project, Habitat acquired eight acres of land in the Upper Ninth. Additional purchase of land was added to the core area. During my June sojourn as a Habitat volunteer in Musician's Village, there were almost forty houses completed with a projection of a total of seventy-three single-family homes, five elder-friendly duplexes, a toddler-friendly park, and the Ellis Marsalis Center for Music. A majority of the completed or nearly completed single houses at the time of my volunteer work had been assigned to musicians. Money for Musician's Village has come from concerts by such groups as the Dave Mathews Band and Little Feat. Corporate sponsors have also donated, including the oil companies BP America and Shell.

Corporate donations, in particular, raise some concerns about Habitat's rather indiscriminate acceptance of such corporate giving, especially in light of the tight regulations over the selection process for applicants for Habitat housing. Something seems a little amiss when Habitat NOLA blithely accepts money from oil companies who have been responsible for such environmental devastation in the New Orleans region. The destruction of wetlands south of New Orleans and the continuing pollution from Baton Rouge to New Orleans in the region known as "Cancer Alley" should have made Habitat, perhaps, a tad more rigorous and environmentally conscious in taking corporate money.

On another level, Habitat's construction operation seems to overlook the contradictions that may accompany the origin of materials used in building Habitat houses or the kind of labor that Habitat employs beyond its volunteers. For example, one day during my volunteer time at Musician's Village our crew unloaded sheetrock for one of the houses that was nearing completion. The Habitat driver who had transported the sheetrock from the warehouse indicated that all the sheetrock was from China. When I inquired about why Habitat would purchase sheetrock from China when there were numerous sheetrock producers in the U. S. employing union labor, I was told that the sheetrock was purchased from a vendor that Habitat regularly utilized. As far as the installation of sheetrock in Habitat homes, this was a matter of subcontracting. According to our Habitat work coordinator on site, the subcontractor was Mexican American, not at all surprising given the large number of Mexican Americans who do drywall. However, it was unclear whether this guy's crew was composed of primarily documented or undocumented workers. Given a 2006 joint study by Boalt Hall and Tulane University about "Labor and Human Rights in New Orleans" which found that twice the numbers of undocumented workers were installing drywall in post-Katrina New Orleans, it was likely that undocumented workers were indirectly employed by Habitat.[10]

Subcontracting other jobs for Habitat houses, such as excavation and laying of the foundations, also opened up the possibility of unfair labor practices. Contractors in the New Orleans region could easily take advantage of the lack of state minimum wage laws and the Bush Administration's rescinding of federal wage standards to hire undocumented workers and pay them one-third to one half what the going rate might be, along with denying them any health care or other benefits. While I was assured by the Habitat communications director that Habitat meets regularly with its qualified subcontractors, the overwhelming number of Latino personnel at Musician's Village helping with excavation and laying of the concrete foundations could easily have been undocumented workers. For an ostensible social justice organization, such as Habitat, to not pay special attention to the treatment and status of its hired help was, to my mind, a grave matter.

Of course, Habitat also relies on its volunteers, both short-term and long-term, to build its houses. As a consequence of the devastation of Katrina and the neglect and incompetence of the federal government in particular, Habitat has grown enormously in the New Orleans area. From a pre-Katrina full-time staff of two to a present fifty with twenty-five AmeriCorps kids, Habitat is a massive operation attracting both church groups and students in large numbers. Especially over the spring break, students in the thousands flocked to New Orleans Habitat. Such interest in service certainly owes something to Habitat's reputation and the continuing tragedy facing New Orleans and the Gulf Region. On the other hand, as noted by Craig Rimmerman, "service activity is devoid of politics and therefore is a relatively empty way of tackling complex structural issues that arise out of the conditions that prompt service activity in the first place."[11] While it may be true that Habitat and many of its volunteers are aware of these complex structural issues on a local, national, and, indeed, global level, the apolitical orientation seems to guarantee that the service rendered is contained within an eleemosynary enclave. In other words, because of its lack of advocacy, Habitat's civic engagement is politically circumscribed.

On the other hand, when corporate CEOs and even President Bush can parachute into the Habitat sites in New Orleans, questions arise about

Habitat's ultimate political and practical efficacy.[12] The constant turnover of volunteers and the participation of unskilled volunteers, like me, create problems for the quick and efficient construction of new houses. There were numerous occasions when many of us working on pounding in joist flooring had to redo the boards because of inexact measurements and certain levels of ineptitude. Beyond the varying levels of skills, the diverse political orientations and sense of mission did not translate into a larger commitment for federal low-income housing programs. In fact, I had a memorable luncheon debate with a conservative financial planner from Tulsa who believed that the private sector was more efficacious when it came to delivering services, something I challenged with a reference to federal programs such as Social Security and private sector companies such as Enron. In any case, irrespective of varying political opinions, people did gravitate to Habitat out of a fundamental concern to help others in need.

Among those drawn to New Orleans Habitat were some who had family connections to the city and others who had either some or no knowledge of New Orleans. I worked with two volunteers, one a medical student at LSU whose family lived in New Orleans and just managed to weather Katrina, and the other a woman with Honduran background who worked in Philadelphia as a physical therapist and whose family lived outside of New Orleans. Both were committed to the idea of rebuilding New Orleans. Those of us who only knew New Orleans previously as tourists came to Habitat because of a commitment to overcoming the lack of low-income housing and to doing something to salvage the city. A group of eight staff members from Berklee School of Music in Boston and ten school employees from outside Minneapolis all seemed dedicated to, in the words of Giri, "come to terms with their identity as citizens and human beings in a society where structural changes in economy and polity in the last two decades have widened the gulf between the two – poverty and plenty – considerably."[13]

Those last two decades for New Orleans have seen increasing poverty and its attendant problems, especially among African-Americans. The 2004 U. S. Census listed the poverty rate in New Orleans at 35%, among the highest in the U. S., with 80% of those being black. While New Orleans and Louisiana state legislators looked to casinos for new revenue sources and quick fixes (and under-the-table bribes), public services and schools were allowed to deteriorate. As a consequence of continued economic hardship and lack of opportunities, crime and the murder rate soared in New Orleans. The poet and New Orleans resident Andrei Codrescu cites the following remarks of one victim of a carjacking who lost her child in the incident: "New Orleans is the most beautiful city in America, the most historic city, and the city with the most potential. But it is a city with a sickness."[14] Even with only half of its pre-Katrina population, homicides continue to plague the city. While I was staying with my cousin in the Bywater area of New Orleans, there were two close-by murders, one in the middle of the day not far from where I walked back from Musician's Village to my cousin's house.

Walking through the Upper Ninth as I did every day, I saw abandoned houses and numerous FEMA trailers which had inhabitants almost two years after Katrina. Katrina had managed to damage areas in New Orleans where over two-thirds of New Orleanians lived. The vast majority of those areas, such as the Lower Ninth, were exclusively inhabited by African-Americans who still remain displaced. There are an estimated 200,000 New Orleanians scattered around the country in cities such as Houston and Atlanta. Many of them previously rented their residences in New Orleans and are still unable to receive any financial help for returning to the city. The lack of affordable housing and the abandonment of public housing altogether only add to the question that I found nagging my pitiful efforts as a Habitat volunteer: "If we build it, for whom and what are we building?"

If the built environment and commitment to racial and economic justice are lacking, the precarious ecology of New Orleans certainly raises other concerns about the long-term viability of the city and the region. While there have been improvements in the levee system and strengthening of floodwalls and pumps, many of the same neighborhoods remain in danger of hurricane storms and surges. Without a serious environmental protection plan, similar to what the Dutch have accomplished with their low-lying landscape, New Orleans faces a bleak future. While New Orleanians, as Dan Baum suggests, "are excellent at the lost art of living in the moment," some future planning must be undertaken by those committed to rebuilding the city not as a playground for the rich or tourists who only care about Bourbon Street, getting drunk, and/or getting laid. A critique of New Orleans as a rebuilt playground can be found in the dystopic vision of Tulane University professor Lawrence Powell:

> Will this quirky and endlessly fascinating place become an X-rated theme park, a Disneyland for adults? Is it fated to be the place where Orlando embraces Las Vegas? That's the American Pompeii I apprehend rising from the toxic sludge deposited by Lake Ponchartain: an ersatz city, a veritable schlock and awe.[15]

Obviously, rebuilding New Orleans as a sustainable and just city will require the kind of imagination and political will and responsibility that, unfortunately, do not appear to exist, at least, among the governing class.

At the grassroots level there are definitely efforts to rebuild a more just and inclusive New Orleans. During the second day of my volunteer time, one of the musicians in Musician's Village gave a lunch break concert from the porch of his brightly colored pastel shot-gun-style house. Although originally Brazilian, he was a New Orleans resident and local musician for the last eight years. As he played to the Habitat volunteers, I was struck by his back-to-back renditions of "Stairway to Heaven" and "Knockin' on Heaven's Door." The latter Dylan lyric, while sung in Portuguese, just seemed to resonate with me at the time and does so even now. Knowing that he, like other Habitat house owners, had put in hundreds of hours of "sweat equity" and feeling the sweat run down my brow during that day and throughout the week, I realized that, even with all the contradictions plaguing Habitat and New Orleans, there were many good folks prepared to hammer on heaven's door in order to bring a little piece of heaven, however battered and compromised, down to that tenuous spot of earth known as New Orleans.

On the other hand, the good folks taking up the hammer to rebuild New Orleans, including the more community-based and radical Common Ground organization, were overwhelmed by the forms of "disaster capitalism" that were immediately employed to further exploit the poor and especially citizens of color in New Orleans. In her discussion of the impact of this "disaster capitalism," Naomi Klein points out that "the poorest citizens in the country subsidized the contractor bonanza twice – first when Katrina relief morphed into unregulated corporate handouts, providing neither decent jobs nor functional public services, and second when the few programs that directly assist the unemployed and working poor nationwide were gutted to pay those bloated bills."[16] The range of corporate parasites feasting on the post-Katrina tragedy of New Orleans, from Halliburton to Blackwater, demonstrated a deep connection to imperial practices in Iraq. However, as noted by one critic of the corporate "reconstruction" efforts, the cultural roots for such "segregation and racialization of space" run deeper than the malfeasance and incompetence of the Bush Administration. In effect, "the destruction and reconstruction of New Orleans compel us to confront the painful truth about how we have been actually governed in this society and to face up to the apocalypse on the installment plan that surrounds us as a result."[17]

The "apocalypse on the installment plan" that not only informs what transpired in New Orleans but also the economic and social devastation unleashed by the implosion of the housing bubble points to continuing contradictions about housing and capitalism which even well-intentioned reformers overlook. It is not surprising that the most dramatic increase in home ownership in modern America was in the period of the establishment of the American Century, a period that followed WWII and demarcated the imperial dominance by the United States.[18] Accompanying this housing boom was the federal funding of an extensive highway system that also helped to facilitate suburbanization. However, that federal funding of home ownership was particularly rife with discriminatory practices that favored whites at the expense of blacks, creating in the process additional inequities. As a consequence of recent predatory lending practices, those inequities have manifested themselves in the extensive foreclosures that have adversely distressed African-American and Latino households. Beyond having been three times more likely to have been victims of predatory loans than whites, African-American and Latino households have lost, according to a 2008 study by United for a Fair Economy, over $200 billion in assets.[19]

While it is hard to imagine how volunteer efforts, such as Habitat for Humanity, can address these overwhelming inequities, it is also difficult to see how providing home ownership to low-income families can expedite a transition away from the environmental unsustainability and cultural mystification that has surrounded such home ownership. Although Habitat's homes are generally a reasonable amount of square footage, "the average new house has doubled in size since 1970, even as the number of people living in it has steadily shrunk and the average density of the most recent housing developments in America is only two people per acre."[20] This is hardly a formula for environmental sustainability! Among the continuing mystifications about home ownership are those endemic to an imperial culture where possessive individualism informs the sense of isolation often sought in what sociologist Zygmunt Bauman calls "islands of intimacy." As he further notes, "homes have turned from shared playgrounds of love and friendship into the sites of territorial skirmishes, and from building sites of togetherness into the assemblies of fortified bunkers."[21] Beyond the slightly sentimental wistfulness of Bauman's insights and the limited efforts of "building sites of togetherness" found in some community-based housing groups, the link between deceptive capitalist practices, mortgages, and the erosion of the public and community by imperial policies is all too evident now. Hence, one must add to Klein's "disaster capitalism" the toxic mix of "deception capitalism."

Such deception capitalism even informs the citizen campaigns in the United States against global sweatshops. Certainly, in trying to take political responsibility as consumers of transnational corporate products, U. S. citizens have engaged in attempts at global solidarity. On the other hand, "a protest model that depends on criteria of consumption and public relations campaigns does not necessarily make garment manufacturing more publicly accountable or improve working conditions."[22] In fact, as we will see from the discussion below, the protests and campaigns against global sweatshops by citizens of the United States have, more often than not, been riddled by numerous strategic and political contradictions, contradictions that have scarred expressions of global solidarity even while undermining the necessary struggle by those in an imperial culture against the privileges and mystifications that define that culture.

The anti-sweatshop movement grew out of an increasing understanding by consumers and trade unions in the United States that corporate apparel manufacturers, driven by the logic of capitalism to lower labor costs, would outsource their factories to countries with poor people and poor working conditions. In the late 1990s Levi Strauss's "reorganization" resulted in closing down its U. S. plants, especially in El Paso, Texas, shedding over 6,000 workers in the process. Levi Strauss then began subcontracting in low-wage countries, including China, where it had previously shut down operations after questions were raised concerning human rights violations.[23] However, the lure of exceedingly low wage rates in China's special economic zones, which a 1998 study found range from 13 to 35 cents an hour, was too tempting to Levi Strauss and a host of other U. S. apparel corporations and retail clothing distributors, including Wal-Mart, Ralph Lauren, Ann Taylor,

Liz Claiborne, K-Mart, J. C. Penney, and the Limited.[24] In turn, many of these U. S. corporations then hid behind the deceptive rationale that they were not responsible for overseeing the conditions in these overseas factories since other contractors were involved. A Disney spokesperson, reacting to criticism concerning a Haitian factory that manufactured Disney apparel, defiantly demurred: "We don't employ anyone in Haiti."[25]

Yet, throughout the developing world, U. S. clothing manufacturers took advantage of the creation of export processing zones (EPZ) that remained invisible to U. S. consumers until the anti-sweatshop campaigns emerged. One example of an EPZ is the walled city of Rosario in the Philippines, ninety miles south of Manila, where manufacturing of such goods as Nike shoes, Gap pajamas, and Old Navy jeans were produced mostly by young women, laboring at least twelve hours a day under harsh conditions. According to one observer, "bathrooms (are) padlocked except during two fifteen minute breaks, during which time all workers have to sign in and out so management can keep track of their nonproductive time. Seamstresses at a factory sewing garments for the Gap, Guess, and Old Navy ... sometimes had to resort to urinating in plastic bags under their machines."[26] Such disciplinary regimes often reflected the orientation of or neglect by the national government.

In fact, many U. S. firms favored countries where the government was under the influence of imperial dominance or authoritarian rule. In this regard, it is instructive to follow the trajectory of Nike as it moved from one lower wage country to the next. As one analysis by an international security company noted: "Nike tends to favor strong governments. For example, Nike was a major producer in both Korea and Taiwan when these countries were under military rule."[27] Furthermore, as both Korea and Taiwan moved away from military rule and U. S. domination and towards independent militant unions, Nike sought out more "stable" governments, essentially moving to authoritarian and low-wage environments in Indonesia, Vietnam, and China. As a consequence of media glare in the United States and a consumer campaign against its labor practices, Nike was forced to deploy a public relations counter-attack that featured a high-profile tour by Andrew Young, former Ambassador to the UN under President Jimmy Carter and a well-known civil rights advocate. While Young reported that all of the Nike factories he visited in Vietnam, Indonesia, and China were without "evidence ... of widespread or systematic abuse or mistreatment of workers," the director of Vietnam Labor Watch, Thuyen Nguyen, commented that Young's "tours were conducted by management, and he talked to workers through Nike interpreters. Workers are not about to complain in front of the boss, especially in authoritarian countries where workers labeled troublemakers can be fired and jailed."[28]

As NGOs continued to contradict Nike's claims, a growing campaign against Nike in the late 1990s led the company to expand its Corporate Social Responsibility (CSR) department to over ninety members. Appearing at global meetings and arranging for audits of their factories, Nike and other U. S. apparel manufacturers engaged in protracted deceptions aimed at defusing and misleading the anti-sweatshop movements in the United States. On the other hand, striking Vietnamese Nike factory workers and labor rights activists in China tried to spotlight the continuing lack of decent wages and working conditions. According to one Chinese observer, "the retailers and their suppliers are playing an elaborate game. They only want to reassure customers, not to improve conditions."[29] There were some instances where Nike, responding to pressure by the anti-sweatshop movement in the U. S., raised their minimum wage, especially in the 1990s in Indonesia. However, when Indonesian workers struck for better conditions, their leaders were fired and denounced as "troublemakers" by Nike in the local press.[30] Thus, Nike, hiding behind its CSR shield in the United States, persisted in making life miserable for its employees abroad.

Another high-profile anti-sweatshop campaign in the 1990s was organized by the U. S.-based National Labor Committee (NLC) against Gap Inc. and its garment supplier in El Salvador, Mandarin International. After the majority women workers at Mandarin established an independent union, the company not only resisted recognition of the union but also retaliated against prominent union members. The NLC-Gap campaign went into high gear, sponsoring a tour in 1995 featuring one of the fired Mandarin International female workers. Feeling the pressure from an effective media campaign, Gap signed an agreement with NLC to oversee the fair resolution of any labor disputes in El Salvador and to work towards humane working conditions at Mandarin. However, according to one study of what actually occurred with the workers on the ground,

> while the campaign, its resolution, and the independent monitoring project have served to assure the integrity of Gap Inc.'s brand name and has made Gap Inc. retail outlets safe once more for progressive-minded shopping, their effects on the shop floor have been either ambiguous or, in some cases, unqualifiedly negative.[31]

In the late 1990s college students took up the fight against global sweatshops which produced their school apparel. The primary national organization that grew out of the local anti-sweatshop campaigns on campuses, United Students Against Sweatshops (USAS), was founded in 1998. Bringing together more than 180 campus groups, USAS activists recognized that, in the words of one student anti-sweatshop protester at University of North Carolina-Chapel Hill, "we can think of the university itself as a brand, a logo that students consume."[32] Beyond the university logo, the centrality of the youth market to consumer capitalism and corporate advertising informed the consciousness and political sensibilities of many of those in USAS. According to Liana Molina from Santa Clara University, "the system is completely dependent on us going out and spending money on all this crap."[33] Nevertheless, by foregrounding the role of the privileged consumer in the United States, such anti-sweatshop campaigns have had the potential to reinforce the notion that agency is based in the United States and that contention occurs only at the heights of political economy. They also potentially reinforce the conception that local conditions are created by global forces rather than through struggles and negotiations in all sites.[34]

On the other hand, because of concerted efforts by North American students to visit global sweatshop sites in the South and to develop on-going relationships with garment industry workers, the actual expressions of solidarity mitigated, to some extent, the belief that anti-sweatshop campaigns were the province alone of privileged U. S. consumers. In addition to traveling to Mexico, Nicaragua, and Honduras during the first half of 2000 to investigate conditions inside and outside garment factories, USAS delegations paid attention to workers' struggles to achieve self-determination on and off the job. Eschewing the discourse of victimization that often accompanies images of third world workers, USAS activist Molly McGrath emphasizes that the organization has "tried to change the rhetoric to show sweatshop workers with more agency and power."[35] Some of the reporting of these visits to the global South on USAS websites highlights the role of specific workers in forming independent unions and reflecting on their involvement as young women and men in labor struggles. "Represented this way, with the emphasis on their humanity and their power rather than on their suffering, sweatshop workers seem more real, even to a privileged First World audience."[36]

In conjunction with the visitations to sweatshops in the global South, USAS activists engaged in a wave of anti-sweatshop sit-ins in 2000. From Penn to Oregon, Wisconsin to Tulane, students demonstrated not only against campus corporate connections to companies like Nike and the selling of their "swoosh" logo to universities but also in favor of college commitments to the Worker Rights Consortium (WRC) instead of the more corporate-friendly Fair Labor Association (FLA). Although many university administrations refused the demand to leave the FLA and join the WRC, some going so far as to break up USAS sit-ins by brutal police intervention, other universities signed up with the WRC. Nonetheless, the economic lobbying and political power of corporations like Nike resulted in applying pressure to enforce their apparel arrangements with specific institutions of higher learning. An especially egregious example of Nike bullying came when CEO Phil Knight withdrew a $30 million dollar offer to the University of Oregon for a new sports stadium after Oregon joined the WRC. After the administration at Oregon reversed its membership in the WRC, Knight revived his offer.[37]

Nike also tried to buy the goodwill of citizens and youth in various cities around the United States from Portland to New York City. Nike proposed a gift of half a million dollars in cash and athletic gear to the deficit-ridden Portland School Board. Although the Board eventually succumbed to Nike's offer, there was intense debate and division. One of the Asian members of the Board confessed his own "moral and ethical dilemma," noting that "Nike contributed the money so my children can have a better education, but at whose expense? At the expense of children who work for six cents an hour?"[38] The contradictions between Nike's operations abroad and conditions in the U. S. are especially evident in depressed inner cities where youth are special targets of Nike marketing and sponsored sports programs. One community organizer in the Bronx contended that

> we got really angry because they (Nike) were taking so much money from us here and then going to other countries and exploiting people even worse. ... We want our kids to see how it affects them here on the streets, but also how here on the streets affects people in Southeast Asia."[39]

As a result of this anger, a campaign was organized by Latino and Black youth from the Bronx and other parts of New York City to collect old Nike shoes and dump them at the Nike Town Store in mid-town Manhattan. At almost the exact same time this high-profile demonstration took place on fashionable Fifth Avenue, a teenage boy murdered another teenager for his Nike Air Jordans elsewhere in the city.[40]

In the face of such tragedies, consumer awareness of Nike's exploitative practices at home and abroad led to increased efforts by cities and towns throughout the United States in the late 1990s to sign on to anti-sweatshop campaigns by passing local ordinances requiring city governments to purchase non-sweatshop manufactured uniforms for its public employees, including members of the police and fire departments.[41] To some extent, USAS and sweatshop garment workers have gained incremental victories against corporate giants like Nike at the site of subcontractors in the global South. One such success was at the Kukdong International factory in Atlixco de Puebla, Mexico. With contracts for Nike and Reebok to produce sweatshirts for numerous universities, including Oregon and Michigan, Kukdong workers, in contact with USAS activists, formed an independent union to voice their grievances about poor food, wages, and working conditions. After the workers went on strike, students from USAS formed picket lines around Nike stores in a number of cities and used the WRC agreements to enlist university administrations to lobby Nike and Reebok. With this pressure and additional political intervention, the Kukdong workers won a collective bargaining agreement.[42] Another example of the symbiotic solidarity of USAS and Mexican garment workers resulted in elevating issues around women workers from inserting language in one independent union contract outlawing sexual harassment and guaranteeing equal representation among union officers.[43]

Certainly, these examples and others reflect an enactment of solidarity that does not diminish the agency of third world people, especially women, in the global sweatshop. On the other hand, certain other high-profile anti-sweatshop campaigns illuminate the contradictions of racialized and gendered imperial consumption and its afflicted solidarities. Perhaps the most notorious case of such contradictions and afflicted solidarity is the consumer campaign that targeted talk show host Kathie Lee Gifford and her clothing line produced at Wal-Mart's subcontracting sweatshops in Central America and the United States.[44] Without going into all of the details of the campaign led by Charles Kernaghan of the NLC in the mid-1990s, what transpired reinforced the sense that the story was ultimately about well-intentioned U. S. consumers and transnational corporations. Instead of emphasizing the agency of Latina and Asian women workers, Gifford became the crucial change agent. As pointedly summarized by academic investigator, Ethel Brooks, "the entire debate, the entire campaign, was translated into one about whether American power, American idealism, and American democratic ideals could be redeemed. The redemption would be symbolic, and it would be embodied by Kathie Lee Gifford," a symbol of how "the aberrant space of the global sweatshop could be civilized through the practice of transnational, redemptive white womanhood."[45]

In displacing the focus from how real solidarity with local struggles and agents in the garment industry of the global South can be developed, U. S. imperial culture and its privileged consumers reinforce the fiction that deception capitalism and its globalist flacks herald concerning lifting the living standard of poor third world people. Again, Brooks punctures the imperial missionary arrogance embedded in such claims: "This process of salvation in solidarity's name is ... a reenactment of earlier (colonial) salvations – of an entire history of 'taking up the white man's burden.'"[46] Against this imperial affliction stands the alternative ethical and political responsibility found in those inspiring moments when USAS activists and their co-workers in the global justice movement could realize, albeit in a temporary manner, the solidaristic connections between the local and global. In their May Day missive to the USAS, the Kukdong workers in Mexico articulated an authentic solidarity of ethical and political responsibility:

> We know that at times our faith is lost, but as long as we are together with each other, we will give each other the spirit to move forward, because we know what we do will be good for others in any part of the world.[47]

This strong sense of solidarity is, thus, related to the fundamental realization that we are significantly now interdependent in such a globalized and transnational existence. Such "genuine solidarity with the poor," argues bell hooks, "is rooted in the recognition that the fate of the poor both locally and globally will to a grave extent determine the quality of life for those who are lucky enough to have class privilege."[48] Alongside that class privilege, one encounters the afflictions of residing in an imperial culture which, in turn, make it difficult to express and act on a sense of mutual solidarity. What is required by those with class privilege is what the sociologist Alberto Melucci calls "altruistic action." He defines altruistic action as "a form of action characterized by a voluntary bond of solidarity among those who participate in it, and by the fact that they do not derive any direct economic benefit for that participation."[49] Yet, even forms of altruistic solidarity cannot overcome the perpetuation of power and privilege embedded in those relationships between citizens of an imperial country and those in third world countries. Moreover, it is hard to enact reciprocal relations that would lead to mutual solidarity in the face of overwhelming social and economic inequities.[50]

On the other hand, altruistic action and compassionate expressions of solidarity, especially with the poor both at home and abroad, reflect a commitment to ethical and political responsibility. Yet, the contradictions of joining citizen campaigns in the global labor market are, nonetheless, imposing. As observed by Naomi Klein,

> the challenges of a global labor market are too vast to be defined – or limited – by our interests as consumers. ... And while Westerners sweat over what kinds of shoes and shirts are most ethical to buy, the people sweating in the factories line their dorm rooms with McDonald's advertisements, paint "NBA Homeboy" murals on their doors and love anything with "Meeckey."[51]

Although our consciousness as ethical consumers may have been raised by the NLC damning documentary, *Mickey Mouse Goes to Haiti*, the continuing depredations and seductions by U. S. corporations and imperial globalization confound and afflict even our best efforts at international or transnational solidarity. Thus, the question of "Whose globalization?", which frames the second part of this book, requires further investigation into how economic and geopolitical imperial policies and practices imperil and entrap citizens around the world. Understanding and contesting the imperial parameters of globalization from above should facilitate the formulation and development of globalization from below, a globalization based on transnational and mutual solidarity.[52]

Part II
Whose globalization?

4 U. S. military imperialism and the pursuit of global dominance

In a new era, we foresee that our military power will remain an essential underpinning of the global balance, but less prominently and in different ways. We see that the more likely demands for the use of our military forces may not involve the Soviet Union and may be in the Third World, where new capabilities and approaches may be required.

National Security Strategy of 1990

The hegemonism of the United States rests far more on its excessive military power than on the advantages of its economic system.

Samir Amin

In his rambling and rambunctious panegyric to the splendors of globalization, *The Lexus and the Olive Tree,* Thomas Friedman recalls the giddy triumphalism of the ideologues of the American Century. Much like Henry Luce, Friedman is convinced that only the United States can provide the leadership necessary to navigate the new computerized world order. Moreover, seemingly channeling Luce, Friedman asserts that "America, at its best, is not just a country. It's a spiritual value and role model."[1] Dating the new era of globalization and superpower dominance of the United States from the fall of the Berlin Wall and the Soviet Union, Friedman embraces the economic logic of neoliberalism with its deregulation and privatization without accounting for the attendant global inequities that follow in its footsteps. (There is more on this in Chapter 5.) On the other hand, Friedman, similar to the neo-conservatives of the New American Century, recognizes and revels in the interconnections between U. S. military prowess and economic power and prestige. "The hidden hand of the market," argues Friedman, "will never work without a hidden fist. McDonald's cannot flourish with McDonnell Douglas, the designer of the U. S. Air Force F-15. And the hidden fist that keeps the world safe for Silicon Valley's technologies to flourish is called the U. S. Army, Air Force, Navy, and Marine Corps."[2]

Implicit in this brazen formulation is the more subtle interrelationship between coercion and consensus that defines the operation of hegemony as a ruling system. In addition, this formulation also reveals the critical dialectic between the macro operation of imperial geopolitics and military strategies and the micro functions of imperial capitalism. Attempting to situate this dialectic in a historical context of the unraveling of U. S. hegemony, beginning in the mid-1970s, and the efforts to restore some forms of global dominance from this period up to the present point will be the focus of this chapter and the following one. While not overlooking those economic functions of capital penetration and financial sabotage (to be covered in Chapter 5), this chapter will examine in some detail the variety of geopolitical military strategies enacted by the United States from the 1970s to the present, especially in Latin America and in the wars with Iraq (up to the 2003 invasion) and Afghanistan. Those strategies have run the gamut from covert operations to low-intensity warfare to outright military intervention. By first surveying certain moments of imperial interference in the sovereignty of other nations, I intend to provide the necessary backdrop to determine the lingering efforts of establishing U. S. imperial and global dominance in a world where U. S. hegemony is withering.

Of course, relying on military strategies, whether through direct or indirect interventions, complicates, if not confounds, the imposition of global hegemony. There can be no doubt that a more emboldened imperialism and militarism have been the hallmarks of recent U. S. geopolitical strategy. Critic Carl Boggs has traced that "revitalized U. S. imperialism and militarism" to a number of factors:

> a growing mood of American exceptionalism in international affairs, the primacy of military force in U. S. policy, arrogation of the right to intervene around the world, the spread of xenophobic patriotism, (and) further consolidation of the permanent war system.[3]

However, as acknowledged by Boggs and other critics of U. S. imperialism, such imperialism and militarism not only exacerbate and/or even create local insurgencies, but also the constant saber-rattling by the U. S. produces global resistance, similar to the massive world-wide mobilization of millions that occurred on the eve of the U. S. military invasion of Iraq in February 2003. In effect, the pursuit of imperial dominance through geopolitical militarism contains contradictions that further undermine hegemony abroad and legitimacy at home, reinforcing, in the process, a crisis of empire. That crisis of empire, argues Walden Bello, "bodes well not only for the rest of the world. It may also benefit the people of the United States. It opens up the possibility of Americans relating to other people as equal and not as masters."[4]

Yet, in reviewing the last several decades of U. S. foreign policy, especially in Latin America and the Middle East, it is clear that the ruling elite in Washington continue to believe in their right to determine the fate of others. In fact, the policies enacted by the decision-makers in DC have become even more harried and brutal in light of those others who have the temerity to exercise their right of self-determination. In the aftermath of the crushing defeat in Vietnam and the crisis of legitimacy confronting the ruling circles in the U. S., imperial policy suffered some setbacks, including the erosion of the pre-rogatives of the imperial presidency with the congressional passage in 1973 of the War Powers Act. Nonetheless, neither presidents nor the Pentagon felt constrained by the congressional restrictions even though the pursuit of geo-political military strategies varied to a certain degree, depending on the soft or hard imperialist policy adopted by particular presidents. However, in Latin America, the bipartisan tradition of intervention often obliterated those differences.

The continuity of Washington's support for counterinsurgency and covert intervention in Latin America was evident in the sponsorship of paramilitary and military death squads in countries like El Salvador and Guatemala in the presidencies of both Kennedy and Reagan. However, while Kennedy's osten-sible support for such death squads was perpetrated as a counter to the influence of Castro-like revolutions, Reagan's support was a more aggressive rollback of any attempt by Latin American governments to stake out an independent policy from U. S. imperial dominance. As argued by historian Greg Grandin,

> It was Central America, and Latin America more broadly, where an insurgent New Right first coalesced, as conservative activists used the region to respond to the crisis of the 1970s, a crisis provoked not only by America's defeat in Vietnam but by a deep economic recession and a culture of skeptical antimilitarism and political dissent that spread in the war's wake.[5]

The roots of the crisis, I want to suggest, can also be traced to the policies of the Nixon Administration in its efforts to reorder the economic and geo-political global framework. As a consequence of the inflationary spiral unleashed by the immense spending on the war in Indochina, Nixon aban-doned the Bretton Woods agreements, going off the gold standard and allowing the U. S. dollar to float. The long-term implication of this "dollar diplomacy" was profound not only for the emergence of U. S.-led casino capitalism with its attendant third world indebtedness (to be discussed in more detail in the next chapter) but also for the primacy of petro-dollars and the impact on capital and oil flows through the Middle East.[6] However, in more immediate geopolitical terms, Nixon and Henry Kissinger, his national security advisor, adopted a strategy of détente that privileged big-power and bi-polar politics while threatening to crush any deviance from allegiances to the two dominant ideological camps. Thus, any attempt by those in Latin America or elsewhere to seek a path outside the U. S. or Soviet orbit was considered a direct challenge to this imperial framework.

In particular, Nixon and Kissinger committed the U. S. to do everything possible to derail the reform government of Salvador Allende in Chile. From the outset of the election of Allende in 1970, Nixon instructed the CIA to organize campaigns of economic subversion and to foster ties to right-wing elements in the Chilean military. Coordinating a vast array of U. S. business interests which had a financial stake in eliminating Allende and various other governmental agencies that could penetrate civil society in Chile, Kissinger oversaw the extensive covert operation to "destabilize" Chile. According to one of Kissinger's staff on the National Security Council, Kissinger "saw Allende as being a far more serious threat than Castro. If Latin America ever became unraveled, it would never happen with a Castro. Allende was a living example of democratic social reform in Latin America … Chile scared him."[7] The dogged and devious actions employed by the Nixon Administration paid off on September 11, 1973 when the military, led by General Augusto Pinochet, overthrew and murdered not only Allende, but thousands of other Chileans. Accompanying the tragic deaths of so many Chileans was the eradication of any reform possibilities and the institutionalization of an ideologically rigid version of "free market" capitalism, designated by Naomi Klein as an economic "shock doctrine."[8]

The overthrow of the Allende government did not, however, impede efforts by others in Latin America from backing insurgencies against unpopular and dictatorial governments. In this regard the victory of the Sandinistas in Nicaragua in 1979 demonstrated that U. S.-favored dictators like the Somozas could not hold back a revolutionary upsurge when it permeated broad sectors of the population. Although the Carter Administration tried to forestall the Sandinistas from coming to power, it was the Reagan Administration that committed itself to doing everything in its power to destroy the potential for the success of Sandinista reforms. Those reforms, aimed in particular at the rural and urban poor, not only overturned decades of elite rule in Nicaragua but also defied the cozy client relationships that the U. S. counted on as part of their imperial dominance in all of Central America. It is not surprising, therefore, that U. S. opponents of the Sandinistas were as blunt about what was at stake in Nicaragua. "Washington believes," pontificated a conservative church advocate for the Reagan Administration,

> that Nicaragua must serve as a warning to the rest of Central America to never again challenge U. S. hegemony, because of the enormous economic and political costs. It's too bad that the (Nicaraguan) poor must suffer, but historically the poor have always suffered. Nicaragua must be a lesson to others.[9]

While the key to undermining the Sandinista government was sponsoring the Contras, a collection of remnants from Somoza's national guard who, with the encouragement of Reagan operatives, wrecked havoc on the country while murdering and torturing Sandinista supporters, the U. S. also pursued a strategy of influencing civil society in order to support and foster political opposition to the Sandinistas. Forced initially into covert campaigns against the Sandinistas because of active domestic opposition from religious and peace groups and their allies in Congress, the Reagan Administration pursued a wide range of activities from economic embargoes to illicit fund-raising and arms brokering (embodied in the notorious Iran-Contra networks) to the internationally condemned mining of Nicaraguan harbors. At the same time, under the guise of "democracy promotion," the Sandinista government was kept under siege, losing in the process much of its capacity to deliver on its promises. Although the machinations of the Reagan Administration did face the resolute opposition by the Sandinistas, its international supporters, and the U. S.-based solidarity networks, such as Witness for Peace, the Reagan Administration eventually managed to bleed Nicaragua and to alienate its besieged population into abandoning the Sandinista government.[10]

While the bleeding in Nicaragua was, as a consequence of so-called low-intensity conflict, insidious but steady, the blood-letting in El Salvador and Guatemala was even more evident and massive during the 1980s. In order to stem the growth of guerilla movements in these two countries, the Reagan Administration relied on supporting atrocious counterinsurgency regimes. Among these was the vicious U. S.-trained Atlacatl Battalion whose 1981 massacre in the Salvadoran town of El Mozote resulted in the brutal execution of over 750 inhabitant, including women and children. Such massacres seemed even more routine in Guatemala. Between the years 1981 and 1983 the Guatemalan military executed over 100,000 indigenous peasants who were alleged to be guerilla supporters and, therefore, deserving of the murderous rage of the military. According to Greg Grandin, "U. S. allies in Central America during Reagan's two terms killed over 300,000 people, tortured hundreds of thousands, and drove millions into exile."[11] All of this horrendous murder and mayhem was rationalized by the Reagan Administration, especially by its U. N. ambassador, Jeanne Kirkpatrick, as absolutely essential to demonstrating the political and moral resolve of the United States to rid the world of those evil forces that fostered nefarious challenges to its imperial dominance.[12]

While outsourcing of imperial violence to military or paramilitary regimes in Latin America gained certain prominence as a strategy to re-assert U. S. dominance in the region, there were moments when outright U. S. military intervention was deemed necessary. When erstwhile ally and CIA protégé, Manuel Noriega, began to insist that Panama be given full control over the Panama Canal with the possible construction by Japan of another canal, President George H. W. Bush ordered 26,000 U. S. troops to invade the country with the ostensible purpose of overthrowing Noriega. In the process, thousands of Panamanian civilians were killed, especially in the indis-criminate bombing of Panama City. Calling the military operation "Just Cause" only further revealed the hypocrisy of a government whose Secretaries of Defense and State, Casper Weinberger and George Shultz, respectively, had been former executives of the American construction company, Bechtel, whose business interests in canal-building would suffer.[13] Beyond this direct and crude instrumental connection, the invasion provided exemplary evidence that the U. S. President would not hesitate to use direct military force in order to prove that the U. S. had the right to intervene militarily. As argued by Greg Grandin, "Just Cause not only broke with Washington's decades-long policy of delegating hemispheric administration to Latin American surrogates" but also facilitated the gearing up of the Pentagon for its mobilization in the first Gulf War.[14]

Although the Pentagon would not launch its attack until January 1991, President George H. W. Bush would be provided with a rationale by Saddam Hussein to go to war against Iraq in the summer of 1990. Saddam had been an ally and even CIA asset going back to the Baath Party's coup in 1963 against a left-wing Iraqi government. During the long war between Iraq and Iran (1980–8), the Reagan Administration had tilted heavily towards Iraq, equipping Saddam with the very chemical weapons and dual-use technology that were used later as a basis for enacting sanctions in the 1990s and for ideological posturing by the Bush Junior Administration. Even after the Iraq–Iran War ended, Saddam Hussein received favored treatment by Washington, despite the very evident human rights abuses, especially against the Kurds in northern Iraq. When Iraq massed tens of thousands of troops along the border with Kuwait in July 1990 as a response to Kuwaiti drilling under Iraqi territory and Kuwait's undercutting of OPEC's set price for crude oil, the U. S. response, conveyed by Ambassador April Glaspie, was that Iraq was justified in seeking to protect its oil production and pricing. On the specific confrontation with Kuwait concerning border matters, Ambassador Glaspie indicated that the U. S. had "no opinion." Viewing this as a "green light" for an invasion, the Iraqi military streamed across the border a week later. As a consequence of that invasion and despite months of attempted open and back-door diplomacy, undermined constantly by the Bush Administration, the U. S. built up a massive military presence in the region. After having achieved a degree of international and national consensus over Saddam's actions in Kuwait, actions distorted by Administration propaganda and mainstream media manipulation, the United States, with several allies, most significantly the British, attacked Iraqi forces and Iraq on January 16, 1991.[15]

The ensuing Gulf War was not just the case of playing international sheriff at the head of an organized posse confronting a universally recognized outlaw. Although clearly a reflection of U. S. bipartisan imperial policy in the region with its obsession with oil flows and the "special relationship" with Israel, the war on Iraq had multiple motivations from diverting attention from domestic crises to satisfying the demands of the insatiable military-industrial complex. That complex, in particular, with the fall of the Soviet Union, required new enemies to justify continuing extravagant expenditures for the Pentagon. Furthermore, the Pentagon and the National Security State were especially obsessed with overcoming what had been called the "Vietnam syndrome," a national reluctance to commit the military to extended geopolitical interventions. Yet, ironically, as noted by Douglas Kellner, what transpired in the Gulf War "was a classic expression of the

Vietnam syndrome, of a militarist compulsion to use U. S. military power to resolve political conflicts."[16] In order to build a consensus among a divided nation and Congress before the war, the Bush Administration and a compliant corporate media had painted Saddam as another Hitler, threatening not only the region but the whole world.

> Against the 'evil' Saddam and threatening Iraqis, the media thus posed images of the 'good' American soldier and powerful U. S. technology. In the nightly repetition of these positive images of U. S. troops valiantly protecting a foreign country from aggression, the need for a strong military was repeatedly pounded into the public's psyche.[17]

While the American public rallied behind its troops, the rest of the world saw the vicious unleashing of techno-war, a form of high-tech slaughter that did much to erode any legitimacy claimed by the Bush Administration for its war-making efforts. This was most evident in the massacre of retreating Iraqis from Kuwait in what became known as the "Highway of Death." Although the U. S. media were highly controlled by the military, images of this massacre did find some fleeting moments in television reporting. CNN showed the vehicular and human carnage littering the road from Kuwait City to the Iraq border. Nonetheless, CNN, at least for its U. S. audience, framed the devastation as just retribution for Iraqi torturers and thieves. Yet, it was clear to other reporters that this fleeing convoy of conscripts and civilians had been repeatedly bombarded by U. S. warplanes using cluster bombs and anti-personnel weapons. Even British military officials decried this slaughter, bridling at how U. S. pilots had boasted about their participation in what they called "The Turkey Shoot."[18]

While the brutal results of techno-war and the political equivocation of the Bush Administration concerning the invasion of Iraq and overthrow of Saddam undermined its claims of moral legitimacy for its actions, the prosecution of the Gulf War also demonstrated the awful long-term physical damage to civilians, soldiers, and the environment of the whole Gulf region. In particular, the use by the Pentagon of depleted uranium, a radioactive substance intended to harden tank and war plane projectiles, caused irreparable harm to all those in the immediate bombardment area. In the Gulf War, according to Professor Doug Rokke, an ex-director of the Pentagon's Depleted Uranium Project,

> well over 300 tons were fired. An A-!0 Warthog attack aircraft fired over 900,000 rounds. Each individual round was 300 grams of solid uranium 238. When a tank fired its shells, each round carried over 4,500 grams of solid uranium. ... What happened in the Gulf was a form of nuclear warfare.[19]

That nuclear warfare contaminated tens of thousands of Iraqi civilians and even U. S. soldiers, giving rise to increased amounts of cancer among Iraqi

children and increased levels of disabilities to Gulf War veterans and defor-
mities to their children. Even though eventually condemned by the United
Nations as a weapon of mass destruction, depleted uranium remained in the
Pentagon's arsenal and was used extensively in the 1999 bombing campaign
by the U. S. in the Balkans.[20]

Beyond the long-term effects of depleted uranium, U. S. policy in Iraq
during the 1990s continued a state of war on the country with the use of
periodic bombing runs and the imposition of economic sanctions, both lacking
in international support with the notable exception of the British government.
Clinton's hard-line position on these air incursions and the controversial
sanctions, estimated by numerous human rights agencies to have resulted in
as many as a half-million deaths of mostly vulnerable children under the age
of 5 years old, did little to dislodge Saddam Hussein from power but much to
harm the Iraqi civilian population. According to Denis Halliday, the U. N.
humanitarian coordinator who resigned in disgust over the continuing sanctions, "We are in the process of destroying an entire society. It is as simple
and as terrifying as that."[21] This slow bleeding of Iraqi society, justified by
Clinton's Secretary of State, Madeleine Albright, as "worth it," was, however,
not enough for the neoconservatives in the Project for a New American Century who, in their 1998 letter to Clinton, pushed for a removal of Saddam's
regime. Arguing that "American policy cannot continue to be crippled by
a misguided insistence on unanimity in the U. N. Security Council," these
neocons would come to power in the disputed election of George W. Bush in
2000. Sidestepping the U. N. Security Council after failing to achieve a
majority vote for its invasion of Iraq, the Bush Administration shifted to a
unilateralism based on "coercion rather than consent, towards a more overtly
imperial vision, and towards reliance upon its unchallengeable military
power."[22]

Although that military power had first been deployed to Afghanistan,
supposedly in response to the Taliban's support for Osama bin Laden, the
history of U. S. involvement in Afghanistan and the actual prosecution of the
war once more demonstrated the duplicity and devastation of an imperial
policy that sought domination in an era of waning hegemony. That policy,
originally rooted in Cold War gamesmanship, had its covert conception in
1979 with the CIA supporting Afghan warlords and Muslim guerillas fighting
against a communist-sponsored government in Kabul. Working in the 1980s
with the Pakistan Inter-Services Intelligence (ISI) agency, the Reagan
Administration began funding those Muslim fundamentalists most favored
by the ISI, included among them, Osama bin Laden. When another virulent
fundamentalist group, the Taliban, began to achieve prominence in the
guerilla war in the 1990s, the U. S. under Clinton continued its support out of
the desire, among other reasons, to help U. S. oil companies construct a
pipeline that would avoid going through Iran.[23] The key U. S. oil company
involved in these dealings with the Taliban and other reactionary governments in Central Asia was Unocal.

Unocal had been actively engaged in doing business with repressive regimes throughout the world in their search for oil and natural gas reserves. From connections to military dictatorships in Burma and Indonesia, Unocal spread its oily tentacles throughout the third world. Having been part of a consortium of U. S. oil firms exploring potential gas and oil reserves in Central Asia, Unocal turned its attention to Afghanistan in the 1990s. Not averse to doing business with the Taliban, Unocal tried unsuccessfully to induce the Taliban as late as the summer of 2001 into making a deal for a major oil pipeline across the country. When talks broke off, there were rumblings in Washington that the Taliban would have to make way for a more pliable government.[24] Conveniently for the militarist-minded and oil-obsessed Bush Administration, bin Laden had located in Afghanistan. Inconveniently for the Afghan people and even former CIA Afghan allies, the Bush Administration needed to wage a demonstration war in Afghanistan that did more than seek retribution against bin Laden and al-Qaeda.

What has been pursued by the United States in Afghanistan is a form of punitive imperialism, which, on the one hand, claims rhetorically to be about precision bombing but, in reality, is about killing without remorse. Over the first year and continuing up to this very moment, various reports of bombings of wedding parties and family gatherings in Afghan villages have accumulated. One such example happened in a village north of Kandahar which was strafed by AC-130 gunships, resulting in the death of at least ninety-three civilians. The blunt response by one Pentagon official was that "the people were dead because we wanted them dead." Trying to avoid any further probing of the incident, then Secretary of Defense, Donald Rumsfeld, said, "I cannot deal with that particular village." In a June 28, 2002 *Los Angeles Times* story about such civilian deaths, one Afghan who had lost his wife, mother, and seven children in the U. S. bombing run of his village angrily lamented: "I put a curse on the Americans who did this. I pray they will have the tragedy in their lives that I have had in mine." Given such indiscriminate killing, it should not be surprising that U. S. policy in Afghanistan has only succeeded in re-legitimizing a guerilla insurgency, led by a renewed Taliban, creating further tragedies for the Afghan people and U. S. imperial policy.[25]

That imperial policy, awash in continuing delusions about the antiseptic precision of U. S. technology and the righteousness of using state terror to punish rogue terrorists, whether ensconced in national regimes or stateless insurgencies, remains a constant of U. S. geopolitical strategy irrespective of the tactical differences in presidential prerogatives. Basking in the short-lived success of the fall of Baghdad in April 2003, President Bush applauded the "new powers of technology" that allowed the U. S. "to strike an enemy force with speed and incredible precision. By a combination of creative strategies and advanced technologies, we are redefining war on our terms."[26] The imperial hubris expressed in such wishful thinking informs fundamental geopolitical thinking for superpowers like the United States and its Middle East strategic ally, Israel, especially in their callous disregard and arrogant

rationalizations for "collateral damage," i.e. devastation of civilian populations. As noted in the following discussion of the parallels of geopolitical
military strategy for the U. S. and Israel,

> the distinction between civilian and military targets and casualties has
> been obliterated, collective punishment has become accepted practice,
> and grotesquely disproportionate response to acts of resistance (think
> Fallujah and Gaza) has become the hallmark not only of the Israeli
> Defense Forces but also of "America under siege." All resistance is
> terrorism. All state violence is self-defense.[27]

Thus, a geopolitical strategy for global dominance becomes obsessed with
any global resistance that defies imperial prerogatives. As argued by Ira
Chernus, "changes anywhere in the world that would challenge U. S. hegemony spell chaos and constant alarm."[28] According to Chernus and other
critics of U. S. imperialism, part of the process of seeking global dominance
results in seeing and, even, of creating monsters to slay. Although the
morphing of those monsters from communists to terrorists marks certain
discursive changes, the continuity for U. S. imperial policy is remarkably
consistent, irrespective of ideological shadings. One of the last Defense
Department directives to be issued by the Bush Administration found support
from President-elect Obama with the assertion that for the "foreseeable future,
winning the Long War against violent extremists will be the central objective
of U. S. policy." Wedded to what can only be construed as permanent war,
U. S. imperial policy garners such consensus precisely because empire has
become an American way of life. A variation on this theme that puts
the Long War into the long trajectory of U. S. imperialism is the following
formulation by Andrew Bacevich:

> the Long War genuinely qualifies as a war to preserve the American way
> of life ... and simultaneously as a war to extend the American imperium
> (centered on dreams of a world re-made in America's image), the former
> widely assumed to require the latter.[29]

While the Long War builds on the deep roots of U. S. imperial militarism,
it also becomes the most recent articulation of seeking global dominance.
That global dominance relies heavily on the forward positioning of military
power throughout the world, but especially in areas laden with oil and other
precious resources essential to the perpetuation of U. S. hegemony. However,
while there may be an economic connection between U. S. imperial policy
and the geopolitics of the extension of U. S. military power, it is important to
understand how that imperial militarism has an inherent logic that drives its
thrust for global dominance. Certainly, if not yet recognized by the American
public, others in those strategically significant parts of the world readily
understand how the presence of the U. S. military, in whatever guise,

embodies the search, whether illusive or not, for global dominance. According to the Indian activist and writer, Arundhati Roy, "It's become clear that the War against Terror is not really about terror, and the War on Iraq not only about oil. It's about a superpower's self-destructive impulse toward supremacy, stranglehold, global hegemony."[30]

To better apprehend the links between military imperialism and the waning goal of U. S. global hegemony, I want to turn to accounting for what Chalmers Johnson has designated as the "empire of bases" with its "five post-Cold War missions" that define that military imperialism. Given the fluctuations and secrecy surrounding the actual number of foreign military bases owned and operated by the Pentagon, the number appears to be between 750 and 800 or more, reaching into 130 countries around the world. The massive costs in maintaining such a far-flung network of military outposts, estimated in the hundreds of billions, is easily rationalized by what U. S. imperial strategists see as the ultimate value of such military bases. According to the 2002 National Security Strategy document,

> The presence of American forces overseas is one of the most profound symbols of the U. S. commitments to allies and friends. Through our willingness to use force in our own defense and the defense of others, the United States demonstrates its resolve to maintain a balance of power that favors freedom.[31]

What that rhetoric of freedom translates into in operational terms for U. S. imperial policy is, according to Johnson, the following five functions:

> imperial policing to ensure that no part of the empire slips the leash; eavesdropping on the communications of citizens, allies, and enemies alike ...; attempting to control as many sources of petroleum as possible ...; providing work and income for the military-industrial complex ...; and ensuring that members of the military and their families live comfortably and are well entertained while serving abroad.[32]

The function of policing areas of oil and gas production has resulted in inserting the U. S. military into parts of Central Asia previously out-of-bounds because those countries were part of the Soviet Union, particularly those countries within the Caspian Basin. Oil and gas fields in this region, strategically close to the voracious China market, are estimated to have around 6 percent of oil and 40 percent of gas reserves. The abysmal human rights records of many of the leaders of these Central Asian republics, such as Uzbekistan and Turkmenistan, have not deterred the Pentagon from utilizing either former Soviet military bases or renting out air facilities for operations in nearby Afghanistan. Especially significant to the establishment of U. S. military bases in the region are the concerted efforts of U. S. energy companies, such as Chevron, Unocal, and Exxon-Mobil, to build pipelines through the countries and region that would bypass both Russia and Iran. In addition, U. S. construction firms, such as Kellogg Brown & Root, have a stake in building new facilities and offering their supply services to whatever arrangements can be made, either temporary or permanent, for U. S. military bases.[33]

Of course, U. S. military intervention in regional conflicts and wars has provided opportunities to establish more permanent military bases. Scores of military bases still remain in Germany, Italy, and Japan, leftovers from World War II but also important Cold War outposts, as well as South Korea where large protests have confronted proposed expansion of U. S. facilities south of Seoul that would replace the former Japanese base in central Seoul that the U. S. military took over in 1945. Periodic demonstrations against other egregious expressions of military imperialism have emerged, especially in the aftermath of crimes committed by U. S. soldiers from Italy to Okinawa under the protection of Status of Force agreements. In Iraq what promised to be an extensive network of permanent U. S. military bases now appears to be another of the evanescent goals of the botched Bush invasion. More successful has been the insertion of the U. S. military into Eastern Europe as part of extending NATO facilities. The U. S. military bases planted in Kosovo and Bosnia in the aftermath of NATO operations in the Balkans may also, according to some critics, have more to do with watching over possible oil pipelines than spreading so-called peace-keeping maneuvers.[34]

Another mode of military imperialism, not bound by terrestrial bases, is the extensive naval operations mounted by the United States that are continuing to expand in the Pentagon's enormous budget, a budget that takes up close to half of the discretionary expenditures by the federal government and equals all of the combined military budgets of every other country in the world. Key to these expanding naval operations are the twelve aircraft carriers that handle hundreds of planes and helicopters, not to mention the military personnel housed on these imperial flotillas. Such floating imperial projections of power are particularly evident in the Persian Gulf and Indian Ocean, regions where control over these waterways has been an essential element of U. S. foreign policy since Carter enunciated his doctrine to repel any force that would threaten the flow of oil. As observed by Arno Mayer,

> Pre-positioned in global bases and constantly patrolling vital sea lanes, the U. S. navy provides the new model empire's spinal cord and arteries. Ships are displacing planes as chief strategic and tactical suppliers of troops and equipment.[35]

Nevertheless, resistance by governments and citizens in various countries has put the Pentagon on notice that institutionalizing U. S. military imperialism on their soil will not always be met with deference. Although efforts by the Pentagon to establish anti-missile facilities in Poland and the Czech Republic have found compliant governments, outraged citizens of those nations have rallied around a desire to be outside the province of an imperial superpower's orbit. One of the most remarkable confrontations with the United States over its military imperialism has come in Ecuador. In the aftermath of the election in 2006 of reform-minded Rafael Correa, he declared his intention not to renew the U. S. lease on the Eloy Alfaro Air Base near the Pacific seaport of Manta when it expired in 2009 unless the U. S. offered Ecuador the right to establish its own military base in Miami. Correa's decision was made even more urgent as a consequence of the March 2008 attack on Colombian insurgents in Ecuador by the Colombian military, aided, presumably, by military intelligence from the Eloy Alfaro Air Base. Also, Correa turned down a request by the United States to establish a base in the Galapagos. Even more provocative moves have been undertaken by President Chávez in Venezuela. Beyond terminating all Venezuelan military connections with the U. S., including any further training at the notorious former School of the Americas renamed in 2000 as the Western Hemisphere Institute for Security Cooperation, Chávez has replaced military contracts with U. S. firms by Russian and Chinese companies and created a new military alliance with Russia that brought Russian naval vessels to Venezuela. In effect, Venezuela and Ecuador have joined a growing list of Latin American countries dedicated now to resisting any U. S. military, and even economic, infringements on their sovereignty.[36]

Nonetheless, the Pentagon persists in finding even more insidious ways to infringe the sovereignty of nations and individuals, especially through far-flung communication outposts that operate as espionage centers. Although obscured in secrecy, these spy networks are overseen by the National Security Agency (NSA) and the National Reconnaissance Office (NRO). Using extensive satellite systems, the NSA is capable of monitoring and intercepting many different forms of electronic communication. The use of fiber-optic cables has encouraged the navy to equip both submarines and their bases world-wide with detecting devices. Some sharing of information with allies, especially through the highly classified "Echelon" program, has intruded into non-military matters, resulting in spying on citizens in the United States and elsewhere throughout the world. As argued by Chalmers Johnson,

> the fatal flaw of Echelon is that it is operated by the intelligence and military establishments of the main English-speaking countries in total secrecy and hence beyond any kind of accountability to representatives of the people it claims to be protecting.[37]

Directly linked to the extensive spy satellite network is the increasing efforts by the Pentagon to militarize space. A leaked 2002 Pentagon paper advocating the establishment of space platforms for missile attacks on terrestrial targets relies heavily on already existing satellites. Mechanisms have been put into operation that have enabled the U. S. Space Command to aid unmanned aircraft flying over Afghanistan and other conflict regions so designated by the military. The Space Command's own definition of its future role highlights the goal to "dominate the space dimension of military operations to protect U. S. interests and investments."[38] It also continues the obsession with further advancements in "techno-war." According to military analyst William Arkin, "no target on the planet would be immune to American attack. The United States could strike without warning, whenever and wherever a threat was perceived."[39]

Another growing aspect in the expansion of military operations and lack of accountability of military imperialism involves the outsourcing and privatization of what had been primary Pentagon responsibilities, such as training foreign military. Such private military contractors, from DynCorp to Vinnell to Blackwater, often staffed with former U. S. military offices, manage, in most instances, to keep their business operations away from public scrutiny. However, certain public incidents, such as attacks on Vinnell employees in Saudi Arabia and the notorious assaults by Blackwater and against Blackwater employees in Iraq, have raised questions about the impunity under which they operate. Because of Blackwater's activities in Iraq, the new Status of Forces agreement appears to make them liable to Iraqi law. However, military privatization continues to garner tax dollars, rising to the hundreds of millions in appropriations. This outsourcing has aroused the anger and scrutiny of some in Congress and some in the military. According to one military critic, "privatization is a way of going around Congress and not telling the public. Foreign policy is made by default by private military consultants motivated by bottom-line profits."[40]

One only has to consider the ramping up of private contractors in the wars in Iraq and Afghanistan to get a better picture of how these countries have become prime outlets for "privatized war and reconstruction."[41] Naomi Klein estimates that in the first Gulf War there was one contractor for every hundred soldiers. After four years of U. S. occupation in Iraq, that ratio was almost one to one. More than just the billions given to Halliburton for no-bid contracts and the extensive security operations mounted by Blackwater and other U. S. firms, the Bush Administration promoted a form of disaster capitalism that utilized U. S. corporations first to destroy infrastructure and then to rebuild that very same infrastructure, albeit often by sloppy and unaccountable methods.[42] Ann Jones reports from Afghanistan that the slipshod training by DynCorp of the Afghan police and military cost U. S. taxpayers close to $2 billion. Even more outlandish was the outlay of money to the Louis Berger Group to rebuild the 389-mile-long Kabul/Kandahar highway. The estimated cost was put at $1 million per mile.[43]

Of course, it is the bottom-line profit with the willing collusion of Congress that continues to stoke the military industrial complex and military imperialism, even if that complex has morphed from military Keynesianism to military neo-liberalism with its attendant privatization and de-regulation. Citing the "Iron Triangle" of interests, i.e. Congress, the defense companies, and military leadership, journalist William Grieder incisively unpacks how the interactions within this Iron Triangle absorb federal tax dollars year after year. Although noting the fluctuations in the Pentagon's budget, Grieder also cites the compelling budgetary commitments that continued even after the demise of the Soviet. Quoting another observer of the military budget process, Grieder underscores how manufacturing for foreign arms sales drives one of the engines of military imperialism.

> A Lockheed official ... testified that the U. S. has to make a multibillion-dollar commitment to the F-22 to counter the widespread proliferation of higher-performance combat aircraft such as the U. S. made F-15 and F-16. ... This argument suggests that with the fall of the Soviet Union, we are effectively engaging in an arms race with ourselves.[44]

The links between that arms race and military imperialism are further accentuated by what economist Ismael Hossein-Zadeh calls "redistributive militarism." He contends that "rising militarization of U. S. foreign policy in recent years is driven not so much by some general/abstract national interests, or by the interests of Big Oil and other non-military transnational corporations ..., as it is by powerful special interests that are vested in the war industry and related war-induced businesses that need an atmosphere of war and militarism in order to justify their lion's share of the public money."[45]

Beyond fueling the staggering U. S. defense budget, estimated close to $1 trillion dollars in 2008 when all the ancillary costs are factored in, the Iron Triangle has managed to capture more than half of the arms sales around the world. Among the leading buyers of U. S. military equipment is Israel whose use of F-16 and Apache aircraft in strafing civilians in Lebanon (2006) and Gaza (2008) gives further meaning to what constitutes a strategic ally in the "war on terror." The transfer of military munitions and equipment to Israel through leading U. S. arms manufacturers can be seen in a 2007 $1.3 billion contract with Raytheon for various missile systems and a 2008 $777 million Boeing contract for uranium-oxide GBU-39 bombs, as well as white phosphorous bombs manufactured by General Dynamics Corporation. The long-term commitment to arms connections between the U. S. and Israel was underscored by the 2007 agreement for $30 billion on arms transfers over the next decade. Is it any wonder that militarization defines the foreign policy imperatives of both Israel and the United States?[46]

The intricate connections that demarcate how military imperialism steers policy both on a global and national scale raise profound questions about the U. S. capacity to sustain imperial dominance and hegemony at home and abroad. It should be clear from the material covered in this chapter and also from Chapter 1 that Thomas Friedman's claim that "America is truly the ultimate benign hegemon and reluctant enforcer" is little more than ideological obfuscation.[47]

Perhaps, more to the point, the geopolitical role of the United States under the disciplinary regime of military imperialism may be seen as an effort to shore up fading economic hegemony. While it is true to a certain extent that transnational capital performs global functions unbound by the nation state, the calculus by which the United States attempts to exercise global dominance and hegemony is firmly rooted in its practice of military imperialism. In fact, at some level, one could agree with the formulation by Emmanuel Todd that the United States

> is battling to maintain its status as the world's financial center by making a symbolic show of its military might in the heart of Eurasia, thereby hoping to forget and have others ignore America's industrial weakness, its financial need, and its predatory character.[48]

For Todd, the U. S. has lost its hegemony and can only flaunt its "theatrical micromilitarism" through the "war on terrorism."[49] Other critics, like Samir Amin, are less sanguine about the disappearance of U. S. hegemony although its expression, noting the similarity with Todd's perspective, "rests far more on its excessive military power than on the advantages of its economic system."[50] He goes on to remark that the

> fight against the imperialism of the United States and its militarist option is everyone's – it's major victims in Asia, Africa, and Latin America, the Japanese and European peoples condemned to subordination, even the North American people.[51]

In *Beyond U. S. Hegemony*, Amin looks to ways of creating "Solidarity in the South" as a potential and real alternative to U. S. imperialism.[52]

While the following chapters will continue to assess the damage done by U. S. imperialism through economic victimization and the alternatives to that imperialism emanating from the South for another possible world, it is necessary to conclude this chapter with a recognition of the ultimate contradictions posed by military imperialism not only for global hegemony but for the perpetuation of the underlying ideological hegemony of the military-industrial complex. Numerous critics have pointed to the demise of the Soviet Union as the historical moment when the United States took advantage of its "unipolar military domination" to seek "a historically unprecedented, global political hegemony."[53] Yet, the following questions posed by Andrew Bacevich seem not to have fully sunk in, especially in light of continuing efforts to assert global dominance and hegemony. Bacevich queries:

> How is it that our widely touted post-Cold War military supremacy has produced not enhanced security but the prospect of open-ended conflict? Why is it that when we flex our muscles on behalf of peace and freedom, the world beyond our borders becomes all the more cantankerous and disorderly?[54]

Certainly, while acknowledging the significance of unipolarity and the asymmetrical power that certain political forces in the United States sought to take advantage of, Gary Dorrien's study of those neoconservative political forces also underscores the continuing delusions shared by rulers and ruled alike about exceptionalism and the denial of the long trajectory of U. S. imperialism.[55] Nonetheless, the ramping up of militarization for the purposes of imperial dominance abroad and certain legitimacy at home does pose a fundamental contradiction as well as a question. As propounded by Carl Boggs,

> If global domination requires broad and firm popular support within the matrix of a stable ... corporate economy, then heavy reliance on military force ... is ultimately counterproductive. If demilitarization of U. S. foreign policy (and society) is the more rational strategy, the problem is that militarism has become so endemic to American society as a whole ... that it will be very difficult to reverse.[56]

Another very real dilemma for U. S. military imperialism, particularly as a consequence of the wars on Iraq and Afghanistan, is imperial overstretch. Both in terms of the eventual costs, estimated in the trillions of dollars just in the case of the war with Iraq, and the continuing drain on military personnel, these wars have further underscored the inherent contradictions of U. S. military imperialism. Even with active troops, counting the National Guard and Reserves, numbering over two million, the U. S. military has so depleted its human resources that it has resorted to extending tours in ways that have lowered morale and created even more internal dissent about deployment. Attempts to offset these problems by higher pay inducements, expansion of the numbers, and use of private contractors have only exacerbated the overall contradictions endemic in maintaining the kind of global garrison embodied by U. S. military imperialism. According to world-systems scholar, Giovanni Arrighi, besides having "jeopardized the credibility of U. S. military might," the war and occupation of Iraq may be one of the key components underlying the "terminal crisis of U. S. hegemony," albeit without diminishing the U. S. role as "the world's pre-eminent military power."[57] Nonetheless, as pointed out by other scholars, imperial overstretch was central to the demise of previous empires and now threatens the death of a U. S. empire also bent on fighting debilitating and self-destructive wars.[58]

Clearly, the pursuit of such wars also engenders resistance abroad and potential dissent at home, the latter, however, contingent on some fundamental understanding of the whys and wherefores of prosecuting war. Certainly, as indicated in this chapter and elsewhere in the book, resistance to a militarized U. S. foreign policy is evident whether in the streets of Caracas or Baghdad. Irrespective of the form such resistance may take, including insurgencies that engage in terror, the U. S. will encounter resistance as long as it insists on imposing its sense of order in the world. In effect, a "system of global domination resting largely on military force, or even the threat of force, cannot in the greater scheme of things consolidate its rule on a foundation of legitimating beliefs or values."[59] On the other hand, U. S. perception of that resistance, whether by the ruling elite, corporate media, or the public at large, is filtered through an ideological smokescreen that either labels that resistance as "terrorism" or some primitive form of know-nothing anti-Americanism. Part of the inability to recognize the reality of what shapes the lives of others is the persistence of a self-image of U. S. benevolence or innocence, even in the face of the realities spawned by U. S. intervention and occupation.[60] Also, what remains both contentious and difficult to face is the degree to which the United States, especially in its pursuit of global dominance through military imperialism, has become, to quote Walter Hixson, a "warfare state, a nation with a propensity for initiating and institutionalizing warfare."[61] For Hixson, the perpetuation of that warfare state requires reaffirming a national identity whose cultural hegemony at home can provide ideological cover for "nation building, succoring vicious regimes, bombing, shelling, contaminating, torturing and killing hundreds of thousands of innocents, and destroying enemy others."[62] As the bodies pile up, however, the ability to maintain hegemony abroad and even at home is eroded.

It is not just the bodies of the dead slain by U. S. military imperialism that haunt the consciousness, if not the conscience, of citizens throughout the world. Many other bodies may be hidden, in fact, by the "invisible hand" of economic imperialism, an imperialism touted by Friedman and the other champions of U. S.-led global dominance. If their victimization is no less real than those destroyed by U. S. military imperialism, their agency is ever more a part of the growing multitudes contesting U. S. imperialism in whatever guise. Turning to that victimization and agency will be the focus of the next chapter.

5   U. S. economic imperialism and global inequities

We will actively work to bring the hope of democracy, development, free markets and free trade to every corner of the world.

2002 U. S. National Security Strategy

Crimes against people, crimes against nature: the impunity enjoyed by the masters of war is shared by their twins, the voracious masters of industry who eat nature on earth and, in the heavens, swallow the ozone layer. The most successful companies in the world are the ones that do the most to murder it; the countries that decide the planet's fate are the same ones that do their best to annihilate it.

Eduardo Galeano

Consider the banana. This once exotic fruit has become a staple of the diet of the average citizen of the United States. Yet, the banana remains, to a great extent, wrapped in mystery; its peel perhaps telegraphing to a discriminating reader of labels something of its national origin and the corporation responsible for bringing the banana to the American consumer. But, what of the intricate web of the relations of production and distribution that accompany the banana from its planting to harvesting to distribution? Beyond the cheap price, do citizens of the United States have any knowledge or concern about the often exploitative and even dangerous conditions that surround the growing and harvesting of the banana? What does it take to peel back those layers and reveal the inequities of which most North Americans are blithely unaware?

Certainly, many in the United States are familiar with the reference to "banana republics" and their reputation as corrupt dictatorial Latin American countries. There may even be a small number of conscientious consumers who know something of the nefarious history of United Fruit from its inception in the late nineteenth century to its role as one of the instigators behind the 1954 CIA coup of the duly elected government of Guatemala. However, the more recent history of the leading U. S. banana corporations, such as Chiquita, Dole and Del Monte, while periodically gaining some notoriety because of their own corrupt business practices, stays under wraps. Thus, to uncover the various implications of the banana for the practice of U. S. economic imperialism provides a direct link to the larger and more contradictory food chain of U. S. transnational corporations, U. S. controlled global financial institutions, such as the International Monetary Fund (IMF), World Bank, and World Trade Organization (WTO), and U. S. economic policies.

Although the banana export business has become more complicated recently as a consequence of subcontracting, the big three U. S. firms, Chiquita, Dole, and Del Monte, still account for the majority of global imports while exercising continuing control of transportation and port facilities. Subcontracting has allowed these companies often to bypass established unions in favor of company unions. Thus, most of the 400,000 Latin American banana workers labor on plantations with indirect ties to the big three. Besides contending with hazardous working conditions and low wages, unionized workers have faced harassment and intimidation from paramilitaries, private security forces, and right-wing death squads, the latter especially rampant in Colombia. One incident in Guatemala in 1999 is indicative of how such paramilitaries operate. Kidnapping several union leaders and scores of members from a Del Monte plantation, the paramilitary threatened the workers unless they renounced their union activities. Fearing for their lives, they denounced the union and fled. Nonetheless, this intimidation did not deter the remaining female union leader who, in the face of death threats, attempted to sustain the organization.[1]

Even more egregious in its support of right-wing military dictatorships and militias is Chiquita, the one-time dominant banana importer in the world. Tracing its lineage to United Fruit's imperial expansion in Latin America in the early twentieth century, along with other extractive firms like Standard Oil and Phelps Dodge, Chiquita inherited an extensive involvement in the infrastructure and politics of specific Latin American countries. Chiquita was deeply implicated in the infamous CIA sponsored coup of the Arbenz government of Guatemala in 1954.[2] However, more recently, Chiquita was caught up in funneling money from 1997 to 2004 to a notorious Colombian right-wing paramilitary group known as the United Self-Defense Forces of Colombia (*Autodefensas Unidas de Colombia* – AUC). After being labeled a terrorist organization in 2001 by the U. S. Justice Department, the AUC still received payments from Chiquita through its Colombian subsidiary, Banadex. According to a former mayor of the largest town in Colombia's main banana-growing region who, herself, was threatened by the AUC, this paramilitary organization "called for the elimination of the left and of all social groups that were supposedly contributing to instability for investors and the multinationals," including, of course, labor unions.[3] In spite of Chiquita's political connections in Washington DC (including a former head of the Security and Exchange Commission who was a law partner at one time with Michael Chertoff, one-time head of the criminal division of the Bush, Jr. Justice Department and then Secretary of Homeland Security), Chiquita was forced to pay $25 million in fines to the U. S. government for its payoffs to the AUC. (Chiquita's attorney in this case was Eric Holder, now Attorney General in the Obama Administration.)[4]

On the other hand, Chiquita had more success with its political connections and lobbying efforts in the 1990s in its challenge to the European Union's tariff regime. While controlling almost a quarter of the world banana trade, Chiquita's overproduction compelled it to seek to export more bananas to Europe. Initially, Chiquita relied on a section of the 1974 U. S. Trade Act to threaten a variety of sanctions against the EU unless it would open its doors to all of Chiquita's exports. With both Republican support and the favor of the Clinton White House (all of which had been stroked by political contributions totaling $2 million during the 1990s), Chiquita approached the World Trade Organization as part of a full-scale attack by the U. S. on EU trade barriers that included not only bananas but also U. S. beef and GMO agricultural products, such as corn and soybeans. Eventually in 1999, the WTO authorized the sanctions imposed by the U. S. government and Chiquita. Although forced into Chapter 11 bankruptcy because of its production problems a short time later, Chiquita gained the upper hand in this financial banana war even though Dole had been able to work out its own deal with the EU.[5]

So, what does this brief case study of the banana tell us about the role of U. S. economic imperialism? First and foremost, U. S. corporations seek out raw materials to extract at the cheapest possible cost to them, exploiting in the process resources and labor in certain geographical regions. (As we will see later in the chapter, it is not just extraction but also new markets and capital flows that consume the attention of imperial economies.) When confronted by challenges to the control over those raw materials, U. S. corporations will rely on either military or economic intervention to protect their investments. However, as David Harvey reminds us, there are two different, if at times overlapping, imperial "logics" operating that distinguish "the politics of state and empire" from the "molecular process of capital accumulation in space and time."[6] In other words, while there may be congruence between the interests of U. S. foreign policy and specific economic sectors and corporations at times, it does not follow that all sectors and all corporations will be supported by the state. Certainly, this congruence was in evidence at certain points in the history of the banana and, specifically, the role of Chiquita. However, there was some variance at particular moments that complicates our understanding of economic imperialism. In effect, the complications of controlling markets and the flow of capital, particularly against the backdrop of contending transnational corporations and interests, may lead to contradictions among a variety of economic and corporate entities.[7] Finally, the extent of resistance to such economic intervention by U. S. capital and corporations will fundamentally alter the degree to which either the state or individual corporations will achieve their economic goals.

As an instance of the latter, I want to turn to two examples of water wars involving U. S.-based corporations in two different regions of the world, one in Bolivia and the other in India. When the Bechtel Corporation, a top-ranked global construction company with over 19,000 projects in 140 countries, took over the public water system in Cochabamba, Bolivia at the end of the 1990s, it met with growing organized resistance.[8] At first, however, the Bolivian government facilitated the privatization of water by Bechtel through prohibiting other mechanisms of water allocation and expanding commodification over all means of water collection, including gathering water from rain. After Bechtel's subsidiary, *Aguas del Tunari*, raised residential water rates that led to spending anywhere between a quarter to a third of the average monthly wage ($60) for water, Bolivians throughout the Cochabamba area began to organize opposition to the new water rates and laws. According to Rosseline Ugarte, a young woman involved with the resistance, "The water laws did not allow you to have your own well in rural communities. You had to pay a certain amount for your own well. How could they charge us for our water? Next it would be air."[9]

Mobilizing on this outrage, rural and urban residents began erecting blockades in January 2000. The main plaza of Cochabamba became the site for the ritual burning of water bills. In response to these protests, the government froze increases but refused to cancel the contract with Bechtel even though close to 100 percent of residents supported the cancellation. As resistance mounted, the government turned to forms of political repression, resulting in the declaration of martial law in April. This did not deter the determined and organized residents of Cochabamba who responded with even more massive mobilizations. As one of the participants recalled,

> All of the neighborhoods in the city were organized. They were overcome with the feeling of resistance ... (They) brought food to those in the city center who were resisting, because the protests raged day and night. ... It was a huge gesture of solidarity.[10]

In the face of such determined opposition, the government canceled the contract. Even though Bechtel then sued for lost revenue, national and worldwide pressure forced the company to drop its claims.

In another instance of combating the exploitation of water resources, women in rural India have challenged Coca-Cola with its insatiable thirst for water for its bottling plants.[11] As a consequence of so-called free market reforms in India in the 1990s, Coke was able to intervene in the Indian market in 1992 and within a year took over a significant percentage of bottling companies and their distribution networks. In 2000 Coke came to Plachimada in the southern state of Kerala. Extracting daily over 1.5 million liters of water, Coke resorted to whole-scale exploitation of the local groundwater, resulting in the drop from 150 to 500 feet in the water table for local wells. In addition, Coke was polluting other local water sources. This resulted in organized opposition by local residents, especially farmers and women who traditionally gathered water for household use. In 2002, these women, under the banner of the People's Collective Against Coca-Cola, led a demonstration to the front gates of the Coke plant in Plachimada. The demonstration soon turned into a permanent picket outside the gates of the plant. Attracting both national and international attention, pressure was mounted on Coke by global networks of environmentalist, labor, and student activists.

By the fall of 2003, Coke was under attack from a number of quarters, including the political and legal institutions in Kerala. On December 16, 2003 the Kerala High Court found in favor of the women protestors and others who charged Coke with pirating Plachimada's water. Ordering Coke to cease and desist, Kerala High Court Justice Balakrishnana Nair rendered the following verdict:

> The public trust doctrine primarily rests on the principle that certain resources like air, sea, waters, and the forests have such a great importance to the people as a whole that it would be wholly unjustified to make them a subject of private ownership. ... The doctrine enjoins upon the government to protect the resources for the enjoyment of the general public rather than to permit their use for private ownership or commercial purpose.[12]

Shortly thereafter, the Kerala government shut down the Coke plant in Plachimada. Although victorious in Kerala, plants run by Coke and Pepsi continue to operate throughout India, generating additional resistance efforts.

Among those efforts was a conference on "Detoxification" that took place on December 2, 2004, drawing attention to the continuing spread of toxins in the environment on the twentieth anniversary of the Bhopal tragedy. It might be instructive to review what transpired at Bhopal and the on-going fallout from another example of the tragic consequences of U. S. economic imperialism. On December 3, 1984, one of the most disastrous industrial accidents ever took place in Bhopal, India after a chemical leak from a pesticide plant owned by Union Carbide led to the death of thousands and severely injured over 150,000 people.[13] Having scrimped on installing any functional safety systems, Union Carbide was responsible for more than twenty-seven tons of deadly gases being released into the atmosphere. Not until 1989 did Union Carbide own up to its culpabilities. Even then, the compensation offered to the victims was no more than the average of $500 and, in return, Carbide escaped any further legal liability. Beyond the immediate deaths by poisoning, tens of thousands of people remain incapacitated twenty years later. In addition, the dumping of other chemicals by Union Carbide has contaminated the drinking water of area residents. After Dow Chemical purchased Union Carbide in 2001, it denied any claims for responsibility and has refused to clean up the sites and to provide compensation for those suffering from the immediate and lingering effects. Moreover, Dow-Carbide continues to hide behind the defense of "trade secrets" in its refusal to divulge important information about the composition and extent of the toxic gasses released on December 3, 1984.

While most people were horrified about the devastating disaster at Bhopal, there were ideological apologists for Union Carbide, especially at the media fountainhead of U. S. economic imperialism, the *Wall Street Journal*. Editorializing in its December 13, 1984 edition, the *Journal* opined:

> It is worthwhile to remember that the Union Carbide insecticide plant and the people surrounding it were where they were for compelling reasons. India's agriculture has been thriving, bringing a better life to millions of rural people, and partly because of the use of modern agricultural technology that includes the applications of insect killers. ... Calcutta-style scenes of human deprivation can be replaced as fast as the country imports the benefits of the West's industrial revolution and market economics.[14]

Apparently, Union Carbide's victims have not been persuaded by the *Journal*'s brief for the benefits of the West's technology and U. S. corporations. Continuing protests to further the legal claims of Bhopal residents, especially punctuated in 2002 by a hunger strike by women survivors, are now part of a global network called the International Campaign for Justice in Bhopal.

Yet, just as the victims of U. S. economic imperialism have found new transnational forums for the articulation of their grievances, so have U. S.-based transnational corporations found additional outlets and allies for continuing exploitation and depredation of the resources of developing nations. What this era of corporate globalization represents is, perhaps, best summarized by economist William Tabb:

> in the last third of the twentieth century large corporations became more single-mindedly transnational in focus, seeing their home country as only one among many profit centers and reorganizing their operations to coincide with this vision of a globalized world economy.[15]

Much of this corporate globalization is now well-known, particularly to those who have lost jobs in the United States as a direct result of the outsourcing of production to developing nations. One sector of that outsourcing, the apparel industry, was discussed in some detail in Chapter 3. As a shorthand example of what such outsourcing has meant, consider the following tragic trail recounted by Jeff Faux:

> Two years after it bought Mr. Coffee in 1998, the Sunbeam Corporation shifted production from Cleveland, where workers who made electric appliances earnd $21 an hour, to Metamoros, Mexico, where they average $2.36. Three years after that, the company moved Mr. Coffee production to China, where they can hire labor at 47 cents an hour.[16]

Instead of additional recounting of the horrors of outsourcing, what I intend to cover in the rest of this chapter is the degree to which the interlocking connections between U. S.-based transnational corporations and international financial institutions, such as the World Trade Organization (WTO) and (IMF), work to promote an economic imperialism that produces on-going global inequities.

Perhaps one obvious place to start is the development of what has been called Structural Adjustment Programs (SAP) in the 1970s and 1980s. As both a class strategy of elite core interests concerned about their falling profits and an imperial strategy to assert additional controls over resources, markets, and capital flows in developing nations, SAP-imposed demands for privatization and deregulation had devastating consequences for numerous countries and their population.[17] Those consequences are dramatically revealed in Mike Davis's brilliant and disturbing book, *Planet of Slums*. As Davis points out, Structural Adjustment Programs, promoted by the IMF and World Bank, not only accelerated the move of the rural poor to growing urban slums, but also eroded, through privatization and debt schemes, the capacity of the state to underwrite public investment and development. Davis cites one researcher's study of the impact of SAPs on agricultural development in Africa:

> Subsidized, improved agricultural input packages and rural infrastructural building were drastically reduced. ... (P)easant farmers were subjected to the international financial institutions' "sink-or-swim" economic strategy. National market deregulation pushed agricultural producers into global commodity markets where middle as well as poor peasants found it hard to compete.[18]

As a further consequence of these economic dynamics, Davis underscores an increasing immiseration and imposed underdevelopment throughout the developing world. "In Luanda," he writes, "where one quarter of the households have per capita consumptions of less than 75 cents per day, child mortality (under five) was a horrifying 320 per thousand in 1993 – the highest in the world."[19] Davis cites the Nigerian author, Fidelis Balogin, on how IMF-mandated SAPs turned into an instrument of "re-enslaving" Nigerians:

> The weird logic of this economic programme seemed to be that to restore life to the dying economy, every juice had first to be SAPed out of the under-privileged majority of the citizens. The middle class rapidly disappeared and the garbage heaps of the increasingly rich few became the food table of the multiplied population of abjectly poor. The brain drain to the oil-rich Arab countries and to the Western world became a flood.[20]

Of course, this flood was not a natural disaster but the logical outcome of the IMF and World Bank dam busters. Behind the IMF and the World Bank stood the U. S. government, eager to find new markets for its subsidized exports and to extend what would become toxic loans to already indebted Third World nations. In 1985, the U. S. Treasury Department enacted what was designated as the Baker Plan (named for James Baker, then Secretary of the Treasury). The Baker Plan called upon the fifteen largest Third World debtors to forgo any state subsidies or provisions for development in order to receive needed international loans. As Davis makes abundantly clear,

> Everywhere the IMF and World Bank – acting as bailiffs for the big banks and backed by the Reagan and George H. W. Bush administra-tions – offered poor countries the same poisoned chalice of devaluation, privatization, removal of import controls and food subsidies, enforced cost-recovery in health and education, and ruthless downsizing of the public sector.[21]

Combined with real natural disasters, like drought, and other manufactured dislocations, like rising interest rates and falling commodity prices, whole continents from Africa to Latin America were subjected to conditions even more devastating than the Great Depression. As a single example of that devastation, Davis sites how a 1991 SAP raised the cost of living in one year by 45 percent in Harare and resulted in the hospitalization of 100,000 for malnutrition.[22]

Even in regions and cities where it seemed that globalization was expand-ing a middle class, much of that immiseration was hidden either in neglected urban slums or social dislocation and worse in the countryside. As one observer noted about the rise of Bangalore's high-tech industry, the "high tech (boom) is a drop in the bucket in a sea of poverty."[23] Citing a variety of sta-tistics and studies, Davis points to the number of street children (90,000) in Bangalore and the lack of clean water and toilet facilities throughout the slums that surround Bangalore. One Bangalore-based UN consultant notes that "children suffered heavily from diarrhea and worm infestations, a high proportion were malnourished, and infant mortality rates in the slums were much higher than the state average."[24] Meanwhile, in the Indian farm-belt state of Andhra Pradesh in July 2004 alone, "500 of its farmers have com-mitted suicide ..., often by drinking the pesticide that was purchased with debts they could not repay."[25]

Behind these suicides, which grew close to 2,000 in a six-month period in 2004 in this one state and over 16,000 in total in all of India in 2004, was another story of SAPs linked to U. S. economic imperialism. As revealed by Indian writer and activist, Vandana Shiva:

> In 1998, the World Bank's structural adjustment policies forced India to open its seed sector to global corporations like Cargill, Monsanto, and Syngenta. The global corporations changed the input economy overnight. Farm-saved seeds were replaced by corporate seeds, which need fertilizers and pesticides and cannot be saved.

She goes on to note that

> corporations prevent seed savings through patents and by engineering seeds with nonrenewable traits. As a result, poor peasants have to buy new seeds for every planting season and what was a traditionally free resource, available by putting aside a small portion of the crop, becomes a commodity. This new expense increases poverty and leads to indebtedness.[26]

In addition, there was the dumping of U. S. agribusiness subsidized cotton in India, as well as cotton-producing countries in Africa, that further undermined the livelihood of small farmers in developing nations. Although some Indian farmers are organizing to find a way out of what Shiva calls the "suicidal/genocidal economy of agribusiness imposed by the WTO and the World Bank,"[27] the majority are still suffering from the effects of economic imperialism and social dislocation.

Another country's agricultural production devastated by U. S. agribusiness, SAPs, and helpful rulings by the WTO was Jamaica. Over several decades through the 1990s, agriculture as a percentage of Jamaican GDP had decreased from 30 percent to less than 8 percent. Although that decline was aided by prolonged drought, the SAPs and other economic impositions on the Jamaican economy led to increased competition from agricultural imports. WTO decisions in favor of U. S.-based banana corporations and in support of U. S.-based beet sugar companies wreacked havoc on the banana and cane sugar industries in Jamaica. As graphically depicted in the 2001 Stephanie Black documentary, *Life and Debt*, small Jamaican farmers, whether in dairy or fruit and vegetable production, were overwhelmed by cheap agricultural imports, predominantly from North America. The privatization and neoliberal policies adopted by the Jamaican government in the 1980s only added fuel to the fires destroying Jamaican agricultural production.[28]

The devastation and disruption wrought by U. S. economic imperialism was obviously co-determined by willing ruling classes in certain countries. In numerous instances, foreign governments and their colluding political and economic elites helped to construct financial and political arrangements conducive to the array of domestic and foreign economic interests and detrimental to the poor majority. For example, in between the near bankruptcy in 1982 and the financial collapse in the mid-1990s, the Mexican government and various bankers aided a "Washington Consensus" that tied the Reagan and Clinton Treasury Departments together with the IMF and private banks. (Under Clinton's Secretary of Treasury, Robert Rubin, a former Citibank and Wall Street manager, private banks, including Citibank, used both the Mexican and U. S. governments to salvage their bad economic investments.) With the full participation of the Mexican presidents during this time, but especially by Carlos Salinas de Gortari, neoliberal policies and programs were adopted that, among other changes, privatized former communal farms and, in the process, forced Mexican peasants into the cities or across the U. S.

border. Furthermore, in taking away land that had been used for subsistence farming and the growing of corn, U. S. corn imports, primarily the less nutritious and even GMO yellow corn, flooded the Mexican markets. NAFTA accelerated U. S.-subsidized agricultural imports in particular, even though it did lead to the emergence and resistance by the Zapatistas and others in Mexican civil society.[29]

On the other hand, absent vocal opposition and combative resistance, the penetration by U. S. economic imperialism has been pervasive, especially in those sectors of the international economy where U. S.-based transnational corporations maintained a leading role. From energy companies to defense industries to financial services and pharmaceuticals, an economic imperialist logic has operated as part of an expanding globalization, albeit with the rise of national and transnational competitors.[30] Especially in developing nations, that imperialist logic has enriched U. S.-based transnationals at the expense of local residents. Energy companies, in particular, such as Exxon Mobil and Texaco, made arrangements with willing governments in countries like Chad and Ecuador that not only added to exorbitant oil profits for those companies but also led to the further impoverishment of the people and despoiling of the land in those countries.[31] In the case of oil and natural gas, as has been demonstrated in the previous chapter, military imperialism is deeply implicated in the search for and protection of those energy resources, especially in the Middle East and Central Asia. However, it is not a mere matter of the extraction of oil for the profit of U. S.-based transnational energy corporations alone, as it is part of a wider context of economic imperialism where capital flows and trading practices come into effect. In addition, there is a close link between energy companies, military imperialism, and so-called reconstruction efforts, or "Oil, Guns, and Money," as evident especially in Iraq. As argued convincingly in *Afflicted Powers*, "it is about Chevron and Texaco, but also about Bechtel, Kellogg, Brown and Root, Chase Manhattan, Enron, Global Crossing, BCCI, and DynCorp."[32]

Beyond these interlocking economic interests, there are specific industries which promote an economic imperialism that exacerbates existent global inequities. Nowhere was that more evident than in the role played by U. S. pharmaceuticals in an Africa desperately trying to contend with the AIDS epidemic affecting upward of forty million people on that continent alone. With the United States government having manipulated trade and patent-enforcement regulations in the international arena in order to protect U. S.-based pharmaceutical corporations and their proprietary "rights," efforts by African countries, especially South Africa, to develop generic drugs for AIDS treatments were met with immediate challenges. Other countries outside Africa, such as Brazil, were taken to the WTO by the U. S. when they attempted to produce and distribute much less expensive AIDS drugs. With righteous indignation AIDS activists in South Africa and around the world began a campaign at the beginning of the twenty-first century that put the spotlight on these pharmaceutical companies and the U. S. government's campaign to protect the profits of those companies. This international pressure has resulted in some concessions by U. S. pharmaceuticals. Nonetheless, the irony of their insistence about protecting their intellectual property rights is particularly apparent in the whole process of bringing research to market. As economist William Tabb argues,

> it is important to note that most drugs for treating AIDS are the result of government-sponsored research. While Glaxo Wellcome claims that it developed AZT, it was the National Cancer Institute working with the staff of Duke University that developed the technology for determining both that AZT could suppress the live AIDS virus in human cells and in what concentration it would affect humans in the desired manner.[33]

Nonetheless, the global inequities around AIDS persist, complicated by the continuing efforts of U. S. pharmaceuticals to defend their prerogatives and profits. According to Salih Booker, the executive director of the American Committee on Africa, "AIDS must be seen for what it is: a consequence of global apartheid, in which basic human rights, including the right to quality healthcare, are denied along the color line."[34]

Of course, to overcome all of the deleterious effects of global apartheid would require not only contesting the imperial policies that shape global apartheid (such as, for example, U. S. resistance to international funding of public water treatment systems) but also challenging the arrogant mindset of U. S. economic policymakers. Among the most vicious manifestations of such a mindset was the notorious memo written by Lawrence Summers in 1991 when he was the chief economist at the World Bank endorsing the dumping of more hazardous waste material and mobile pollution to third world countries, specifically in Africa. (Summers went on to become Secretary of the Treasury under Clinton and is now the chief economic advisor to President Barack Obama.) The memo deserves to be quoted at length for what it reveals about the arrogance of Summers and the U. S. economic imperialist thinking he reflected:

> The measurements of the cost of health impairing pollution depends on the foregone earnings from increased morbidity and mortality. From this point of view a given amount of health impairing pollution should be done in the country with the lowest cost, which will be the country with the lowest wages. I think the economic logic behind dumping a load of toxic waste in the lowest wage country is impeccable and we should face up to that.
>
> The costs of pollution are likely to be non-linear as the initial increments of pollution probably have very low cost. I've always thought that under-populated countries in Africa are vastly UNDER-polluted, their air quality is probably vastly inefficiently low compared to Los Angeles or Mexico City. Only the lamentable facts that so much pollution is

generated by non-tradable industries (transport, electrical generation) and that the unit transport costs of solid waste as so high prevent world welfare enhancing trade in air pollution and waste.

The demand for a clean environment for aesthetic and health reasons is likely to have very high income elasticity. The concern over an agent that causes a one in a million changes in the odds of prostate cancer is obviously going to be much higher in a country where people survive to get prostate cancer than in a country where under 5 mortality is 200 per thousand. Also, much of the concern over industrial atmosphere discharge is about visibility impairing particulates. These discharges may have very little direct health impact. Clearly trade in goods that embody aesthetic pollution concerns could be welfare enhancing. While production is mobile the consumption of pretty air is a non-tradable.[35]

While the memo speaks for itself, the hidden dimensions of the imperial inequities between the U. S. and developing nations need to be revealed and factored into the full national and global implications of economic imperialism. It is estimated by some that the average inhabitant of the United States uses 250 times the resources of the average Nigerian. That average U. S. inhabitant, if a baby born in the 1990s who reaches 75 years of age, will have generated fifty-two tons of garbage while utilizing close to 4,000 barrels of oil. The amount of energy consumed by that average U. S. resident would be equivalent to 531 Ethiopians. Meanwhile, tens of thousands of children in the developing world die each day from contaminated water.[36] These inequities tell us as much about the history of U. S. economic imperialism as they do about the continuing underdevelopment of third world countries. When UNICEF reports, as it did in 2002, that ten million children under the age of 5 died each year from preventable causes, such as malnutrition, unsafe water, and the lack of the most basic heath care, we should, in the words of ethics philosopher Peter Singer, "know that others are in much greater need ... and learn to think critically about the forces that lead to high levels of consumption and to be aware of the environmental costs of this way of living."[37]

Certainly, there are environmentalists who are thinking about the interconnections between the legacy of cheap and imperial energy resources that fuel non-sustainable agricultural production in the United States, as well as our overall "way of life." The calculations of this reliance on diminishing and polluting fossil fuels are unmistakably manifested in the following critique by Bill McKibben of U. S. industrial farming:

It takes half a gallon of oil to produce a bushel of Midwestern hybrid corn; a quarter of it is used to make fertilizer, 35 percent to power the farm machinery, 7 percent to irrigate the field, and the rest to make pesticides, to dry grain, and to perform all the other tasks of industrial farming.[38]

If McKibben and other U. S. environmentalists are not always as cognizant of the role of U. S. economic imperialism and its repercussions abroad and at home, they do provide the basis for an understanding of how de-emphasizing and deconstructing an imperial lifestyle, fed by oil transnationals, is essential to the long-term survival of the planet.

On the other hand, the more immediate ramifications of U. S. economic imperialism are felt, in particular, by those struggling to escape the traps set by U. S. transnational corporations and the international financial institutions which have, for the most part, done the bidding of U. S. companies and the U. S. government. As noted by Vandana Shiva: "Instead of a culture of abundance, profit-driven globalization creates cultures of exclusion, dispossession, and scarcity. In fact, globalization's transformation of all beings and resources into commodities robs diverse species and people of their rightful share of ecological, cultural, economic, and political space."[39] The desire to look beyond U. S.-imposed economic arrangements, whether in the form of SAPs, or IMF, WTO, and World Bank directives, and to reclaim one's own ecological, cultural, economic, and political space is evident around the globe. In Brazil, members of the Landless Peasant Movement have mobilized to contest failed IMF policies. One of the organizers of the Brazilian Landless Peasant Movement, Rogerio Mauro, explained this motivation to resist this U. S. globalized capitalism: "We want to fight this hypocritical globalization of capital and instead globalize our struggle to determine the future of our country."[40] From another perspective, an Oxfam spokesperson noted, "When only poor countries have to open their markets, it's not free trade, it's global plantation."[41] Although not alone in turning the planet into its own plantation, U. S. economic imperialism, especially since World War II and before in the case of certain commodities like bananas, has been the primary agent in both the global plantation and global apartheid.

Now, it appears that the chickens are coming home to roost. Although U. S. economic imperialism has not collapsed, the ability to sustain that economic imperialism is being eroded by numerous forces from transnational competitors to national and transnational resisters to the ultimate contradictions of the U. S. system of financial capitalism itself. Especially in the production of manufactured goods, there has been a precipitous decline from the post-World War II period. Close to 60 percent of manufactured goods world-wide were produced in the United States in 1950. By the end of the twentieth century, that had fallen to 25 percent. Although the United States had dominated industrial production in electronics and electrical equipment at mid-century, by the beginning of the twenty-first century, non-U. S. corporations occupied nine out of the top ten positions. Even in the banking sector, nineteen of the top twenty-five banks in the world were located outside the United States.[42]

While the dollar still remains the primary reserve currency in the world, the recent massive international financial failures are a direct result of financialization that was promoted by U. S. economic imperialism from the

1970s onward. The impact of the imperial logic before the collapse was noted by Will Hutton:

> by pushing the scope of U. S. financial autonomy outward, enlarging the role of the New York markets as financial intermediaries and insisting on the pivotal role of the dollar, the United States has created an environment in which essentially the rest of the world adjusts to U. S. economic choices and becomes enslaved to the prevalent U. S. financial and economic ideology.[43]

Now that those financial arrangements have turned toxic, even the formerly enthralled slaves are in revolt. Uprisings have led to the fall of governments in Iceland and Latvia. Protestors have taken to the streets from Greece to Martinique to contest their governments' complicity in the imposition of the flawed logic of the U. S.-dominated global system.

As a way of closing this chapter and foreshadowing a more detailed discussion in the conclusion of the book, I want to highlight in a very brief manner the key economic components of U. S. imperial capitalism that led up to the recent global financial crisis. The systemic and deeply rooted problems made manifest in collapsing banks and investment firms are related to economic strategies which came to prominence in the 1970s and 1980s. In particular, the strategy of financialization informed all of the speculative practices that have been part and parcel of the neoliberalism of the last third of the twentieth century and beginning of the twenty-first century. Losses of trillions of dollars in capital assets, especially in the United States, are directly attributable to the implosion of structured debt mechanisms with their so-called sophisticated and technological approaches to collateralized and securitized debt. In effect, the crude efforts to impose additional debt on developing nations, leading to massive social dislocation and a planet of slums, and the monetarist strategies to rationalize increasing consumer debt, while adopting tax policies that benefited the wealthiest at the expense of the poor and working class in the U. S., backfired. What is now better understood as the latest version of a pyramid scheme came crashing down.[44]

The imperial capitalist search for new markets and the attendant exploitation and marginalization of working multitudes abroad and at home certainly shifted wealth to those at the very top in the United States. As a consequence of domestic economic policies, especially from Reagan through Bush junior, the top 1 percent of the population in the U. S. owns over twice as much as the bottom 80 percent. In turn, as a consequence of continuous, albeit waning, economic imperialism, the income of the top 10 percent of the U. S. population, according to a 2002 United Nations Development report, is equivalent to that of the poorest 43 percent of the world population. According to calculations by the International Labor Organization, around three billion people languish in poverty, with the gap between the richest and poorest doubling in the last forty years.[45]

In ravaging the planet as part of an obsessive-compulsive drive for cheaper raw materials and goods, along with the desperate search for new markets, U. S. economic imperialism has left a legacy of devastation and despair. Yet, out of that despair have come shining examples of resistance from Indian women to Mexican peasants. (More discussion of this resistance will occur in Part III.) However, an even more insidious form of imperialism has managed to seduce many of those victimized by U. S. economic imperialism. Whether through the entertainment industry or through American-style consumption patterns, U. S. cultural imperialism has injected values and habits into the globalized world. As Eduardo Galeano mordantly observes: "The world, which puts on a banquet for all, then slams the door in the noses of so many, is simultaneously equalizing and unequal: equalizing in the ideas and habits it imposes and unequal in the opportunities it offers."[46] Trying to discern how those injections of ideas and habits have been part of U. S. cultural imperialism over the last third of the century and the ways that they have been mediated and mitigated will be the focus of the next chapter.

6 U. S. cultural imperialism and global dissonance

Released in 2001 by Twentieth Century Fox, Australian director Baz Luhr-mann's *Moulin Rouge* is a musical swirling with the influences of global popular culture, a culture with distinctive American features but decidedly hybrid in its overall make-up. Yet, for all its Bollywood bricolage, the film incorporates extensive fragments of American popular songs known to both musical theater *aficionados* and MTV devotees. Ranging from musical numbers made famous by Broadway and Hollywood stars like Carol Channing and Marilyn Monroe ("Diamonds are a Girl's Best Friend") to pop rock's Monroe wannabe, Madonna ("Like a Virgin") to Nirvana's grunge rock ("Smells Like Teen Spirit"), the musical pastiche woven together by Luhr-mann borders on sensory overload. Viewers are swept along not only by the pulsating sounds but also by the choreography that traverses distances from Paris (the Can-Can) to Buenos Aires (a Tango danced to "Roxanne") to India. At its core, however, *Moulin Rouge* is a tragic love story in operatic style with hints of thematic connections to the Greek myth of Orpheus and Verdi's *Traviata*. Given its eclectic roots and grand pretensions, the film still manages to convey its own postmodern nostalgic love affair with the Hollywood musical, especially in its brief and fragmentary allusions to *The Sound of Music*.[1]

The Sound of Music appears in another tragic musical released only a year earlier, but as a more complete and ironic reference. Directed by the Danish filmmaker, Lars von Trier, *Dancer in the Dark* not only subverts the happy escapism of classic Hollywood musicals but also challenges the subtext of the American Dream that informed many of those musicals and the broader cul-tural contexts. The protagonist of von Trier's film, Selma, played by the Ice-landic world music phenomenon, Bjork, has left her European birthplace in Czechoslovakia to seek a new life in the United States in the early 1960s with her young son. Although suffering from a congenital disease affecting the loss of her eyesight, she is determined to save money for an operation which could prevent her son from experiencing the same loss. Unfortunately, her hard-earned savings are stolen by her neighbor and landlord, Bill, an American sheriff desperate for cash. When Selma confronts him with his crime, there is a scuffle that results in his own gun accidentally wounding him. Bill begs Selma to put him out of his misery and she obliges in a grief-stricken panic. Eventually captured, charged with first-degree murder, and then condemned to death in a trial that bristles with anti-communist and anti-immigrant rhetoric from the prosecuting attorney, Selma is locked on death row, await-ing her execution by hanging.

In no way does the above brief plot summary capture all of the film's melodramatic twists and turns. Neither can it do justice to the brilliance of the fantasy sequences shot by von Trier which happen during Selma's day-dreaming, sparked by the stunning songs of Bjork. However, what must be confronted is how and why von Trier uses *The Sound of Music* as the linchpin in his critique of the Hollywood musical and its ideological baggage. As part of her limited free time, Selma has joined an amateur cast in the production of *The Sound of Music*. Struggling to manage her part as Maria in the after-math of Bill's death, Selma is arrested during a rehearsal of the musical. While in prison facing her own death, she wistfully sings the song, "These Are a Few of My Favorite Things." Unlike Maria's escape and happy ending, America and its musicals can only doom Selma to her tragic demise.

What can these brief diversions into two contemporary musicals directed by two non-U. S. directors reveal about U. S. cultural imperialism, other than that Baz Luhrmann appears to be a fan of U. S. pop culture and musicals and Lars von Trier in this (and numerous other Danish Dogma films) is a dogged critic of U. S. imperialism and culture? When one considers the connecting thread of *The Sound of Music* and what has transpired not just to the allu-sions to that musical but to the predominant role of U. S. culture in the world, one gets a sense of a more complicated and dissonant picture of U. S. cultural imperialism than either its proponents or critics are prepared to admit. Just consider that when *The Sound of Music* first appeared on Broad-way in 1959, the United States, in general, and New York, in particular, were seen as the cultural center of the world. Moreover, when the film version was released by Hollywood in 1965, the U. S. and its military and economic pro-wess seemed invincible and Hollywood studios and U. S.-made cultural arti-facts reigned supreme. Much has transpired in the half century since *The Sound of Music* rang from various hilltop theaters around the globe. Besides the erosion of U. S. global dominance and the transnational ownership of much of the global culture industry, the question of the continuing allure of and resistance to U. S. culture is certainly a more debatable matter than during the heyday of *The Sound of Music*.

So, how do we handle a problem like ... U. S. cultural imperialism? Per-haps one way of approaching the issue of cultural imperialism in general is to continue to focus on the production of music, or from an even more elemental perspective, the creation and dissemination of songs. Songs emanate from people's experiences and traditions and express a cultural repertoire of values and lifestyles. Since songs are in constant flux as part of cross-cultural exchanges, they are often transformed in subtle and not-so-subtle ways. In effect, the change in melodies and lyrics of any song adds to a new mix which may, in turn, lead to hybrid songs that engender greater dissonance rather than harmony. However, as songs become part of a music industry, considerations of power, privilege, and cultural homogenization endemic to the structural arrangements of the industry take precedence. With the aid of new techniques of transmission, a certain song may generate a privileged hearing, establishing what can be called a limited and contested hegemony. It is at that point that we arrive at a form of cultural imperialism, especially if that song operates in conjunction with particular instruments of transmission that reinforce the frequency and volume of a song.[2]

Leaving behind, for a moment, the emphasis on song, what can now be said about the larger issue of cultural imperialism? Following John Tomlinson's working definition, we can characterize cultural imperialism as "*essentially* about the exalting and spreading of values and habits – a practice in which *economic* power plays an instrumental role."[3] In the exalting and spreading of specific cultures or cultural products, the role of hegemony is critical. Thus, the degree to which any culture, often itself a result of different influences, achieves that hegemony is reflective of its capacity to render a privileged transmission and reception, albeit that reception is never one-dimensional and without potential resistances. "This hegemonic culture in powerful states may, under certain circumstances, act 'imperial' when extended beyond the borders of the country in question. Acknowledging that the dynamics of 'imperialism' have become more complex and internally contradictory in the latter part of the twentieth century does not mean that we should abandon the exploration of underlying power differences and forms of inequality."[4] Thus, while globalization certainly complicates hegemonic and imperial constructions of culture, it does not eliminate attempts at cultural imperialism and our efforts to understand, in particular, the transmission and impact of U. S. cultural imperialism.[5]

It is important to keep in mind that the transmission and impact of U. S. cultural imperialism is intimately connected to U. S. economic imperialism in its myriad forms, whether government-sponsored or as part of the strategies of U. S.-based transnational corporation. Concerning that role of the U. S. government in "promoting cultural exports," Mel van Elteren identifies the connections "not only as a source of export income, but also as a means of exporting beliefs, values, and practices that inherently favor U. S.-based corporate capitalism."[6] However, as noted in the previous chapter, there are certainly cross-purposes and contradictions in the links between the U. S. government and particular transnational corporations or interests at any historical moment. On the other hand, another insight by van Elteren conveys the more universalist pretensions of U. S. cultural imperialism. "The global dissemination of Americanized cultural goods and practices involves the spread of social visions of U. S.-style development with its heavy emphasis on 'progress' in the form of unlimited, quantitative growth and economic-technological expansion."[7] Given these universalist pretensions, there is the sense, deeply shared by U. S.-based transnational corporations, their huckster advertisers and promoters, members of the political elite, and by many citizens that "American values are, or will soon be, shared by all humankind."[8]

It might be instructive at this point to follow up on the connections between U. S. commercial culture and the transmission of certain habits and values embedded in U. S. cultural imperialism through the example of the "Coca-Colonization" of the world.[9] We have previously encountered the pernicious impact of the commercial practices of Coca-Cola in India (Chapter 5). On the other hand, Coke sees itself as a purveyor of a drink that everyone on the planet should want. In their 1993 annual report, Coca-Cola asserted:

> All of us in the Coca-Cola family wake up each morning knowing that every single one of the world's 5.6 billion people will get thirsty that day. ... If we make it impossible for these 5.6 billion people to escape Coca-Cola ... then we assure our future success for many years to come. Doing anything else is not an option.[10]

Beyond the corporate pep-talk and commercial imperatives, Coke has designed advertising jingles that are intended to capture the attention of prospective consumers of Coke. In an early 1970s Coke musical advertisement this brand of cola drink is promoted not only as something to quench one's thirst but also as an example of bringing the world together in "perfect harmony." In the visual rendition of the musical advertisement, the ideal of perfect harmony is reinforced by scores of identifiable ethnic types in their native dress all singing about "teaching the world to sing in perfect harmony," while consuming, of course, the perfect drink – Coca-Cola.

The ideology of this advertisement not only reveals some interesting contradictions about U. S. cultural imperialism but also about the role of advertising in spreading the habit of drinking Coke and the value of being an Americanized consumer. This Coke ad emerged at almost exactly the same time as the defeat of the United States in Vietnam in 1973. That war, with its massive imperial destruction of a third world country and millions of its people, certainly sullied the reputation of the United States throughout the world. On one level, the Coke ad attempts to recuperate a vision of peace, love, and understanding for an American product by obliterating the reality of the U. S. devastation of Southeast Asia and substituting the idealized and utopian vision of a diverse world in perfect harmony. Coke, thus, promotes itself as an instrument to heal the world, or, at least, make it whole for purposes of commodity fetishism and cultural homogenization. Ironically, the jingle also conveys the idea that Coke is a "gift" from some disembodied individual among the ethnically and culturally diverse chorus. Of course, Coke does not arrive as a gift but as a commercial product to be purchased, often at the expense of one's indigenous resources and overall nutrition. Thus, the musical advertisement hopes to seduce the listener and viewer to become a habitual consumer of Coke, along with its subliminal cultural imperialist agenda.[11]

The intricate interpenetrations of consumerism, commercial practices, like advertising, and the entertainment industry constitute the structural and ideological parameters of cultural imperialism. In order to explore those parameters in greater depth, I want to turn to two differing interpretations of U. S. cultural imperialism, especially probing their contrasting perspectives on McDonald's, film, television, and popular music. The author of one of the texts, *Weapons of Mass Distraction*, Matthew Fraser, is a conservative Canadian political scientist and journalist whose views on U. S. cultural influence in the world are congruent with those of American triumphalists, Henry Luce and Thomas Friedman. On the other hand, Ziauddin Sardar and Merryl Wyn Davies, authors of *Why Do People Hate America?*, are cultural studies scholars in Great Britain, well-versed in Islam and the accompanying Orientalist ideologies of the West, whose book is unremitting in its criticisms of all aspects of U. S. imperialism. While both books offer important insights into U. S. cultural imperialism, their overdetermined readings of the impact of that cultural imperialism should provide the necessary outer borders from which we can better discern the inner dialectical play of cultural production and reception.[12]

Before turning to their specific and differing analyses of the topics delineated in the previous paragraph, it is essential to highlight their theoretical perspectives on cultural imperialism. Fraser expands on the key metaphor of U. S. political scientist, Joseph Nye, on American "soft power," which Nye defines as "the ability to achieve desired outcomes in international affairs through attraction rather than coercion (18)." (This bifurcation of soft and hard power overlooks the degree to which U. S. imperial policies are often a combination of both at the same time.) For Fraser, then, "soft power has become increasingly instrumental in the emerging world order dominated by an American Empire (9)." Identifying the cultural components of soft power as "movies, pop music, television, fast food, fashion, theme parks," Fraser, in a nod to Tomlinson, acknowledges that the cultural imperialism of soft power "spreads, validates, and reinforces common norms, values, beliefs, and life styles" in a manner that "seduces" and "persuades" (10). While American soft power "incites awe and envy," it also "provokes resentment and hostility (11)." Since Fraser is convinced, not unlike Luce and Friedman, that the world is pre-ordained to desire and want American culture in all its myriad forms, he is eager to affirm "that American soft power … promotes the values and beliefs that, while contentious, are ultimately good for the world (260)."

On the other hand, Sardar and Davies insist that U. S. cultural imperialism is not only bad for the world, but is so overpowering and totalistic in its influence that there is little capacity to resist. While the irresistible nature of U. S. cultural imperialism may seem to be a common thread in both books, Sardar and Davies allude to metaphors that underscore the malevolent nature of that cultural imperialism. From the Australian science author and cultural critic, Margaret Wertheim, they cite her references to comparing

> American culture to the AIDS virus, HIV. Like that brilliantly adapted organism, U. S. culture is endlessly self-replicating and alarmingly adept at co-opting the production machinery of its hosts. ... So too, American fast food culture, pop music, films and television infect the cultural body of other nations, co-opting local production machinery to focus their efforts on mimicry (117).

According to Sardar and Davies, the patterns of viral replication are so insidious because of the universal appeals of American abundance and affluence (117–18).

> To replicate American abundance – the choice of goods, the service and lifestyle it permits – does not involve a free choice of means, but adaptation to the constraints of the "virus": a particular kind of economic organisation, particular political and social forms, that inevitably compromise the "immune system" of the host (118).

In effect, Sardar and Davies deny any possibility for the host to withstand the virus of U. S. cultural imperialism, thus eliminating the role of agency.

Reinforcing the helplessness and even complicity of the victim of U. S. cultural imperialism, Sardar and Davies cite the British sociologist, Steve Fuller's metaphor of "bioterrorism," (118) a metaphor that Fraser contends is representative of "anti-American extremists" (256). As Fuller points out, bioterrorism leads to "victims ... who infect each other with the germ or virus in their day-to-day interactions." Applying his model of bioterrorism to McDonald's, Fuller notes that

> the proliferation of burgers has had a devastating effect on most of the world – from forcing the natives to adopt the practices of American culture to blighting their cultural and physical landscapes. In fact, when the natives start behaving more like the burger giants, and start infecting themselves with their attitudes and behaviour (impatience, obesity, heart disease, etc.), they become even more susceptible to even more American interventions (131).[13]

Given the widespread proliferation of McDonald's restaurants, estimated in 2007 as more than 30,000 in close to 120 countries world-wide with revenues of around 23 billion dollars, the pernicious influence is evident, if not at the over-the-top metaphorical level of bioterrorism.

While Fraser does not deny the global impact of McDonald's, he spells out the local adaptations by McDonald's to varying cultural tastes, something Sardar and Davies skeptically skip over in their analysis. From "McQuesos" in Uruguay (251) to "teriyaki burgers" in Japan (255), one sees the influence of hybridity in the global market which certainly dilutes U. S. cultural imperialism.[14] On the other hand, Fraser appears blind to connections between McDonald's and the "phenomenon of rationalized modernization, part and parcel of the mass society with its frenzied pace and standardized consumption and production."[15] Embedded in this production is the larger issue of industrial farming and the related environmental concerns about destruction of rain forests and the immense consumption and pollution of resources that accompany the raising and slaughter of cattle that Fraser completely neglects. Fraser seems so taken with explaining the symbolic allure of McDonald's as a positive element of U. S. culture that he obfuscates what is the cultural logic of contemporary consumerism and its connections to U. S. cultural imperialism.[16]

Although cognizant of the interrelationship between consumerism and U. S. cultural imperialism, Sardar and Davies also elevate the lowly hamburger to metaphorical status in their extended discussion of American fast food and McDonald's. As they assert,

> A true hamburger is a superabundant, multi-layered compound entity. It is the degree to which America proclaims and glories in itself as a compound whole that makes the hamburger such a powerful metaphor for the nation, and such a potent symbol and focus for criticism of America in the rest of the world (103).

However, Sardar and Davies, as well as Fraser, completely overlook the very real issue of nutritional value at the core of American fast food and its export as junk to the rest of the world. According to a consultant to the World Health Organization,

> Not only are McDonald's encouraging the use of a style of food which is closely associated with the risk of cancer and heart disease, whilst health professionals are trying to reduce the risks to Western populations, but they are actively promoting to the same cultures where at present these diseases are not a problem.[17]

Because of his focus on the symbolic role of McDonald's, Fraser claims that the "nutritional merits of Big Macs ... misses the point." Dismissing those who focus on the "nutritional deficiencies" of "American fast-food imperialism" as cranks and even "anti-American extremists" (256), Fraser obscures one of the essential critiques of both American fast-food imperialism and McDonald's.

Even more pernicious in Fraser's discussion of McDonald's is his tendentious and ideologically crude attack on one of the leading global critics of McDonald's and McDonaldization, José Bové. Bové's 1999 assault on a McDonald's site in the French town of Millau, close to Bové's farm where he produced Roquefort cheese, propelled him into the spotlight as a key critic and activist against imperial globalization. Lumping Bové with those who object to U. S. cultural imperialism out of "commercial protectionism" (243), Fraser goes on to label Bové as a "canny publicity seeker" and "jet-setting" member of the "radical ranks of the anti-globalization movement (246–7)." While acknowledging Bové's role in fighting corporate globalization, at least Sardar and Davies refer to Bové's co-authoring a book "which outlines an alternative vision of sustainable and humane farming (117)." By using Bové as an ideological punching bag to ridicule those activists and critics of the wholesomeness of McDonald's, Fraser maligns any substantive critique of and alternative to U. S. cultural imperialism.

Yet, Fraser is not unaware of the narrow nationalist practices of U. S. cultural imperialism, especially when it comes to the exporting of Hollywood films. In recounting the Cold War promotion of cultural imperialism by the U. S. government, Fraser cites the creation of a State Department office, the Informational Media Guaranty, which helped subsidize the export of Hollywood films that positively portrayed American values (60). Later, in the 1970s, tax incentives and shelters allowed Hollywood to expand their markets worldwide (66–7) where revenues from film exports reached as much as half of the total profits. When that expansion ran up against trade barriers by specific countries attempting to protect their own film industry, e.g. France, Hollywood used its powerful world-wide distribution networks to place blockbuster films in theaters around the globe (68–70). Ironically, Hollywood became a target in the 1990s for foreign banks and corporations, such as the French bank, Credit Lyonnais, and the Japanese company, Sony, transforming Hollywood into a more transnational site of a globalized entertainment industry.

Nevertheless, some Hollywood companies remained powerful vehicles of U. S. cultural imperialism. From its founding, Disney, under the leadership of Walt Disney, proclaimed its commitment to help export the American way of life. Seeming to channel Henry Luce, Disney, as Fraser notes, asserted that "it was America's destiny to export values, institutions, and politics of democracy and capitalism to achieve peaceful dominion over the rest of the world (78)." After Disney's death, his company began its transformation into a prominent global giant in the entertainment industry. Under Michael Eisner, Disney expanded its operations in the 1980s and 1990s into a wide-ranging entertainment network that included its theme parks, cruise liners, and retail stores (79). Although the theme parks attracted millions of visitors, they, also, especially EuroDisney in France, encountered protest and cultural clashes (86–9). One such denunciation of EuroDisney labeled it a "construction of hardened chewing gum and idiotic folklore taken straight out of comic books written for obese Americans (87)."

Another Disney firestorm of controversy occurred with the international distribution in 1993 of the animated film, *Aladdin*, with its demeaning portrayals of Arabs. Although Fraser duly notes the criticisms by Arab countries and the American-Arab Anti-Discrimination Committee, especially after additional films, such as *Rules of Engagement,* perpetrated further pejorative stereotypes (79), he skips lightly over one of the prime functions of cultural imperialism, i.e. the facilitation of ideological hegemony within domestic U. S. culture.[18] Sardar and Davies, however, examine *Rules of Engagement*, its anti-Arab message, and U. S. audience response in more depth (41–4). Citing one review of the film that reported the audience cheering Marines as they fired into a crowd of Yemeni civilians, containing women and children (41), Sardar and Davies conclude their own review of the film with an indictment that this movie and other Hollywood films convey simple-minded stereotypes that reinforce cultural biases and clichés about Arabs, in particular, and racial others, in general (44). Unfortunately, there is still a tendency in their review of this film and other media constructions to neglect any interpretive ambiguity, especially when it comes to the multiple meanings that audiences often take away from media constructions.[19]

The impact of Hollywood images may no longer carry the same hegemonic weight they carried in the past as a consequence of the role of globalization and the emergence of film competitors to Hollywood. Sardar and Davies appear to be incapable of recognizing this development, especially persisting in the belief that "American-led globalization (121)" is so overwhelming and totalistic that it allows no space for the flourishing of other cultures and their creations. They reduce the success of Bollywood to the mere imitation of the "production values" of Hollywood (121). While Fraser admits that recently "Bollywood has followed Hollywood's example of churning out more escapist fare (107)," he does provide a more balanced overview of the emergence of Bollywood and its Indian cultural roots. On the other hand, he is too quick to attribute anti-Hollywood sentiments in India to narrow-minded Hindu nationalism (106–8). Moreover, he too glibly dismisses the possibility that Bollywood might have any rival impact on the global film industry beyond the Indian diasporic community (108). Apparently, Fraser shares with Sardar and Davies an ignorance of the kind of "critical transculturalism" that Bollywood and other hybridized cultural products spread around the world, influencing, as noted in the opening paragraph of this chapter, non-Indian films like *Moulin Rouge*.[20]

When it comes to the influence of U. S. television, Sardar and Davies decry the dumping of American TV programs around the world with the attendant ideological contamination and hyper-consumerism (122–4). Fraser provides more insight into the corporate sponsorship of such consumerism, albeit with his own implicit endorsement of the culture and lifestyle accompanying such consumerism. He quotes a senior executive with ABC international concerning the link between television and consumerism: "It is highly desirable from the standpoint of the economies of these countries that television be brought in, so it can fulfill its natural function as a giant pump fueling the machine of consumer demand (118)." Unlike Sardar and Davies, Fraser is more skeptical of the ideological impact of U. S. television on global audiences, arguing that the "cultural influence via television was diverse, complex, and multilayered (134)." Yet Fraser is too quick to reject the connections between U. S. television and cultural imperialism. His argument that the "influence of American culture is sometimes a welcome antidote to local cultural suffocation (166)" does not negate the larger promotion of a capitalist modernity embedded in U. S. cultural imperialism.[21] On the other hand, his recognition that television "has been the subject of considerable cross-cultural hybridization and regional exchanges" (166) captures the more complicated and contradictory nature of U. S. cultural imperialism in a globalized world.

Of course, the fact that there are more diverse influences and competitors to the predominance of U. S. cultural imperialism does not preclude the desire of the U. S. entertainment industry to achieve pre-eminence in market share. Noting the global aspirations of MTV and its Washington supporters, Fraser cites the head of MTV declaring in the early 1990s that "our goal is to be in every home in the world." As part of that goal, MTV adopted a campaign reminiscent of the 1970s Coke commercial: "One Planet, One Music" (193). For Sardar and Davies MTV's orientation to youth culture and its commodified musical tastes is part of "the pursuit of endless consumption, the withdrawal of all collective, communal and social responsibility (125)." Furthermore, they see indigenous music as being overwhelmed by Western popular music, torn from its roots and homogenized to appeal to the pop music sensibilities of youth culture (125–6). Once again they allow no room for a dialectical interaction of critical transculturalism with the active involvement of varying agents. On this point, Fraser occupies a more solid and agency-oriented position. "Music," he contends, "is subject to a complex interaction of styles, forms, trends, and influences that do not obey – and indeed often defy – reductionist theories about one-way cultural 'hegemony' (187)."

Nevertheless, Fraser does examine the efforts of those in the music industry and their Washington boosters to spread the values and beliefs of U. S. culture. Referring to MTV as a "pulsing electronic extension of the American Empire," Fraser describes MTV's efforts, helped along by the Bush Administration, to tap into the Islamic world with its own brand of world music (172). As part of a campaign to "win the hearts and minds of Moslem youths (172)," this musical appeal was connected to the larger propaganda effort by the Bush Administration to allay the fears, suspicions, and antagonisms of the Arab and Islamic world. Another aspect of that strategy took place in 2002 when then Secretary of State, Colin Powell, appeared on MTV. When he was asked about his response to being associated with the "Great Satan," Powell's retort was that "far from being a Great Satan, I think we are the Great Protector (221)." (This from the man who once boasted that he wanted the United States to be "the bully on the block.")

Ironically, the Great Protector was incapable of protecting the domination of the music industry by U. S. companies. Throughout the Cold War period, the music industry, the State Department, and the Voice of America spread jazz throughout the world as a way of showcasing African-American culture and artists even while their fellow African-Americans during the 1950s and 1960s were still treated as second-class citizens. As the influence of jazz waned and the sounds of rock-and-roll pervaded the airwaves, the U. S.-based music industry was unchallenged in its global hegemony. However, by 2003 only one of the big five global music companies was American (Warner). The others were German (BMG), Japanese (SONY), British (EMI), and French (Universal) (186). It seems that the Great Protector had become, in more ways than one, the Great Pretender. And like that oldie-but-goodie from the 1950s sung by the Platters, one line from the lyrics seemed particularly pertinent not only to what had become of the dominance of the U. S. music industry, but to the vaunted power and prestige of U. S. cultural imperialism: "I seem to be what I'm not you see."

Like other illusions that leave traces and residues of an evanescent reality, U. S. cultural imperialism still lives on in the fantasies and dreams generated not just by the American entertainment industry but also by the fading allure of capitalist modernity. As noted by French cultural critic Jean Baudrillard, U. S. film and other cultural artifacts have been integral to the promotion of the ideology of abundance and affluence. "Whatever happens," Baudrillard muses,

> and whatever one thinks of the arrogance of the dollar and multi-nationals, it is this culture which, the world over, fascinates those very people who suffer most at its hands, and it does so through the deep insane conviction that it has made all their dreams come true.[22]

Certainly, Sardar and Davies are convinced that the dreams spread by U. S. cultural imperialism are responsible for only creating nightmares from which there is no escape. They too readily assume either the incapacity of resistance or its futility. On the other hand, Fraser touts the goodness and emancipatory qualities of U. S. culture for a global populace hungry for its products. Even his ideological soul-mate, Thomas Friedman, recognizes the partly illusory nature of that cultural global spread. According to Friedman, "globalization is a means for spreading the fantasy of America around the world. In today's global village people know there is another way to live, they know about the American lifestyle, and many of them want as big a slice of it as they can get with all the toppings."[23]

However, the reality evaded by Fraser and Friedman is the degree to which the desire for another way of life is integral to the "global diffusion of consumerist beliefs and practices" and the contingent role played in that diffusion by U. S. cultural imperialism.[24] For Friedman and Fraser, the U. S. is a "benevolent hegemon" (263) which remains essential for the betterment of humankind. Their cultural and ideological blinders not only make them incapable of understanding the underbelly of globalization with its exclusions and depredations but also of recognizing the persistence of the local in the face of U. S. consumerism and cultural homogenization. In the latter belief, they share common ground with Sardar and Davies who also see the disappearance of the local. As a response to such a totalistic orientation to globalization, Manfred Steger contends that "rather than being obliterated by Western consumerist forces of homogenization, local difference and particularity evolve into new cultural constellations and discourses."[25] It is those new cultural constellations and discourses, articulated by other publics and represented in other worlds, that will be explored in detail in Part III. For now, I want to conclude this chapter with a brief discussion of a man and his songs that expressed new musical constellations which emanated from local particularities but resonated around the globe.

At about the exact time that Coke was distributing its musical jingle about keeping the world company in perfect harmony, an album was released by Island Records called *Catch a Fire*, featuring Bob Marley and the Wailers from Jamaica. The sounds and songs of this album, while a hybrid mix of U. S. R&B and Soul, Jamaican ska and rock steady, and even Asian-Caribbean influences, were expressions of a new and compelling musical idiom, reggae. Growing out of experiences with oppression and exploitation, reggae formulated lyrics that conveyed not only protest of oppressive conditions but also the desire and hopes for redemption. Tied to those desires for redemption, reggae and some of its leading exponents, like Bob Marley, endorsed Rastafarianism, a Jamaican-based cultural revitalization movement which believed that the former emperor of Ethiopia, Haile Selassie, was a divine figure and that ganga (marijuana) was a sacred plant to be used for sacramental purposes. While these Rastafarian beliefs were not always understood by listeners to the music, especially those outside Jamaica or the black diasporic communities in Great Britain and elsewhere, the fact was that reggae, and particularly its crown prince, Bob Marley, gained a world-wide hearing and following.[26]

Marley's musical skills and charismatic performances garnered such global prominence as a consequence of the seductive qualities of reggae music and its protest lyrics which did resonate with a diverse population around the world. One protest anthem is the song, "Get Up, Stand Up" from the 1973 album, *Burnin'*, which contains the lyrics that encourage its listeners to "stand up for your rights," a very different message than the Coke musical commercial making the rounds that same year. Additional lyrics from the same song carry a critique of the allure of wealth. Embedded in these lyrics and the overall posture of Marley's reggae music is also, according to Paul Gilroy, "a critique of the economy of time and space which is identified with the world of work and wages from which blacks are excluded and from which they, as a result, announce and celebrate their exclusion."[27]

One of the most compelling of Marley's songs of that racial exclusion amounted to a direct challenge to the global apartheid that condemned people of color to inferior positions. Transforming an address given by Haile Selassie before the United Nations in October 1963, Marley produces a lyrical condemnation of the denial of rights for people of color and the inevitable conflict that will result from that denial in the song, "War," released as part of the 1976 album, *Rastaman Vibration*. Among the most pertinent lines from Selassie's speech are the following:

> That until the philosophy which holds one race superior and another inferior is finally and permanently discredited and abandoned; That until there are no longer first-class and second-class citizens of any nation; That until the color of a man's skin is of no more significance than the color of his eyes; That until the basic human rights are equally guaranteed to all without regard to race; That until that day, the dream of lasting peace and world citizenship and the rule of international morality will remain a fleeting illusion, to be pursued but never attained.

While not eschewing the healing power of love and the hope for redemption, Marley was clearly in tune with both local and global aspirations to "stand up for your rights." Whether that stand was against racial oppression or the pernicious effects of colonialism and imperialism, Marley and his music became an alternative beacon to the imposition of any form of imperialism, economic or cultural. He shared what Gustavo Esteva and Madhi Suri Prakash call a form of "political humility" that

> struggles for the dignity of all peoples, embracing the premise which rejects the supposed superiority of any culture, any ideology, any political position, over the others. It dreams of a world in which everyone can pose and propose their views and intentions to others, but no one can impose their own on others.[28]

The world Bob Marley dreamed of was not the spurious and ahistorical Coke-sponsored one of perfect harmony, but a historically rooted vision that sought a way out of "mental slavery" and other kinds of cognitive and bodily oppression. Struggling to find redemption in an oppressive world, Marley sang about not being intimidated or persuaded by the power of Babylon, or, its more recent incarnation, the United States. Having spent time in the United States in the mid-1960s, Marley complained that "everything was too fast, too noisy, too rush-rush."[29] Although attracted to the sounds of U. S. popular music, especially the soulful Sam Cooke, Marley found a way to craft his own musical style, trumping in the process the rule and role of any external culture. In turn, his listeners, especially in "post-imperial Britain," found in "his egalitarianism, Ethiopianism and anti-imperialism, his critique of law and the types of work ... meanings with which to make sense of their lives."[30]

Marley's songs and legacy certainly contradict the perspective that there is only one form of globalization. As we will see in Part III, alternative voices and visions challenge globalization from above. So, we must close this chapter and Part II with the understanding that no one nation or culture or even class owns globalization even though nations, most recently the United States with its imperial culture, and new classes, such as an emergent transnational class, attempt to direct and control that globalization. Nevertheless, forces from below guarantee that globalization will remain contested territory, constantly open to the eruptions of global dissonance and dissidence.

Part III
Other publics, other worlds

7 Transnational counterpublics and the globalization of resistance

> Wherever there is domination, there is resistance to domination. Wherever there is imposition of meaning, there are projects of alternative meaning. And the realms of this resistance, and this autonomous meaning are ubiquitous.
>
> Manuel Castells

> If there is any hope, it must depend on a new way of thinking, and a new way of taking action. We must spike the lies of political life, and surmount every constraint. We must mount an international general strike against war.
>
> Petra Kelly

Writing in the midst of the violent proxy wars waged by U. S. sponsored military regimes and guerrillas in the 1980s in Central America, Noam Chomsky bemoaned the fact that the "highly refined ideological institutions (in the United States) protect us from seeing the plight (of) ... millions of suffering and tormented people through much of the Third World ... and our role in maintaining it, except sporadically." Proceeding to decry the lack of "honesty and moral courage" in "hearing the cries of the victims," Chomsky challenged the mainstream media to present the actual suffering of others to citizens of the United States. Envisioning such a change of media focus, he imagined the following:

> We would turn on the radio in the morning and listen to the voices of the people who escaped the massacres in Quiche province and the Guazapa mountains, and the daily press would carry front-page pictures of children dying of malnutrition and disease in the countries where order reigns and crops and beef are exported to the American market, with an explanation of why this is so. We would listen to the extensive and detailed record of terror and torture in our dependencies compiled by Amnesty International, Americas Watch, Survival International, and other human rights organizations.

Realizing, however, that "we successfully insulate ourselves from the grim reality," Chomsky charges "we sink to a level of moral depravity that has few counterparts in the modern world."[1]

In many respects, the suffering of millions as a consequence of the imperial policies of the United States and its internationally controlled organizations still remains invisible to U. S. citizens. On the other hand, the expansion of global communication networks and alternative media, especially through the World Wide Web and the internet, has made the plight of the oppressed and the poor throughout the world more accessible to people around the globe, and, in particular, to the highly wired U. S. Acting on that information and with a sense of moral urgency, the very human rights agencies cited by Chomsky and other new transnational networks have grown rapidly. The interconnections of a globalized world that have facilitated the penetration of micro-imperial economic and cultural policies have also produced growing awareness and activism not only on the part of citizens of the U. S. and global North, but also by those who Chomsky portrayed as somewhat passive victims. Utilizing the very tools first invented in imperial America as an extension of its geopolitical dominance, specifically the internet, global networks have emerged that challenge U. S. imperialism while creating new sites of political engagement and resistance in what Manuel Castells calls "grassrooting the space of flows."[2]

In order to understand the development of those transnational spaces of political engagement and resistance, it is first necessary to determine how those sites are constituted. One way of conceptualizing the crystallization of such sites is through the idea of counterpublics. Following the work of feminist political philosopher, Nancy Fraser, counterpublics articulate alternative forms of public discourse and political action, contesting in the process the privileged constitution and constituency of the legitimatized public sphere.[3] Transnational counterpublics, hence, act to widen and democratize the already enlarged social spaces created by "the accelerated space of transnational practices that become routine practices in social life."[4] Transnational counterpublics, then, are less like social movements, although such movements often constitute important elements of counterpublics, than mobilized networks of globally conscious individuals who share a "perception of the interconnectedness of the world and of humanity."[5] Furthermore, transnational counterpublics are not the same as Non-Governmental Organizations (NGOs) because they lack the bureaucratic and institutional links to dominant publics. Yet, in contesting how the dominant publics are constructed and the political frames within which they operate, transnational counterpublics reveal the limitations and contradictions of both the dominant discourse and its vehicles of transmission.[6]

That contestation by transnational counterpublics is linked to what Christopher Chase-Dunn and Barry Gills call the "globalization of resistance." Beyond challenging globalization from above, such "globalization of resistance" nurtures the kind of grassroots participatory democracy that attempts "to build bridges and solidarities." What Chase-Dunn and Gills identify as "core values" of the "new social movements of resistance" are also among the essential defining characteristics of the transnational counterpublics that will be highlighted in this chapter: "nonviolent struggles, democratic practice, social justice ... peace, solidarity ... and equality (including opposition to patriarchal forms of oppression against women as well as class, caste, and ethnic-based discrimination)."[7] It should be clear that the kinds of solidarity enacted by transnational counterpublics differ from the forms of afflicted solidarities discussed in Chapter 3. As a consequence of the transnational connections embedded in globalization of resistance, such solidarity "invokes empathy with, rather than sympathy for, other struggles leading to a solidarity ... based on reciprocity and a sense of ultimately interconnected fates."[8]

What I want to explore in this chapter are the particular social spaces and political sites around which transnational counterpublics coalesce and the means by which they articulate and enact those core values. As a way of introducing this focus, I want to return to Chomsky's references to the horrific U. S.-sponsored tragedies engulfing Central America during the 1980s and the emergence of solidarity networks and transnational counterpublics involved with the situation in Central America and Central American migrants and refugees. In particular, Salvadoran and Guatemalan migrants, along with religious and political networks in the United States, organized a number of human rights and solidarity groups in the 1980s that addressed the human rights abuses in Central America and the problems encountered by refugees and migrants from these countries. Those organizations included the Committee in Solidarity with the People of El Salvador (CISPES) and the Network in Solidarity with the People of Guatemala (NISGUA). Given their stated solidarity efforts, continuing right-wing hysteria about "communism," and budding government obsession with "international terrorism," CISPES and other Central American solidarity activists were subjected to surveillance and even harassment and intimidation. While many of these organizations fell by the wayside after peace arrangements were negotiated in the 1990s in El Salvador and Guatemala, others took up the concerns directly related to conditions in the *maquila* industries in Central America. Confronting the labor repression in the U. S.-supported free trade zones, activists in Central America and the United States worked towards transnational solidarity through a variety of campaigns. While not always successful or even considerate of the full context of the economic exploitation and political oppression, labor and human rights activists did manage to create a transnational counterpublic which contested exploitative and oppressive conditions in Central America.[9]

Before moving on to more substantive examples of transnational counterpublics, I want to make some tentative remarks about the context and mechanisms underlying the Central American transnational counterpublic cited above. Although before the public deployment of the internet, the communications network was extensively developed and reinforced by the flow of migrants and refugees from Central America. Institutional connections from churches to unions to college campuses provided important sites where all of the issues related to Central America, from escaping death squads to finding work, could be articulated. Hence, the exchange and distribution of vital and compelling information was circulated throughout an emergent transnational counterpublic. As one study of the "transnational character of the Central

America solidarity movement of the 1980s" notes: "Missionaries, church workers, and Central American opposition leaders and refugees were all part of a transnational network that opposed U. S. policy toward the region and provided firsthand information that sometimes contradicted that given by the Reagan administration and the mainstream media."[10]

The fact that the Reagan Administration made Central America a prime target of its foreign policy meant that their framing of the public debates and the mainstream media parroting of Administration claims created an obvious opportunity to challenge and repudiate their ideological assertions.[11] In effect, this particular transnational counterpublic was as much a consequence of the attempts by the Reagan Administration to set the public agenda as it was a result of the transnational interactions between Central America and the United States. It was out of this mobilized transnational counterpublic that key oppositional movements developed around Reagan's Central American policy. In addition to those mentioned above, three specific organizations – Sanctuary, Witness for Peace, and the Pledge of Resistance – mobilized tens of thousands of U. S. citizens who were prepared to transgress whatever legal and/or legislative restrictions the Reagan administration tried to impose in order to manifest the highest expression of transnational solidarity.[12]

Another transnational counterpublic owed its coalescence to a different aspect of Reagan's foreign policy. As a direct response to Reagan's intent to expand the placement of nuclear weapons in Western Europe, the traditional peace movements in the United States and Europe saw an explosion in their ranks.[13] Although the new weapons systems, such as the MX and Pershing II missiles, had been given the green light by the Carter Administration in the late 1970s, Reagan entered the presidency in 1981 committed to ramping up not only the development and deployment of these and other new nuclear weapons systems but also the Cold War rhetoric. In particular, the unilateral and belli-cose assertion by the Reagan Administration to deploy Pershing II and ground-launched cruise missiles in a number of Western European countries as a warning about U. S. first-strike capabilities aroused massive opposition, result-ing in demonstrations in late 1981 and early 1982 of hundreds of thousands in Bonn, London, Paris, Rome, and Amsterdam. For peace activists in the United States, such European activism operated as a potential catalyst. Wrote one such activist: "This movement has created hope and therein lies the hope for us all. They send us a challenge: Why do you not scream, America?"[14]

Certainly, the Western European demonstrations and subsequent anti-nuke campaigns inspired U. S. peace activists as well as garnering attention by the mainstream media.[15] As the U. S. Nuclear Freeze campaign kicked into gear and mobilized for what would be the spectacular demonstration in June 1982 of one million people in New York City, it appeared that a significant transnational counterpublic would emerge. However, there were clear limitations on the Nuclear Freeze movement that prevented it from developing a sense of global resistance, unlike what transpired in Western Europe. Constrained by a "sociopolitical environment" that "made it difficult for the (Freeze) to move beyond a bilateral Cold War orientation," the transnational perspective of the U. S. anti-nuke campaign was impeded.[16] In highlighting some of the developments and limitations of the Freeze movement, as well as particular eruptions within the peace activist networks in the United States and Europe during this time, I want to explore the degree to which transnational counterpublics were either able to emerge or hampered in their emergence. Such an investigation should provide further insight into the formation of transnational solidarity and the globalization of resistance before the arrival of the internet and other computer-mediated methods of communication.

Of course, print communication and global exchanges by peace activists at the time provided vehicles for constituting transnational counterpublics. Such intellectuals and activists like British historian E. P. Thompson and Australian pediatrician Helen Caldicott could be seen as transnational counterpublic catalysts in their work. Thompson wrote an impassioned essay in the January 1981 edition of the U. S. progressive journal, *The Nation*, which implored citizens of the U. S. to mobilize against the installation of cruise missiles in Europe.[17] While there were many more voices added to his, the eloquence of his plea and persistence of the work of the organization he belonged to, the Campaign for Nuclear Disarmament (CND), definitely inspired activists in the United States. (It was certainly formative in my own eventual engagement with the anti-nuke movement. In 1983, I became part of a group of peace and anti-nuke activists in the greater Detroit area who attempted to blockade the entrance to a local manufacturer that made engines for the cruise missile.) Caldicott's revival of the organization, Physicians for Social Responsibility, and her outspoken dramatic appeals against nuclear weapons and nuclear power had a major impact on public awareness.[18]

However, to the degree that public awareness was also shaped by the mainstream media, it placed certain constraints on the Freeze movement and its capacity to project its own political analysis and strategies. As the movement gained momentum in 1982, especially at the grassroots level with New England town meetings passing freeze resolutions aimed at calling on the U. S. and USSR to impose a freeze on the production, testing, and deployment of nuclear weapons and missiles, the mainstream media began to run extensive new stories that actually helped to generate public sympathy and support. Nonetheless, many of those stories conveyed a media frame that trivialized and distorted the Freeze movement in a way that depoliticized that movement and added to its own internal contradictions.[19] Although those contradictions were evident with the emergence of the Freeze as a public campaign to attract the middle class and lobby Congress for arms control measures,

> the media had legitimated and appropriated the nuclear fear underlying much freeze support and had translated it into a humanitarian concern that had little to do with policy. This concern was expressed as so moderate and apolitical that it could continue to demonstrate very high levels of support in public opinion polls without having any effect on politics or policy.[20]

Certainly, for those who had been among the founders of the Freeze movement, such as Randall Forsberg, their vision of the movement did embody a more radical and transnational approach. In her presentation to the World Council of Churches' International Public Hearing on Nuclear Weapons and Disarmament in November 1981, Forsberg discussed the need to "mobilize the middle class, to give them hope and to bring them actively into the ranks of those who oppose the arms race." Such a mobilization, then,

> would show that human beings can direct their own destiny; that we can harness the arms race; that together, we are stronger than the military industrial complex; that human will can prevail over the technological imperative. It would demonstrate that we can 'democratize' and therefore eventually abolish the ancient, pernicious, elite institutions of warfare and exploitative foreign policy.[21]

Yet, Forsberg's idealistic rhetoric came crashing down around the narrowly constructed class constituency of the white middle class and the almost exclusive focus on lobbying Congress and electoral politics. While gaining legitimacy and creating a national agenda around arms control, the Freeze deliberately distanced itself from those peace and justice activists who wanted a broader and more radical agenda. This was especially evident in the June 1982 demonstration when voices urging denunciation of Israel's invasion of Lebanon and condemnation of U. S. intervention throughout the third world were dismissed.[22] In effect, the Freeze created a public awareness and movement with limited national goals while constraining those who wished to generate a transnational counterpublic linked to global resistance.

On the other hand, the context out of which the Freeze operated did motivate other groups and networks, some of which existed prior to the Freeze, to move towards that transnational counterpublic. One such group was the Women's Pentagon Actions (WPA). Growing out of the radical pacifist organization, the War Resister's League, the WPA mounted its first demonstration in November 1980, shortly after the election of Reagan. Poet and activist Grace Paley announced their solidarity with women and oppressed people around the planet, underscoring in the process their desire to build another world. The second demonstration in November 1981, built on the inspiration of the activism in Western Europe, linked their efforts to express a feminist anti-militarism with a larger political perspective. As one of the participants acknowledged,

> Again and again we reminded ourselves that our symbolic protest would develop in significance only if we live out our politics in our lives. The WPA expressed a global vision and a determination to end the obscenity of racist, women hating, death wish governments.[23]

While the WPA with its global vision was central to an emergent transnational counterpublic, it was, nevertheless, marginal to the larger anti-nuke movement in the United States. On the other hand, what materialized in Western Europe did qualify as a transnational counterpublic. As a consequence of its ability to look beyond the bilateralism and Cold War politics that constrained the anti-nuke forces in the United States, those in Western Europe, such as the CND in Great Britain, the Interchurch Peace Council in the Netherlands, and the Green Party in West Germany, were able not only to challenge the deployment of cruise and Pershing II missiles in the countries but also to mobilize around a global vision of disarmament and peace. In Great Britain, women set up a peace camp outside the Greenham Common U. S. Air Force base in 1981 that became a lightning rod for several years thereafter for transnational women's peace networks and activists. In West Germany, a traditional Easter Peace March dating back to 1960 that had been almost moribund gained momentum in the 1980s, reaching half a million by 1986.[24] Hence, at local and national levels, transnational counterpublics were flourishing in Western Europe as a response to the nuclear threat.

One of the most significant catalysts for that mobilization and for a transnational counterpublic was one of the founders of the West German Green Party, Petra Kelly. Born in 1947 in Bavaria, Kelly adopted her last name from her stepfather, an American Army officer. Educated in both Germany and the United States, Kelly became the perfect bridge to connect counterpublics after she returned to West Germany in 1970 and began her work with the Greens at the end of the decade. That involvement and its connections to the anti-nuke movement, chronicled in the compilation of her writings and speeches in *Fighting for Hope*, offer further insights into the political parameters of the transnational counterpublic in this arena.[25]

Having spent extensive time in the United States and thoroughly versed in on-going political activities among Catholic anti-nuke activists, Petra Kelly acknowledges the necessary links to America.

> The changes that have been taking place in the United States, especially among American Catholics, have not sunk in yet over here. But we should look towards America with hope as well as apprehension. Over there, security is not necessarily identical with weapons, and people have not yet surrendered to a provincial cynicism where sentimentality is mistaken for morality, as is so often the case here (7).

For Kelly, then, the moral witnessing and dramatic actions by Catholic activists should serve as an inspiration to those in Germany. Throughout her writings, Kelly cites the civil disobedience of priests, Daniel and Philip Berrigan (61–2), Molly Rush (62), their fellow Catholic co-conspirator who entered a General Electric weapons factory to hammer on a missile nose cone, and several Catholic Bishops, Hunthausen of Seattle (59–60) and Matthiessen of Amarillo (64), who have not only urged their parishioners to refuse to work in any nuclear weapons facility but have also declared, in the case of Hunthausen, a refusal to pay part of federal taxes as a protest against

Pentagon weapons manufacturing. She also quotes from the long statement made at the first Women's Pentagon Action in November 1980. All of these instances are intended to move her German compatriots to new levels of militancy against the weapons of nuclear war being installed in their own backyard.

On the other hand, Kelly is also cognizant that there is a global movement embracing the power of non-violence not only as a form of resistance but also as a new way of living. In her essay, "The Power of Non-Violence" (27–32), Kelly cites both well-known classic and lesser-known recent advocates of non-violence from Thoreau to Gandhi to King to César Chávez and German Catholic women activists, Dorothee Solle and Ingeborg Drewitz. In addition, she alludes to wide-ranging examples of non-violent resistance from Poland to Bolivia, all of which reinforce her point about the constitutive role of non-violence in shaping what I have called transnational counterpublics. Bringing all of this home to the emergent political movement in West Germany, the Greens, that Kelly is helping to build, she posits:

> The Greens seek a new life-style for the Western world, as well as in their own personal lives. They would like to see an alternative way of life without exploitation, and they aim for non-violent relationships with others and with themselves ..., relationships free from fear and based on mutual support (20).

Beyond those personal and social transformations, Kelly envisions the Greens as a different kind of political party, one she designates as an "anti-party party" (17).[26] Clearly, there is some thought being given to thinking and acting outside a limited institutional framework. As she notes,

> Nuclear energy, the nuclear state, and the growing use of military force threaten our lives. We feel obliged to take public, non-violent action and to engage in civil disobedience outside and inside parliament, throwing a spotlight on the inhumanity of the system (18).

For Kelly, it is the job of the Greens to expand and revitalize democracy through counterpublics connected to global resistance. "We are living at a time when authoritarian ruling elites are devoting more and more attention to their own prospects," Kelly contends, "and less and less to the future of mankind. We have no option but to take a plunge into greater democracy (11)."

At almost the exact same time as Kelly is articulating the need for greater democracy, a leading intellectual luminary of the Hungarian democratic opposition, George Konrad, is completing his book, *Anti-Politics*, which shares similar sentiments about war and peace and the need to get beyond the rule by authoritarian elites, whether in the East or West. "Anti-politics," argues Konrad, offers a radical alternative to the philosophy of a nuclear *ultima ratio*. ... Anti-politics is the ethos of civil society and civil society is the antithesis of military society. There are more or less militarized societies – societies under the sway of nation-states whose officials consider total war one of the possible moves in the game. Thus, military society is the reality, civil society is the utopia.[27]

Along with other Eastern European dissident intellectuals, from Adam Michnik in Poland to Vaclav Havel in Czechoslovakia, civil society becomes the beacon around which counterpublics are mobilized. Looking beyond the confrontation with national authoritarian institutions and elites, Konrad envisions an "international public sphere ... (which can) curb the tendency of the state to be omnipresent."[28]

Linking the emergent ideas about civil society in Eastern Europe with the ferment in Western Europe around war and peace in the early 1980s, Mary Kaldor sees the common thread of a demand to end the stultifying politics of the Cold War and to develop a mutual solidarity in the creation of another world.[29] For her, E. P. Thompson provides the clearest articulation of this need for mutual solidarity. "We must defend and extend the right of all citizens, East and West, to take part in this common movement and to engage in every kind of exchange," asserts Thompson. "We must learn to be loyal not to 'East' or 'West' but to each other and must disregard the prohibitions and limitations imposed by any national state."[30] Returning to Konrad, one finds an amazing foreshadowing of what will become that transnational counterpublic and global space of resistance, the World Social Forum. Writing in 1982, Konrad looks forward to the

> existence of a world forum (which) favours the emergence of the eccentric, of those who stand out. ... The international alliance of dissenters and avant-gardists takes under its wing those few people who, in their various ways, think their thoughts through to the end.[31]

From Kaldor's perspective, the political ferment unleashed by thinking beyond the binaries of the Cold War and the reinvention of civil society in a transnational context opened up new frames of meaning and new opportunity structures for citizens and non-state actors to intervene on the global level. Thus, the fall of the Berlin Wall in 1989 had been prepared by the dismantling of Cold War mental blockades. According to Kaldor,

> the year 1989 did represent a profound rupture with the past that is difficult for us to comprehend. In the stirrings of thought that developed beneath the structures of the Cold War were the beginnings of some new concepts and practices that can help us analyze our immensely complex contemporary world.[32]

For Kaldor, the key concept is global civil society which "offers a way of understanding the process of globalization in terms of subjective human agency instead of a disembodied deterministic process of 'interconnectedness.'"[33] Thus, new actors in a variety of formats and from diverse sites were prepared to engender and expand transnational counterpublics.

Perhaps nowhere was this more evident than in the massive global demonstrations that mobilized tens of millions of people world-wide on February 15, 2003. As a response to the Bush Administration's threats to attack Iraq, protest marches were organized with the aid of new networks and technology that facilitated what has been called the first truly global anti-war demonstration or, rather, globalized resistance by transnational counterpublics. From Barcelona to Berlin to Buenos Aires to Bangkok, from Manila to Mexico City to Moscow to Madrid, from Nairobi to New York, from São Paulo to Sydney to Seoul to San Francisco, from Toronto to Tokyo to Tel Aviv to Tegucigalpa, in short, in hundreds of cities around the world, on every continent, millions marched. According to Joss Hands,

> the sheer diversity of participants across the globe was self-evidently not sharing a specific set of localized reasons for action but rather, on a global level, the marches were coordinated through an orchestration of aims, which were loose enough to mobilize the common interests of all participants: peace, democracy, and human rights, all made concrete by the injustice and illegality of the pending war.[34]

While the forthcoming war was the common focus, the global mobilization was undoubtedly aided by the new information and communication technologies, specifically the internet and cell phones. In fact, as noted by W. Lance Bennett,

> deeper levels of coordination involved sharing open-source communication technologies, establishing web links, and agreeing on common messages that would encourage inclusiveness and maximize turnout. … The technological links and social software common to many sites facilitated the diffusion of posters, banners, slogans, information about gathering points, transportation, computer matching of socially comfortable (affinity) groups for different types of people to join, guides to protest tactics, and information and internet news reports on the war and the pending protests.[35]

Such new technologies not only facilitate quick, intense, and extensive protests, but, given the nature of how such protests are constituted by these new technologies, demonstrations can be evanescent events.[36] Being a participant in the February 15, 2003 demonstration in New York City, estimated to be close to one million people, the use of cell phones by the vast majority of demonstrators did allow for on-the-spot tactical maneuvers, such as transgressing police barricades and swarming into the streets. Conveying which streets were available to occupation gave the crowd a sort of guiding intelligence for improvised tactics. Yet, once people occupied the streets they seemed so preoccupied with talking on their cell phones that their presence was merely a matter of technological transience rather than purposeful protest. It was as if having expedited the taking of the streets, the use of cell phones reverted to instruments of spectral reportage, turning a counterpublic into a consuming public.

On the other hand, the internet and new information/communication media provided an incredible link between indigenous insurgents in the jungles of Chiapas Mexico and a transnational counterpublic willing and able to disseminate the resistance messages of the Zapatistas. Since those messages will be explored in more depth in the next chapter, I want to concentrate here briefly on how the internet bolstered the creation of a transnational counterpublic and the globalization of resistance in the aftermath of the dramatic appearance in 1994 of the Zapatistas. In particular, the internet assisted in traversing the social and cultural distances at surprising speed as the Zapatista network radiated out from Chiapas to Mexico City and then around the globe in the following years. As one of the key activists and theorists within this network noted:

> It is quite clear that the internet is making possible a level of organization, a speed of organization that we have never seen before ... it is a qualitative difference that has to do with a quantitative change ... just like the Zapatista mobilization against the Mexican government, in Mexico 200,000–300,000 people would gather at the Zocalo (the main square in Mexico City), but around the world it was happening in 40 countries and 100 cities, and it was having effect, and it would not have been possible without the internet.[37]

Nevertheless, that same activist, Harry Cleaver, understands that the "availability of information and a vehicle of connection does not guarantee either that a connection will be made or that it will be effective in generating complimentary action."[38] In effect, what was required to deploy the internet was a transnational Zapatista solidarity network that created and disseminated information by and about the Zapatistas.

Of course, the Zapatistas themselves, at least in the incarnation of Subcomandante Marcos, realized the novelty and importance of the internet for reaching out to a transnational counterpublic. "A new space, a novel space, that was so new that no one thought a guerrilla could enter into it," opined Marcos, "is the information superhighway, the internet. It was a terrain not occupied by anyone."[39] Perhaps more important to the Zapatista's deployment of the internet than the perspectives of Marcos was the role of a Mexican women's internet network called *La Neta* and the training sessions it established in Chiapas. From those sessions in the mid-1990s, the Zapatistas built on their face-to-face *encuentro* in Chiapas in 1996 to issue a call to create an "international network of resistance, recognizing differences and acknowledging similarities" which "will strive to find itself in other resistances around the world."[40] Out of that call was born the People's Global Action (PGA) in Geneva in 1998, a transnational grassroots network committed to putting into effect counterpublics that would globalize resistance through nonviolent direct action.[41]

Building on prior involvement in local, national, and transnational encounters, the 300 delegates in Geneva created a context for mutual solidarity and a launching pad for global confrontations from Seattle to India. As noted by Lesley Wood, the

> PGA would build a communicative structure that linked a wave of direct action protests across the planet. United around their rejection of neo-liberal policy and institutions and their refusal to engage in traditional lobbying, the organizations that participated in the PGA appeared to have little else in common.[42]

Yet, the PGA did share a commitment to a common set of principles. Among those principles were the following:

> We reject all forms and systems of domination and discrimination including, but not limited to, patriarchy, racism and religious funda-mentalism of all creeds. We embrace the full dignity of all human beings. ... A call to direct action and civil disobedience, support for social movements' struggles, advocating forms of resistance which maximize respect for life and oppressed peoples' rights, as well as the construction of local alternatives to global capitalism.[43]

Adopting an "organizational philosophy based on decentralization and autonomy," the PGA was able to attract thousands of delegates and hundreds of organizations to its three international conferences. Over 1,500 diverse groups took part in the "global days of action" in the late 1990s and early twenty-first century. A number of these actions were coordinated PGA protests at the sites of the WTO, IMF, and World Bank meetings. Although pulling together diverse groups for such actions was a testament to the PGA nurturance of its transnational counterpublics, there were, nonetheless, orga-nizational tensions, especially around the divisions between participants from the global North and South and the resultant agenda-setting for PGA.

> "These tensions," surmised Wood, "are reflected in debates about num-bers of participants at meetings, organizational process, and the role of the informal European-dominated 'support group,' which has helped with the logistics of conferences, the maintenance of communication infrastructure, and fund-raising."[44]

On the other hand, the common and dedicated commitment by PGA aligned groups to eschew a reliance on hierarchical forms and to create the most democratic ethos possible brought together diverse networks from the global North and South. One of those groups from the global South, the Karnataka State Farmers Association of India, articulated their perspective on such organizational obligations:

> This means that the final objective ... is the realization of the 'Village Republic,' a form of social, political and economic organization based on direct democracy, on economic and political autonomy and self-reliance, on the participation of all members of the community in decision-making about the common affairs that affect them.

These pledges to direct democracy and autonomy were echoed in the Montreal-based *Convergence de Luttes Anti-capitalistes* (CLAC): "The CLAC is autonomous, decentralized, and non-hierarchical. In favor of direct democracy, we encourage the involvement of anyone who agrees with this statement of principles."[45] With a degree of mutual respect and mutual solidarity, enhanced by computer-mediated communications and face-to-face interactions and activities, the PGA embodies the capabilities of transnational counterpublics to globalize their resistance.

Although various groups and sectors of transnational counterpublics retain their autonomy from NGOs, states, and international bodies, other counterpublics emerge in a different context that allows for significant influence on international organizations. For example, the Global Campaign for Women's Human Rights materialized as a transnational network organizing around the 1993 UN Conference on Human Rights. The network helped to solicit testimony about abuses perpetrated against women from torture to slavery, coalescing around the position that "violence against women violates human rights." By challenging the institutional efforts to obscure women's rights behind a veil of domestic privacy, issues were investigated that resulted in the adoption of the 1994 UN Declaration on the Elimination of Violence Against Women. The agenda for women's human rights was expanded in 1995 by focusing on the economic and social dislocations caused by U. S. underwritten structural adjustment programs. Playing a significant role in highlighting such economic injustices was a transnational network from the Global South, Development Alternatives with Women for a New Era (DAWN).[46]

Dating back to the 1985 UN Third World Conference on Women in Nairobi, DAWN by the late 1990s was utilizing internet connections that allowed it to relocate its secretariat to the small Pacific Island nation of Fiji. Extending its reach through research and communication with other transnational women's networks, DAWN was part of a counterpublic that provided women "with an alternative identity." Beyond this identity, however, DAWN, like so many other women's transnational organizations, created:

spaces for women from different racial and ethnic groups, countries, classes, and occupational backgrounds to meet on a consistent and continuous basis. ... They gave birth to issue-based networks at local, regional, and global levels, which in turn provided the research and analysis that served to empower women's advocacy.[47]

That advocacy crossed over not only into the public consciousness but also into policy directives from international and human rights organizations, turning women's global resistance into significant global reform.

As a final exploration of the impact of transnational campaigns for change, I want to return to the issue of disarmament and focus specifically on the advocacy by NGOs, in particular, for bans on landmines and cluster munitions. In the case of the campaign to ban landmines and the resultant international treaty,

> most of the operational NGOs that became involved in the campaign did so out of a desire to effect substantive change for those affected by landmines on the ground. Generally more reluctant to be seen as political, the operational NGOs were more concerned with removing mines than with fostering a paradigm shift in global governance.[48]

Yet, in their organizing efforts, the international campaign to ban landmines found a number of prominent people, from human rights advocate Jody Williams to international celebrity Princess Diana to Canadian foreign minister Lloyd Axworthy, who acted as significant non-state and state actors in promoting the international ban. On top of this, the campaign successfully deployed email lobbying and internet-based collaborative efforts to achieve ratification and operationalization of a landmine ban treaty in 1998 and 1999.[49]

The tenth anniversary of the Mine Treaty Ban was celebrated on March 1, 2009. This treaty, sometimes also referred to as the Ottawa Convention, outlawed the production, maintenance, and distribution of anti-personnel landmines. The United States has consistently refused to join the now 156 countries that have signed the treaty, proving once again that U. S. military imperialism pays scant attention to international law irrespective of the party or president in power. In addition to the aforementioned prohibitions, the Mine Ban Treaty also legally binds the parties to search for and clear known landmine sites and offer assistance to the victims. Although the treaty lacked enforcement provisions, the impact has been significant with diminished landmine injuries, the destruction of tens of millions of stockpiled landmines, and the stigmatizing of continued use of landmines. Nonetheless, the U. S., Russia, and China, with stockpiles of over 160 million units, refuse to ban landmines, although the U. S. has not used this particular type of landmine in the last two decades.[50]

On the other hand, the U. S. has relied on the more deadly and sophisticated cluster munitions. On December 3, 2008, ninety-four countries became signatories to an international treaty banning cluster munitions. That treaty grew out of an international coalition of groups seeking a ban on such weapons, particularly in the aftermath of their extensive use by Israel in 2007 during its invasion of Lebanon. Once again, the United States was the most intransigent opponent of any legally binding treaty, arguing at one point in the face of massive evidence to the contrary that cluster bombs would exact less collateral damage than other kinds of ordnance. Having used such weapons in Afghanistan and Iraq, with extensive stockpiles estimated to be in the range of hundreds of millions of units, the U. S. remained an outlaw nation even though President George W. Bush, under international pressure, signed congressional legislation in December 2007 that eliminated the sales of such cluster munitions for one year. Congress has recently developed legislation that proscribes, but does not fully prohibit, the use of cluster bombs except in heavily populated areas. It remains to be seen whether Congress can pass and the Obama administration will join the international community in its ban on cluster bombs.[51]

It should be clear from the examples cited in this chapter that transnational counterpublics and global resistance networks and campaigns have been able to arouse not only other public actors but even, on some occasions and under certain circumstances, governments and international agencies. To the degree that transnational counterpublics can inject compelling voices into the virtual and public sphere, especially as that public sphere fragments and more media channels proliferate, there will be increasing recognition for issues and campaigns that may start out on the political margins. Moreover, specific advocacy campaigns from NGOs with limited political goals have achieved and will probably continue to attain certain success.[52] While there remain critical differences between NGOs and transnational counterpublics, especially around organizational matters such as centralized and bureaucratic structures and strategic objectives such as lobbying governments, there will be productive overlaps, enhanced in many respects by the new communication and computer-mediated technologies. It should be noted, however, that "it is not the technology alone that creates rapidly expanding action networks – it is the capacity to move easily between on- and off-line relationships that makes the scale shift to transnational activism possible."[53] And, as we will see in the next chapter, that transnational activism is motivated also by grounded visions and enacted practices for possible new and better worlds.

8   Is another world possible?

We can build a new path, one where living means life with dignity and freedom. To build this alternative is possible and necessary. It is necessary because
on it depends the future of humanity.

Subcomandante Marcos

All revolutionaries, regardless of sex, are the smashers of myths and the
destroyers of illusion. They have always died and lived again to build new
myths. They dare to dream of a utopia, a new kind of synthesis and equilibrium.

Pat Robinson, Patricia Haden, and Donna Middleton

The insistent cry of the global justice and resistance movements is: "Another
World is Possible!" Yet, even though major attempts have been mounted to
articulate and pre-figure that other and better world, there are still significant impediments, not the least of which is the continuing insistence by
the United States that it can arrogate to itself the leadership of the world.
Whether in the form of hard or soft imperialism, the international operations of the United States either explicitly or implicitly often blunt fundamental efforts to realize another world. Moreover, when one considers the
role of the United States as the leading per capita polluter in the world,
the very possibility of another world seems choked off at its most sensitive
ecological site. What I want to investigate in this chapter is both the imaginative and actual configurations of realizing another world. That is, what
I propose to explore in the first part of the chapter will be the role of a
utopian imaginary in fiction and in political philosophy, specifically in
Marge Piercy's utopian novel, *Woman on the Edge of Time*, and then the
liberation theology of Gustavo Gutiérrez. Following the thread of the role of
the poor of the global South, I will consider the universal emancipatory
meaning of the Zapatistas and the World Social Forum, especially against
the backdrop of U. S. imperialism, neoliberal globalization, and globalization from below. Finally, I will consider the possibilities in developing the
links between these utopian visions and insurgent social and political praxis
required in realizing a new or another world.

To probe the utopian moments of building another world also requires some understanding of the dystopian elements of this and future worlds. In order to comprehend the utopian/dystopian dialectic, one needs to define that dialectic in ways that underscore the fictive and real nature of that dialectic as it contends with forces of domination and emancipation. Following Russell Jacoby, I want to suggest that "utopias seek to emancipate by envisioning a world based on new, neglected, or spurned ideas; dystopias seek to frighten by accentuating contemporary trends that threaten freedom."[1] I first intend to explore the utopian/dystopian dialectic in Marge Piercy's 1976 novel, *Woman on the Edge of Time*. Although a work of political imagination, Piercy's novel reflects the world historical insurrections of the 1960s that still resonate today. I will then address the utopian aspirations in the political philosophy represented by Liberation Theology. By examining the imaginative projections of other worlds, this chapter will indicate the ways that utopian visions are ineluctably immersed in the question of whether a better, or another, world is possible.

Imagining another world is, of course, central to utopian literature. As an act of imagination, utopian literature seeks to critique the dominant relationships of the world inhabited by the writer of such literature while projecting an alternative time and/or space which may be thought of as the incubator of a new and better world. In effect, utopian literature is a form of social and visionary dreaming that can mobilize the critical consciousness of its readers. At its most compelling moments, fictive utopianism provides another form of political engagement. Drawing upon a variety of social movements and contestations of the 1960s and 1970s, Marge Piercy's *Woman on the Edge of Time* engages our political imagination precisely along those points of contestation that remind us of what impedes our utopian desires for freedom and the realization of emancipatory projects. In effect, *Woman on the Edge of Time* enacts what one interpreter of literary utopias calls its "two-fold strategy: ... the unmasking of prevailing forms of social manipulation, domination, and containment ... and the projection of a utopian dream in which all forms of alienation and manipulation are dramatically reversed or negated."[2]

The protagonist of *Woman on the Edge of Time*, Connie Ramos, a poor Chicana, spends much of her time in the novel alternating between the dystopian reality of a mental hospital and a utopian future of a twenty-second-century Massachusetts village called Mattapoisett. In her struggle to emancipate herself from becoming an experimental subject for mind control by the white male medical establishment of the Rockover State Mental Hospital, Connie can be seen as a representative of the global South in its confrontations with a form of Yankee imperialism, masked in the ideological frame of humanitarian intervention. Those doctors who have selected Connie, along with other supposed social deviants, for their experiment to implant neurotransmitters to control the alleged irrational violence of their subjects are more than the obvious repressive patriarchal order; they are the epitome of the well-intentioned elite rulers of the United States for whom the disorderly activities of potentially menacing others must be controlled. Arguing that accepting the beneficent control of the implants would be in her best interest, one of these doctors imperiously informs Connie that the "more you resist, the more you punish yourself. Because when you fight us, we can't help you (262)." While the doctors have obviously convinced themselves of their altruistic motives, it becomes clearer and clearer to Connie that her freedom and very sovereign identity are threatened by such disciplinary regimes.

Connie's illumination about the ulterior motives of the doctors and her own capacity to contest their so-called enlightened rule are facilitated by a resident sender of the future Mattapoisett named, appropriately enough, Luciente. It is the intervention of Luciente and the mental voyages that Connie makes to Mattapoisett that heighten her awareness of her ability to struggle against the depressing and repressive reality she inhabits. While initially skeptical of a village that on its surface looks a little like her "Tio Manuel's in Texas (69)," Connie becomes increasingly won over by living arrangements that are both human scale and humanizing, equalitarian yet respectful of individual and collective diversity. Certainly, some of the most radical and revolutionary feminist breaks with the past, such as artificial birth and breast-feeding and co-mothering men, shock both Connie and the reader into that sense of estrangement which utopian literature cultivates. On the other hand, Connie comes to recognize the insight shared by one resident of Mattapoisett about what constitutes the real social evils of the past that "center around power and greed – taking from other people their food, their liberty, their health, their land, their customs, their pride (139)."

While it is not surprising that Luciente and the residents of the future refer to Connie's time as the "Age of Greed and Waste," Connie must be schooled in the ecological and political economic arrangements of Mattapoisett to appreciate fully the utopian alternatives. Among those are the elimination of the capitalist cash nexus with its attendant exploitation of human beings – "we don't buy or sell anything (64)" – and the intimate relationship with the surrounding environment, including especially the kind of humility and skepticism that are foreign to the mechanistic and technocratic order touted in the past by Western science and the political empires of the West, most recently embodied by U. S. imperial rule. As Luciente notes, "We're cautious about gross experiments. 'In biosystems, all factors are not knowable.' First rule we learn when we study living beings in relation (97)." Those environmental and human interrelationships, something so often abused by U. S. multinationals in the developing world, are at the core of Mattapoisett's utopian ethos. Eventually, Connie recognizes that the utopian future is not about "more ... more things, or even more money (328)," but about self-determination and self-sufficiency.

Connie's realization that "more" is not the measure of anything, let alone all things in the utopian future, contains an implicit critique of the imperial and consumer culture that Mattapoisett transcends. Military historian Andrew Bacevich identifies "more" as the key to an American identity that "centers on a relentless personal quest to acquire, consume, to indulge, and to shed whatever constraints might interfere with those endeavors."[3] With an understanding that resources are limited and nothing must be wasted, residents of Mattapoisett embody a stark alternative to compulsive drives to gain and consume. Another perspective on "more" can be found in a recent essay by American novelist, Barbara Kingsolver, who opines that "our empire (is built) on the presumption of the endlessness of certain resources, which we are now running out of: more forests, more easily exploited oil, more economic growth based on more untapped markets for our goods."[4]

Beyond the utopian sense of self-sufficiency in Mattapoisett, Piercy's obvious embrace of an ecological sensibility merges with Bill McKibben's recent critique of the mania with "more" in *Deep Economy: The Wealth of Communities and the Durable Future*. Where Mattapoisett practices being "ownfed (70)" or self-sufficient in food production, McKibben touts the values of eating locally from smaller farms, citing a report from the USDA Census of Agriculture that "smaller farms produce more food per acre, whether you measure in tons, calories, or dollars. They use land, water, and oil much more efficiently."[5] Just as Mattapoisett and the other small communities of the future are the realization of McKibben's localism, so his critique of the global economic waste and inefficiencies mirrors that found in *Woman on the Edge of Time*. When Luciente and her co-mothered child Dawn return with Connie to the present, Dawn is insistent about seeing some of those polluting internal combustion monsters. From Dawn's perspective, the people of Connie's time "all set out in their private autocars to go some place at the same time and got stuck in jams and breathed poisons and got sick (245)." While Piercy's ecological sensibility about the profligacy of fossil fuels was in its infancy as she was writing the novel, McKibben has been able to catalogue the wanton waste and massive pollution destroying the planet and heralding global dystopian catastrophe.

On the other hand, *Woman on the Edge of Time* does present a dystopian future that appears to be the extension of the mind-controlled and hierarchal society embodied in the Rockover State Mental Hospital experiments. Connie finds herself in a future metropolis, heavily polluted and controlled exclusively by multinationals where cybernetic production engenders both robocops and other artificial entities from prostitutes to produce. Piercy is obviously extrapolating the dystopian realities of an imperial America that descends into the worst sort of oppressive society. Such an extrapolation, according to Tom Moylan, is a world where

> social justice is replaced by social control. … As corporate greed and military expenditure reduce the financial resources available …, the state must respond by cutting back services and further dehumanizing its citizens by use of cybernetic technology that makes people less able to determine their own lives and the direction of society, rendering them passive in the face of corporate domination.[6]

Connie's efforts to combat that passivity, reinforced by the constant administration of tranquillizers in Rockover State Mental Hospital, require her to enact a willed transformation that is integral to the utopian sensibility, a sensibility stoked by her encounters with the future Mattapoisett. After maneuvering for a short-leave in the care of her Anglicized brother, Luis, she returns to the hospital with a vial of poison from his nursery business. (One interesting irony may be that the herbicide Connie procures is very similar to those once sprayed by U. S. patrols on the coca fields in Bolivia before Morales ended such interference.) Regarding her situation as similar to a war where violence was the only recourse, reminiscent of the third world national liberation struggles that inflamed the passions of the 1960s acti-vists like Piercy, Connie pours the poison into the morning coffee intended for the head doctors. Although Piercy deliberately leaves the reader hanging concerning the ultimate ramifications of Connie's act of resistance, it is obvious that without radical action there will not be an alternative future. As Luciente wisely contends, "Those of your time who fought hard for change, often they had myths that a revolution was inevitable. But nothing is! All things interlock. We are only one possible future (177)."

To realize that future, Connie has to be convinced that her own struggle, especially given her situation as a poor, marginalized, and institutionalized Chicana, is central to transforming her own world, as well as the larger one. Recalling a moment in her past when as a "young and naïve" poor person she became active in the "War on Poverty," Connie bitterly remonstrates that she "ended up with nothing but feeling sore and ripped off (154)." To which Luciente replies: "You lose until you win – that's a saying those who changed our world left us. Poor people *did* get together (154)." On the other hand, one of the other residents of Mattapoisett acknowledges, "You individually may fail to understand us or to struggle in your own life and time. You of your time may fail to struggle together (197)." Connie demurs and says: "What good can I do? Who could have less power (198)?" In response, another Mattapoisett figure points out that the "powerful don't make revolutions (198)." Still not convinced, Connie dismisses the idea of revolution as "honchos marching around in imitation uniforms (198)." The rebuttal is that it is precisely people like Connie who are the most authentic agents of historical change.

Drawing on the oppositional movements of the late 1960s for inspiration, Marge Piercy animates Connie's revolutionary role as an agent of historical change. Especially exemplary for Piercy's formulation of the historical role Connie can and must play as a poor woman of color is the emergence in the late 1960s of radical welfare rights movements led by African-American women. Among those black women were Pat Robinson, Patricia Haden, and Donna Middleton. Writing about their own class and racial experiences, Robinson, Haden, and Middleton asserted: "Only we, the politically conscious oppressed can find out how we were molded, brainwashed, and literally produced like any manufactured product to plastically cooperate in *our* own oppression. This is *our* historical responsibility (authors' emphasis)." Reflecting on that responsi-bility, they went on to urge throwing off the dead weight of the past and looking towards a revolutionary break, one that dared "to dream of a utopia."[7]

That vision of historical agency coming from the ranks of the poor and oppressed is central to liberation theology in general and the writings of one of its leading advocates, Gustavo Gutiérrez. A mestizo priest, living and working in the slums of Lima, Peru, Gutiérrez was at the forefront of the development of liberation theology, especially after its emergence at the Latin American Bishops Conference in Medellín, Colombia in 1968. In the aftermath of that Conference, Gutiérrez articulated a theology of liberation that "was to shift the discussion of the Latin American predicament from the misleading concept of development ... to a multifaceted notion of human agency."[8] In highlighting the links between the poor and oppressed as agents of change through a series of essays collected in *The Power of the Poor in History*, Gutiérrez not only fleshed out the political project of liberation theology but also underscored its utopian content and aspirations in building a new and better world.

Gutiérrez described liberation as "a process of human emancipation, aiming at turning a society where men and women are truly free from servitude, and where they are active shapers of their own destiny." That destiny not only led to a "radical transformation of structures" but beyond to a "creation of a wholly new way for men and women to be human (29)." For Gutiérrez, however, those men and woman were not abstract creatures or some disembodied universal figures, highly spiritualized as in more traditional theology. According to him, "the theology of liberation is an attempt to understand the faith within the concrete historical, liberating, and subversive praxis of the poor of this world – the exploited classes, despised ethnic groups, and marginalized cultures (37)."

Decrying the very system of "imperialist capitalism" (41), "headed by the United States" and aided by reactionary powers in Latin America (83–5) that exploited and oppressed the poor and marginalized, Gutiérrez identified the poor "as a by-product of the system in which we live and for which we are responsible." The poor, then, from Gutiérrez's perspective are

> the oppressed, exploited proletariat, robbed of the fruit of their labor and despoiled of their humanity. Hence the poverty of the poor is not a call to a generous relief action, but a demand that we go and build a different social order (44).

In order to build that "different social order," Gutiérrez realized that this required a revolutionary, and, indeed, utopian social praxis. "Latin American misery and injustice," he asserted,

> go too deep to be responsive to palliatives. Hence we speak of social revolution, not reform: of liberation, not development; of socialism, not modernization of the prevailing system. "Realists" call these statements romantic and utopian. And they should, for the rationality of these statements is of a kind quite unfamiliar to them (45).

Elaborating further on the connection between utopia and a new historical reality, Gutiérrez notes that such

> utopianism clashes with the realism of the oppressor, who is incapable of appreciating the kind of historical rationality that springs from the power of the poor. In the final analysis, there is nothing more revolutionary, nothing more charged with liberative utopianism than the ancient deep-seated oppression suffered by the poor of Latin America (81).

Beyond the theological and historical grounding of utopian liberation in the poor of Latin America, such formulation recalls the contention of anthropologist James Scott that "most traditional utopian beliefs can, in fact, be understood as a more or less systematic negation of an existing pattern of exploitation and status degradation as it is experienced by subordinate groups."[9] In effect, Gutiérrez's preference for the poor is a reflection of not only a radicalized theology but also a political articulation of the utopian aspirations of Latin American subordinate groups.

In the predictable clash between the poor and their oppressors, Gutiérrez named both the system of oppression and the role of all of those seeking to overcome that oppression. As noted by one interpreter of Gutiérrez's writings on liberation theology, it "inevitably entailed a collision between Latin Americans and the capitalist countries which dominated them as well as 'with their natural allies; our national oligarchies.' "[10] In the "struggles and hopes" of the poor, according to Gutiérrez, one finds "the condition of an authentic solidarity with everyone (129)." Therefore, as the historical agent of real change, the poor of Latin America have created a new and transformative social praxis. "Latin Americans have found in their grassroots community life," contends Gutiérrez, "a rich vein of faith and vitality, and have found a way to carry forward their combat against social injustice, their struggle for liberation, and their experience of the gospel (151)." Such "social appropriation of the gospel" and "militant reading of the Bible" (208) was not just the province of theologians, such as Gutiérrez, but what he called the different and new "interlocutors" (91–2), the poor of Latin America.

During my 1984 visit to Nicaragua as a member of Witness for Peace, I observed this remarkable "social appropriation of the gospel" and "militant reading of the Bible" in a peasant cooperative where what were called "Delegates of the Word," i.e. lay preachers, inspired by Nicaragua's version of liberation theology, presented their own interpretation of a passage from the Old Testament concerning the struggle of the poor. In their exegesis of this passage, the man and woman of this peasant cooperative expressed not only the joy of overcoming their previous illiteracy and becoming "delegates of the word," but also their own sense of empowerment. For them, the Bible, thus, provided inspiration for confronting and overcoming oppression and exploitation. Embodying the central tenet from liberation theology of the poor appropriating history for purposes of radical transformation, these two, among many others, were living examples of the political project of liberation theology.[11]

Although the impact of liberation theology abated throughout Latin America as a consequence of papal chastisement, political repression and disenchantment, and the rise of evangelical Protestantism, the core call to "the exploited classes, despised ethnic groups, and marginalized cultures" persisted. Its next iteration took place on January 1, 1994 in an amazing community insurrection by thousands of indigenous men and women, mostly armed, in San Cristobal in the state of Chiapas, Mexico. While primarily a response to the debt crisis and neoliberal policies in Mexico, including the implementation of NAFTA, which, in turn, drove those on the margins into further economic and political deprivation, the Zapatista Army of National Liberation (*Ejército Zapatista de Liberación Nacional* – EZLN) opened another front against global inequities. Embracing the legacy of political struggles from the Mexican past, the Zapatistas also looked forward to creating a new and better world. In the January 1 missive that accompanied their occupation in Chiapas, the legacy of past conflicts acknowledged the role of the poor, despised, and marginalized:

> We are the product of 500 years of struggles: first against slavery, in the War of Independence against Spain led by the insurgents, then to keep from being absorbed by U. S. expansionism, then to enact our Constitution and expel the French Empire from our land, then the Porfiro Diaz dictatorship prevented the just application of the Reform laws and the people rebelled, developing their own leadership, Villa and Zapata emerged, poor men like ourselves.[12]

After close to a year of public engagement that saw the intervention of the Mexican army and the establishment of a wary truce, the EZLN issued another declaration about their political intentions: "The Zapatista plan today remains the same as always: to change the world to make it better, more just, more free, more democratic, that is, more human."[13]

Although the Zapatistas had been organizing for a decade prior to their dramatic public insurgency, the first years of that public existence, marked with much bad faith from the government, did manage to create waves far beyond the Mexican shore. In fact, the Zapatistas electrified a global audience not only with the audacity of their action critique against neoliberalism but also with their new ways of doing politics, from the use of the internet to their invitations to dialogue to their eschewing of seeking power for themselves. One of the EZLN's most prominent spokespersons, Subcomandante Marcos, expressed the desire and hope for that new politics:

> In the midst of this navigating from pain to hope, the political struggle finds itself bereft of the worn-out clothes bequeathed to it by pain; it is

hope which obliges it to seek new forms of struggle, new ways of being political, of doing politics. A new politics, a new political ethic is not just a wish, it is the only way to advance, to jump to the other side.[14]

The hope expressed in Zapatista pronouncements and political praxis is not an abstract longing but what the philosopher of hope, Ernst Bloch, calls "concrete hope," that which "leads ... towards the radical termination of the contents of fear."[15] As noted by one of the foremost scholars of the Zapatistas, "Hope is central to the Zapatista uprising, but it is not a hope that springs from the certainty of the end result, but from confidence in the necessity of the project. Hope is dignity, the struggle to walk upright in a world which pushes us down."[16]

The universal aspirations to realize another world expressed in the Zapatista movement caught the attention of millions around the world struggling against neoliberal globalization and for the creation of equitable alternatives. "Zapatismo is not a movement restricted to Mexico," argues John Holloway, "but is central to the struggle of thousands of millions of people all over the world to live a human life against and in an increasingly inhuman society."[17] On the other hand, the Zapatistas were able to bring an indigenous and pre-modern sensibility to the postmodern task of imagining and creating a world that not only validates the desire for autonomy but also for emancipatory politics. As noted by anthropologist June Nash,

> the discourse of the Zapatistas reflects primordial roots of both inspiration and identification: their strategies reflect a sure sense of the political process in which they are situated and which they are trying to push to new levels of pluricultural existence.[18]

Certainly, the conditions in Mexico that produced the EZLN are important to recognize, as well as the transformations and efficacy of the Zapatista's various campaigns in that country. However, what I want to concentrate on is the universal appeal that the Zapatistas embody and inspire in order to underscore the various configurations underlying the political project of building another world.[19] As articulated by one EZLN spokesperson: "In the world that the Zapatistas want, all skin colors fit, all the languages and all the paths. The good world has many ways and many paths. And in those paths there is respect and dignity."[20] Another way that the Zapatistas discovered to make that appeal was through the construction of a symbolic figure, Votan Zapata. According to one interpreter of the role that figure played, "Votan Zapata is projected not only as a symbol of struggle for indigenous peoples of Chiapas, but for all people living in misery, without rights, justice, democracy or liberty and who support the struggle to obtain these goals."[21]

Even more significant to the projection of the political alternative represented by the Zapatistas was the real figure of *subcomandante* Marcos. Marcos deliberately played with a kind of shape-shifting universal oppressed person, especially evident in the following communiqué:

> Marcos is gay in San Francisco, a black in South Africa, Asian in Europe, a Chicano in San Isidro, an anarchist in Spain, a Palestinian in Israel, an indigenous person in the streets of San Cristobal. ... In other words, Marcos is a human being in this world. Marcos is every untolerated, oppressed, exploited minority that is resisting and saying "Enough!"[22]

While embracing those who were despised and marginalized, both Marcos and the Zapatistas made clear their insistence that they sought mutual solidarity rather than charity. At one of the Zapatista *encuentros* (encounters), a speech was given which asked to "not see us as someone who must be helped, poor things, out of pity, out of alms, out of charity."[23] Instead, the Zapatistas called for joining forces around the globe in a common, but diverse, endeavor for insurrection. For Marcos, the rebellion promoted by the Zapatistas was an invitation to listen to a

> network of voices ..., a network that covers the five continents and helps to resist the death promised to us by Power. ... There follows the reproduction of resistances, the I do not conform, the I rebel. There follows the world with many worlds which the world needs. There follows humanity recognizing itself to be plural, different, inclusive, tolerant of itself, with hope.[24]

The network of voices inspired by Marcos and the Zapatistas certainly led to the articulation of shared resistance and mutual solidarity, perhaps most succinctly articulated in the slogan of "One No, Many Yeses!" Seeking ways to valorize that resistance and mutual solidarity, the Zapatistas provided a critical voice in their national intervention against global neoliberalism. Beyond that intervention, they offered a new way of connecting to a vision and practice of globalization from below. By invoking a global consciousness for the excluded, the Zapatistas opened up the possibility of projecting another world or even other worlds where dignity would reign. As noted by Fiona Jeffries,

> In the Zapatismo mirror, solidarity is the building of alternative resistance networks around the world through the practice of radical democracy, liberty, and social justice with a related emphasis on localism, autonomy, and horizontal relationships among all the participating groups and organizations.[25]

Whether or whatever possible alternative future is realized as a political imaginary or political reality is intimately connected to transforming a radical and contingent political imaginary into a practical incubator for another or other worlds. Certainly, the emergence of the World Social Forum (WSF) as an extension of the challenges to U. S. imperialism, corporate domination, and the destruction of various sovereignties opened up the utopian possibilities for an alternative future. According to Boaventura de Sousa Santos, the "WSF is the first critical utopia of the twenty-first century and aims to break with the tradition of the critical utopias of Western modernity, many of which turned into conservative utopias: from claiming utopian alternatives to denying alternatives under the excuse that the fulfillment of utopia was under way. The openness of the utopian dimension of the WSF is its attempt to escape this perversion."[26]

Furthermore, as de Sousa Santos makes clear, the WSF "represents a stark departure from the old internationalism that dominated anti-capitalist politics throughout the twentieth century," especially in the privileging of specific historical agents, their organizations, and the strategies and certitudes articulated by those in the North.[27] Hence, the earlier discussion of this chapter presented agents (as in Piercy and Gutiérrez) and organizations and strategies (Zapatismo) from the global South as a way of decentering that old internationalism while foregrounding the significance of those who had been marginalized even in the political projections of an older left. In effect, the World Social Forum can be seen as a culmination of the new struggles of movements and resistances against domination from the global North and for new approaches to changing the world.

It is not surprising that de Sousa Santos sees the close alignment between the WSF and a utopian imagination. Santos defines utopia as

> the exploration of new modes of human possibility and styles of will, and the use of the imagination to confront the apparent inevitability of whatever exists with something radically better that is worth fighting for, and to which humankind is fully entitled.[28]

Certainly, the WSF provides the necessary social space for wrestling with both the theory and practice of achieving a new and better world. As announced in its founding Charter of Principles:

> The World Social Forum is an open meeting place for reflective thinking, democratic debate of ideas, formulation of proposals, free exchange of experiences and interlinking for effective action, by groups and movements of civil society that are opposed to neoliberalism and the domination of the world by capital and any form of imperialism, and are committed to building a planetary society directed towards fruitful relationships among Humankind and between it and the Earth.[29]

That open space at the WSF was particularly evident when I attended the 2006 World Social Forum in Caracas, Venezuela. Tens of thousands of attendees brought a wide variety of interests and concerns to how to create a new world. Yet, the degree to which those attending could reach consensus about that other world was open to contention. In fact, following what de Sousa Santos identifies as a series of "cleavages" in the WSF that create tension in the projection of another and better world or worlds, I will try to highlight how those cleavages were embedded in the moments of contestation and critical utopianism I encountered in order to discern how ideas about realizing another world were articulated.

The 2006 World Social Forum (WSF) meetings in Caracas from January 23–29 took place amidst continuing leftward trends in South America. It was not surprising, therefore, that these trends, reflected in the Venezuelan Bolivarian experiments and the electoral victory of indigenous leader, Evo Morales, in Bolivia, played a prominent role in formal presentations and informal discussions. Although preliminary plans for the WSF had delineated six thematic areas, two themes – "imperial strategies and people's resistance," and "power, politics, and the struggle for social emancipation" seemed to dominate most of the sessions, or at least, the sessions I managed to attend.

The program for the Caracas 2006 WSF touted the event as a "space for encounter and debate ... for sharing ideas, proposals and experiences, for developing strategies and for articulating struggles around the world." Certainly, the carnivalesque atmosphere in some of the venues in Caracas suggested not only lively discursive encounters but also celebrations of South American social movements. The opening march on January 23 of tens of thousands of WSF participants and supporters through the streets of Caracas under myriad banners focused, in particular, on the theme of anti-imperialism. Passing the guarded burial site of Simon Bolivar, one chant exploded from contingent after contingent of Latin Americans: "With the spear of Bolivar, we will march through Latin America."

While the celebratory mood in the streets was swept along by the currents of radical change in South America, the question of the degree to which these currents challenged the hegemonic models of neoliberalism and imperialism was part of the debates and discussions throughout the week. Whether, as the program suggested, the WSF was the breeding ground for "new alternatives to the actual model of imperialist domination" and "a new way of doing politics, one that is anti-hegemonic and a true alternative to the dominant social model," had much to do with the emergent perspectives found throughout the WSF. In particular, debates about the degree to which South American social movements compelled or were constrained by their leftist governments, as well as the rhetoric and practice of anti-imperialism, raised profound questions concerning realizing another world.

Given the particular location and role of the state in Latin American resistance movements, cleavages identified by de Sousa Santos of the state as "enemy or potential ally," as well as the primacy of "national or global struggles," could be seen in the aforementioned events and program.[30] Even prior to the Caracas WSF, there were movements, such as the Movement for National Democracy in the Philippines, which chastised the WSF for its somewhat remote distance from these national struggles. Charging that "the World Social Forum still floats somewhere above, seeing and trying yet really unable to address actual conditions of poverty and powerlessness brought about by imperialist globalization in many countries," this group protested that "national struggles against globalization are and should provide the anchor to any anti-globalization initiative at the international level."[31] In an earlier WSF meeting, one delegate urged a direct confrontation with U. S. imperialism by tying together local, national, and global forces under an anti-imperialist banner. "To beat U. S. imperialism," argued Achin Vanaik from India, "we must help struggles and resistances develop within each country. And we must recognize and explain to the people that there is a direct connection between U. S. empire-building, war, and globalization."[32]

In fact, numerous contingents in the 2006 WSF hoisted the banner of resistance to U. S. military intervention. The large contingent of Colombians spotlighted the nefarious activities of Plan Colombia, a joint initiative of the Colombian government and the U. S. to ostensibly stop drug-trafficking but mainly to forestall insurgent movements throughout Colombia. Lila Solano, a candidate for the Colombian parliament, identified the new edition of Plan Colombia, called Plan Patriot, as "state terrorism financed by Washington." On the last day of the WSF the International Assembly of Social Movements announced a day of international protests against the U. S. occupation of Iraq, March 18, and a follow-up conference on March 24–27 in Cairo. Undertaking such pointed political action suggests that the WSF is morphing from what was its primary focus on neoliberal globalization to one that recognizes the dystopian realities spread by U. S. imperialism.

On the other hand, the critique of neoliberalism remained at the core of the International Assembly of Social Movements and the 2006 WSF. The Assembly issued a document that lambasted privatization, expressing, in turn, support for the protection of water, land, and energy as public goods. One of the most eloquent analyses of neoliberalism at the WSF came from indigenous leader Blanca Chancoso from Ecuador. Accusing neoliberals of wanting "to base society only on the economy and also on the idea that only certain people are fit to rule," Chancoso also condemned the social dislocation that resulted from neoliberal policies throughout Latin America. Lauding the efforts of Cuban solidarity and Venezuelan reciprocity, she proposed that such efforts could become "the basis of a new economy, a plurinational, pluricultural state that we can build together."

In fact, the whole question of how revolutionary governments can be within the world system of capital and the internal contradictions of political traditions was of primary concern to practically all participations in the 2006 WSF in Caracas. One of the leaders of the MST (Landless Workers Movement) from Brazil, Ricardo Gebrim, noted that

> no political party, no matter how left-wing they are, has been able to take
> political power without succumbing to the dynamics of electoralism

and moving to the right. What we need to build is a powerful united political movement, like in Bolivia, that will take power at the right revolutionary moment.

Certainly, in Bolivia the crescendo of activities engaged in by various social movements propelled Morales to power. On the other hand, the whole question of how counter-hegemonic movements could achieve state power and then transform the state to realize "another world" is open to the kind of debate and discussion seen throughout the WSF.

Although many at the 2006 WSF would agree with the Uruguayan women's activist, Lilian Celiberti, that "it is important for governments to create mechanisms for participation to translate demands into public policies," how closely aligned social movements should be with governments is another matter. Moreover, the whole question of the relationship of the WSF to particular governments, in this case the Chávez government of Venezuela, proved disconcerting to some, including a small group of anarchists who sponsored an Alternative Social Forum in Caracas under the slogan of "No compromise with power!"

Indeed, the whole question of the relationship to power is at the core of both imagining and building another and better world. As seen earlier in the struggle of Connie Ramos to contest the oppressive power of the doctors who arrogated to themselves the right to determine Connie's life, their power over Connie was reinforced by the institutional status and privilege accorded them. With the aid of the utopian inspiration of Mattapoisett, Connie was able to challenge and overthrow their entrenched power over. Through liberation theology, Gustavo Gutiérrez and his followers throughout Latin America took on the established power of the state and imperial formations propping up the national ruling elites in theory and in praxis in order to achieve a degree of emancipation and dignity not afforded them under their particular ruling regimes. In turn, liberation theology provided a springboard to those marginalized and despised to seek alternative routes to overturning the structures of power that abused them, whether in Peru, Nicaragua, or Mexico.[33] In the Zapatistas' confrontation with imperial and Mexican policies, they found a new way to refuse to compromise with power and, in the words of *subcomandante* Marcos, to "globalize hope." In his September 2003 message to the anti-globalization conference in Cancun, Mexico, Marcos spelled out the divisions between globalization from above, "those who globalize conformism, cynicism, stupidity, war, death and destruction," and globalization from below, "those who globalize rebellion, hope, creativity, intelligence, imagination, life, memory, and the construction of a world that we can all fit in, a world with democracy, liberty, and justice."[34]

Extrapolating from the Zapatista experience, John Holloway envisions the construction of an "antipower, something that is radically different from power over."[35] In reformulating the relationship to power, Marcos provides the guidelines and inspiration behind Holloway's sense of antipower and those global movements dedicated to reconfiguring power and instigating new forms of radical democracy. "It is not only that we do not set ourselves the task of taking power," Marcos insisted in a 1999 interview, "but we propose that the very relationship of power with society must itself change. It must invent itself, or turn itself around in some form."[36] In their insistence on defending their autonomy and eschewing compromise with power, the Zapatistas embody that antipower and a form of grassroots democracy, a democracy that is radical and emancipatory.

The continuing efforts by the World Social Forum and its many spin-offs to enact an "emancipatory democracy" as the "process of changing power relations into relations of shared authority" finds numerous outlets around the globe.[37] Local and national variations of the WSF are exploring how to enact radical politics that flow from grassroots efforts. However, even in the WSF the process of changing power relations runs up against the persistence of certain hierarchies and exclusions, especially in the lack of equal involvement of women and the poor. In fact, there are those who charge that the WSF is less about globalization from below than about globalization from the middle.[38] Nonetheless, the global consciousness and mutual solidarity manifested through the World Social Forum and the regional representations of the Forum pre-figure a world without power over.

In addition, in raising the banner of "Another World is Possible," the WSF has recognized that "the other possible world is a utopian aspiration that comprises several possible worlds."[39] To fuse utopian aspirations with forms of global resistance and rebellion is at the core of the WSF and the fundamental desire to eliminate all vestiges of imperialism and global power over. It is instructive to note that the WSF was central to the massive global response of millions in February 2003 to the threatened U. S. war on Iraq.[40] Obviously, that moment of global resistance was but a fleeting vision of united multitudes seeking a world without the "war, death, and destruction" denounced by Marcos and repeated loudly by millions around the world. Those voices were raised out of a sense of existential faith and utopian longing that another world is possible. That utopian longing, represented through acts of imagination and social practice, also contains the sobering realization that, unlike the conservative and closed utopias of the past, including the visions of an American and New American Century, there is no absolute guarantee of a better, let alone perfect world.[41] Writing in the midst of the fears and hopes of the early twenty-first century and cognizant of the struggle between those seeking another world free from power over, Noam Chomsky discerned

> two trajectories in current history: one aiming toward hegemony, acting rationally within a lunatic doctrinal framework as it threatens survival; the other dedicated to the belief that 'another world is possible,' ... challenging the reigning ideological system and seeking to create constructive alternatives of thought, action, and institutions. Which trajectory will dominate, no one can foretell.[42]

If no one can foretell the future, it is also the case that no one can control the future. Certainly, as we will see in the Conclusion, there are signs indicating certain positive and ominous trends in the world. What will emerge after the disastrous Bush years is yet to be determined not only for the role of U. S. imperialism but also for those seeking to resist that imperialism and to create another and better world. In commending the appropriation of agency and meaningful intervention in the world, one global justice activist contends: "With agency and meaning reclaimed, perhaps it is possible to imagine tomorrow today and to be wary of desires that can only be fulfilled by the future. In that moment of creation, the need for certainty is subsumed by the joy of doing, and the doing is filled with meaning."[43] Together with all of the aforementioned agents struggling for self-determination, liberation, and emancipation, we can take solace in the fact that our mutual solidarities, resistances, and rebellions are themselves an answer to the question of whether another world is possible.

Beyond envisioning that other world, of course, lies the daunting task of building another or other better worlds. We can take tremendous inspiration from the examples, especially emanating from the global South, that, although imperial impediments persist, people in different regions and nations, from different cultures and from the most despised and marginalized classes, have managed to construct alternative ways of resisting and living. And in these alternative paths, one sees the beginnings of a world without the exploitative and oppressive conditions imposed by imperial regimes. While there are certainly critical challenges ahead for both humanity and the survival of the planet, a web of global resistances and reciprocal solidarities, indeed, augur another possible world.

As a way of concluding and bringing together the various threads in this chapter, I want to highlight one of many living models of how to sustain oneself and the planet while creating a version of that better world. Although still small and seemingly local in orientation, the women of Lijjat Papad have built a food production and distribution network throughout India that has 40,000 members in over sixty-three branches. Their commitment to common ownership, non-discrimination, autonomy, and independence reflects what Indian environmental activist and writer, Vandana Shiva, sees as essential components of "living economies" which, in turn, "rejuvenate ecological processes while reactivating people's creativity, solidarity, and interdependence."[44] Shiva points to Lijjat Papad and other local efforts to be part of another world as instances of what she calls "Earth Democracy." Those examples grow out of "struggles of the disadvantaged and excluded," not unlike Connie Ramos, the poor empowered by liberation theology, and the Zapatistas, who challenge the imperial hubris and elite arrogance of treating them as "disposable people."[45] Furthermore, as claimed by Shiva, "Earth Democracy is not just about the next protest or next World Social Forum; it is about what we do in between. It addresses the global in our everyday lives, our everyday realities, and creates change globally by making change locally."[46]

The doing of the "in between" as the concrete and grounded prefiguring of that other world can be found replicated around the planet. It is the "possible" of that other world, the bridge to a realizable utopia that is needed now more than ever, not just for the realization of a better world but for the survival of the planet. Overthrowing empire and confronting power over require more than insurrectionary fervor and utopian will. What we do in the here-and-now, necessarily motivated by the anticipatory and transformative moments of Bloch's concrete utopia, is an on-going challenge.[47] As one of the characters from the future says to Connie Ramos, "We must fight to come to exist, to remain in existence, to be the future that happens (197–8)." For that future to happen, for that other possible world to come into existence, we must struggle daily with the dystopian realties that confront us and strive for that concrete utopia in ways both large and small. Perhaps we too may fail, doomed like Sisyphus to push a boulder up a hill, only to fall short of the summit. However, to turn away from the effort, to eschew our existential need for creativity, solidarity, and interdependence is to abandon the hopes and needs of our fellow global citizens.

Conclusion

It's the end of the world as we know it

> There is no prospect of a return to the imperial world of the past, let alone the prospect of a lasting global imperial hegemony, unprecedented in history, by a single state, such as America, however great its military force. The age of empires is dead. We shall have to find another way of organizing the globalized world of the twenty-first century.
>
> Eric Hobsbawm

When Alexis de Tocqueville, the astute French diplomat and essayist, reflected on his travels throughout the United States during the early 1830s, there were few national and cultural idiosyncrasies that escaped his attention. From the policies of Indian removal to the "peculiar" institution of slavery, Tocqueville perceived a young country in the midst of a dynamic and anxiety-ridden growth. As the country continued its expansion westward, what had once been the North American outpost of the British Empire was in the process of building its own empire. That historical progression would soon be ideologically ordained as "manifest destiny." For Tocqueville, however, there was a curious constraint on this restless American, one that seemed to presage a form of national and cultural solipsism. "Every one shuts himself up in his own breast," observed Tocqueville, "and affects from that point to judge the world."[1]

Over 150 years later, on the California coast of the nation about to become the one remaining superpower in the world, another French essayist and cultural critic, Jean Baudrillard, jotted down his musings on his travels in the United States. Sharing the same fascination with Tocqueville about American novelties, Baudrillard, in contrast, wrote against the backdrop of an imperial America that had only recently intimidated Europe with its nuclear arsenal, violated the sovereignty of a small Central American and Caribbean nation, and imposed, through the long reach of its financial institutions, structural adjustment programs that literally sapped the well-being of numerous countries and their precarious populations. Baudrillard also detected the presence of a national and cultural solipsism, this time coming at the closing stages rather than the beginning of an American Empire. "Nothing evokes the end of the world more than a man running straight ahead on a beach," Baudrillard contemplated, swathed in the sounds of his walkman, cocooned in the solitary sacrifice of his energy, indifferent even to catastrophes since he expects destruction to come only as the fruit of his own efforts, from exhausting the energy of a body that has in his own eyes become useless.[2]

One of the objectives of this book has been to puncture that smug self-enclosure that looks out on the rest of the world from a blinkered view. Whether out of nationalist dogma, ideological certitude, cultural projection, or "knowledgeable ignorance," Americans have failed to apprehend the complexities of the world and the contradictions of the U. S. imperial role in that world. As noted by historian Marilyn Young, the U. S. national story is based on the "conviction that an American empire, as opposed to those established by other nations, is democratic, that American interests are consonant with the last, best hopes of all mankind." This self-righteous belief "occludes both the fact of U. S. power and the effects of its exercise."[3] Although polemical at times, the intention of *Dying Empire* has been to investigate with a critical eye all of the dimensions (economic, geopolitical, ideological/cultural) of U. S. power, especially in the aftermath of World War II with the emergence of American global hegemon and, more particularly, in the face of challenges to and declension of that hegemony, beginning in the 1970s.[4]

Scattered throughout the book have been the analytical perspectives of those scholars who have traced the rise and fall of the American Empire. From U. S. diplomatic historians (Michael Hunt, William Appleman Williams, and Marilyn Young) to military historians and political science critics of militarism (Andrew Bacevich to Carl Boggs, Chalmers Johnson, and Gabriel Kolko) to Marxist economists and geographers (Samir Amin, John Bellamy Foster, William Tabb, and Ellen Meiskins Wood to David Harvey and Neil Smith) to world systems analysts (Giovanni Arrighi and Immanuel Wallerstein) to foreign and domestic cultural critics of empire (Walden Bello, Emmanuel Todd, Zillah Eisenstein, and Arundhati Roy to Morris Berman, Rashid Khalidi, Michael Mann, and Cornel West), there is broad consensus that the American Empire is in decline. How quickly that decline will lead to a demise of the American Empire, however, continues to be in contention. Moreover, the degree to which global resistance to the American Empire will ultimately expedite the erosion and termination of its global hegemony and power is also open to question, even as it has been a consistent thread throughout this book.

Another consistent thread in *Dying Empire* is the basic understanding, culled from the historian William Appleman Williams, that empire is a "way of life." Following Williams's definition of the "way of life" as "the combination of patterns of thought and action that, as it becomes habitual and institutionalized, defines the thrust and character of a culture and society," I have critically explored those patterns of thought and action both abroad and at home.[5] I have considered in both Parts I and II how the institutionalized exercise of imperial power abroad has operated with specific deleterious effects while generating particular instances of resistance. I have also described the habitual patterns of thought and action of an imperial culture at home in Chapters 2 and 3 which have created a paranoid community and made difficult acts of transformative and transnational solidarity. With Williams in mind, I have probed the "imperial way of life" and its underlying "economic factors as well as politics, ideas, and psychology."[6] Before delineating the most recent economic, geopolitical, and ideological/cultural factors evident in the dying American Empire, I want to turn to specific psychological perspectives on the denial of death as it relates to that Empire.

As a practicing psychiatrist and psycho-historian, Robert Jay Lifton is well-versed in the denial of death and what he identifies as the "illusion of invulnerability" that breeds a "superpower syndrome" with its "death anxiety."[7] In the case of the United States, the insistence on the "ownership of history" projects a fantasy of "infinite power and control … that is as self-destructive as it is dazzling – still another version of the ownership of death."[8] Contending that the "American superpower is an artificial construct, widely perceived as illegitimate," Lifton also asserts that its "reign is … inherently unstable … and its reach for full-scale world domination marks the beginning of its decline."[9] For both the health of its citizens and the planet, the "superpower syndrome" must be rejected and with it the "claim to an exclusive power over life and death."[10]

Probably the classic psychological study of death and dying emerged from the clinical work of Elisabeth Kubler-Ross. Although focused on individual patients, Kubler-Ross also reflected on societal denial of death. "If a whole nation, a whole society suffers from … a denial of death," she originally wrote in 1969 in the midst of the war in Southeast Asia and the aftermath of urban uprisings, "it has to use defenses which can only be destructive. Wars, riots, and increasing numbers of murders and other crimes may be indicators of our decreasing ability to face death with acceptance and dignity."[11] Kubler-Ross's well-known stages of dealing with death prior to acceptance run the gamut from denial to anger to bargaining and depression. While cognizant of psychological reductionism, I think it is appropriate to suggest that the American Empire's political leaders and their followers are mostly stuck in the first two stages of denial and anger with a feint now and then towards bargaining, the latter evident in some of the policies of Bill Clinton and now Barack Obama.

Given the denial of death and the belief in the ownership of history, it is not surprising that the wielding of power by the managers of the American Empire continues to frustrate as much as it satisfies the demands of the institutional networks in which those managers are embedded. According to Gabriel Kolko, the

> U. S. obsession with power and its failure to create the world order it idealizes has been its defining characteristic for at least a half-century. … All presidents, whether Democrats or Republicans, have sought to shape the contours of politics worldwide. This global mission and fascination with military power has entangled its priorities and stretched its resources over and over again.[12]

Although imperial overstretch is even more pronounced in the aftermath of the recent world-wide economic crisis (more on this below), the fundamental bi-partisan commitment by the political elite to exercising, in the words of Barack Obama, "global leadership" will continue unabated.[13] Of course, there will be nuances in the exercise of that global leadership. Given the egregious violations of international and U. S. laws by the Bush Administration, from abrogation of the Geneva Conventions to renditions to torture and domestic spying, it is not surprising to see President Obama repudiate torture, renditions (albeit still utilizing the state secrets act from the Bush era), and to begin the closure of Guantanamo prison. Although the adoption of these positions by President Obama is certainly part of the restoration of U. S. standing in the international arena, this new administration is wedded to prosecuting war aggressively in Afghanistan with the expansion of U. S. troops and in Pakistan with increasing attacks by U. S. drones and forays by U. S. Special Forces while still retaining redefined combat troops and military contractors in Iraq.[14]

The imperatives of U. S. military and economic imperialism with commitments to sustaining the global garrison of U. S. troops, facilitating the predatory spread of private contractors, and protecting the oil and gas regions of the Middle East and Central Asia portend the imperial presence in these aforementioned regions irrespective of President Obama's articulation of "smart power" or the massive deficits incurred by the United States. While there have been congressional calls for severely reducing the budget for the Pentagon, that budget, submitted and signed by Obama, continued to expand, albeit by a minimal amount, 4 percent, by previous Bush benchmarks. Even in the face of the 2008 National Intelligence Council's surprising report on "Global Trends 2025" with its projection that "the United States relative strength – even in the military realm – will decline and U. S. leverage will become more constrained," there will be an imperial dedication to guarding increasingly scarce energy resources.[15] As Tom Engelhardt points out, such military and economic imperialism will prolong an "Empire-speak" from Washington that, on one hand, "offers official Washington a kind of 'plausible deniability'" and, on the other, persists in preventing "imperial officials from imagining a world not in their own image."[16]

The contradiction of carrying on imperial wars, with weaponry named for death-dispensing creatures like Predators and Reapers, in the face of what Chalmers Johnson has called an "economic death spiral at the Pentagon," seems overwhelming. From Johnson's perspective the U. S. faces a

> double crisis at the Pentagon: we can no longer afford the pretense of being the Earth's sole superpower, and we cannot afford to perpetuate a system in which the military-industrial complex makes its fortune off inferior, poorly designed weapons.

Johnson cites a former civilian manager in the Pentagon's Office of Systems Analysis who wrote in December 2008 that "patterns of repetitive habitual behavior in the Pentagon have created a self-destructive decision-making process. This process has produced a death spiral." Another former senior official in the Department of Defense decried the decades-old patterns of faulty and over-budgeted procurement:

> Unless someone is willing to stand up and point out that the emperor has no clothes, the U. S. military will continue to hemorrhage taxpayer dollars and critical years while acquiring equipment that falls short of meeting the needs of troops in the field.

While there may be some modest efforts to reign in the more expensive and outlandish weapons systems, as long as military imperialism persists and with it the military-industrial's Iron Triangle of interests, there will be a spiraling of economic death not only at the Pentagon but throughout a debilitated U. S. economy.[17]

Attributing the debilitation of the U. S. economy to a mortgage crisis or the collapse of the housing market misses the truly epochal crisis in the world economy and, indeed, in capitalism itself. As economist Michael Hudson contends, "the financial 'wealth creation' game is over. Economies emerged from World War II relatively free of debt, but the 60-year global run-up has run its course. Financial capitalism is in a state of collapse, and marginal palliatives cannot revive it." According to Hudson, among those palliatives is an ironic variant of the IMF strategies imposed on developing nations.

> The new twist is a variant on the IMF 'stabilization' plans that lend money to central banks to support their currencies – for long enough to enable local oligarchs and foreign investors to move their savings and investments offshore at a good exchange rate.

The continuity between these IMF plans and the Obama administration's fealty to Wall Street can be seen in the person of Lawrence Summers, now the chief economic advisor to Obama. As further noted by Hudson,

> the Obama bank bailout is arranged much like an IMF loan to support the exchange rate of foreign currency, but with the Treasury supporting financial asset prices for U. S. banks and other financial institutions ... Private-sector debt will be moved onto the U. S. Government balance sheet, where "taxpayers" will bear losses.[18]

So, here we have another variation of the working poor getting sapped by the economic elite! In fact, one estimate of U. S. federal government support to the elite financial institutions is in the range of $10 trillion dollars, a heist of unimaginable proportions.[19]

Given the massive indebtedness of the United States, its reliance on foreign support of that debt by countries like China, which has close to $2 trillion tied up in treasury bills and other investments, a long-term crisis of profit-ability, overproduction, and offshoring of essential manufacturing, it does not appear that the United States and, perhaps, even the capitalist system can avoid collapse. Certainly, there are Marxist economists and world-systems analysts who are convinced that the collapse is inevitable although it may take several generations to complete. The question becomes whether a dying system can be resuscitated or if something else can be put in its place. One of the most prominent world-systems scholars, Immanuel Wallerstein, puts the long-term crisis of capitalism and the alternatives in the following perspective:

> Because the system we have known for 500 years is no longer able to guarantee long-term prospects of capital accumulation, we have entered a period of world chaos. Wild (and largely uncontrollable) swings in the economic, political, and military situations are leading to a systemic bifurcation, that is, to a world collective choice about the kind of new system the world will construct over the next fifty years. The new system will not be a capitalist system, but it could be one of two kinds: a differ-ent system that is equally or more hierarchical and inequalitarian, or one that is substantially democratic and equalitarian.[20]

Predictions about the ultimate collapse of capitalism, even based on solid historical evidence, may still be too mired in Marxist crisis theory and the stages of history. On the other hand, Wallerstein may be too sanguine about or too oblivious to environmental calamities, especially in the face of con-tinuous overexploitation and maldistribution of essential resources, such as water, which could, in turn, lead to a planetary catastrophe.[21]

While Wallerstein and many of the Marxist critics of capitalism correctly identify the long-term structural crisis of capitalism and offer important insights into the need for more democratic and equalitarian systems, they often fail to realize other critical predicaments that have plagued human societies in the past and persist in even more life-threatening ways today. Among those predicaments are the power trips of civilization and environ-mental destructiveness. Such power trips can be seen through the sedi-mentation of power over in the reign of patriarchal systems and an evolutionary selection for that power over which contaminates society and social relationships. Certainly, many of those predicaments can also be attributed to a 5,000-year history of the intersection of empire and civiliza-tion. Anthropologist Kajsa Ekholm Friedman analyzes that intersection and its impact in the Bronze Age as an "imperialist project ..., dependent upon trade and ultimately upon war ... (in) the struggle for resources."[22] How-ever, over the long rule of empire and especially within the last 500 years of the global aspirations of various empires, "no state or empire," observes historian Eric Hobsbawm, "has been large, rich, or powerful enough to maintain hegemony over the political world, let alone to establish political and military supremacy over the globe."[23] Since World War II, however, the

United States has attempted to maintain global hegemony, relying as much or more on its military supremacy than on its economic prowess.

Certainly, a deeply rooted expansionist and exceptionalist ideology has been an essential part of the American imperial project, justifying in the minds of the ruling class, the political elite, and the majority of U. S. citizens myriad military interventions. While those interventions have shifted geographically, the intensity seems almost to be inversely proportional to decreasing economic power. Hence, numerous critics cited throughout the book have drawn attention to the fact that militarism and wars have tried to substitute for waning economic and political influence in the world. While this habituated turn to war is a consequence of a variety of structural factors, the commitment to the imperial project and a dying empire appears at times to be profoundly irrational.[24]

Although war and trade still remain key components of the imperial project today and pretensions for global supremacy persist in the United States, what is just as threatening to the world as we know it is the overexploitation and abuse of environmental resources. Jared Diamond brilliantly reveals how habituated attitudes and values precluded the necessary recognition of environmental degradation which, in turn, led to the collapse of vastly different civilizations, societies, and cultures throughout recorded history.[25] He identifies twelve contemporary environmental challenges which pose grave dangers to the planet and its inhabitants. Among these are the destruction of natural habitats (rainforests, wetlands, etc.); species extinction; soil erosion; depletion of fossil fuels and underground water aquifers; toxic pollution; and climate change, especially attributable to the use of fossil fuels.[26] As we have seen in Chapter 5, U. S. economic imperialism has played a direct role in environmental degradation, whether in McDonald's resource destruction of rainforests in Latin America, Coca-Cola's exploitation of underground water aquifers in India, or Union Carbide's toxic pollution in India. On the other hand, if we are seeing "the demise of the fossil-fuel economy," as argued by Anthony Giddens, then we must address the on-going environmental and economic calamities unleashed by globalization from above.[27]

Beyond the links between empire, globalization from above, and environmental destruction, unless we also clearly understand and combat the connections between empire and unending growth with its attendant "accumulation by dispossession," we may very well doom ourselves to extinction. According to James Gustave Speth, Dean of the Yale School of Forestry and Environmental Studies, the macro obsession with growth is also intimately related to our micro habituated ways of living. "Parallel to transcending our growth fetish," Speth argues,

> we must move beyond our consumerism and hyperventilating lifestyles. ...
> This reluctance to challenge consumption has been a big mistake, given
> the mounting environmental and social costs of American "affluenza,"
> extravagance and wastefulness.[28]

Of course, there are significant class and ethnic/racial differences in consumerism and lifestyle in the United States. However, as highlighted in Chapter 5, even more vast differences and inequities obtain between the U. S. and the developing world. It is those inequities that led Eduardo Galeano to conclude that "consumer society is a booby trap. Those at the controls feign ignorance, but anybody with eyes in his head can see that the great majority of people necessarily must consume not much, very little, or nothing at all in order to save the bit of nature we have left."[29] In addition, from Vandana Shiva's perspective, "unless worldviews and lifestyles are restructured ecologically, peace and justice will continue to be violated and, ultimately, the very survival of humanity will be threatened."[30]

For Shiva and other global agents of resistance, the ecological and peace and justice imperatives require us to act in the here and now. Her vision of "Earth Democracy" with its emphasis on balancing authentic needs with a local ecology and democratic economy provides an essential guidepost to what we can all do to stop the ravaging of the environment and to salvage the planet. As she contends, "In the face of a world of greed, inequality, and overconsumption, Earth Democracy globalizes compassion, justice, and sustainability."

The local, national, and transnational struggles and visions of change, elaborated in Part III and other sections of this book, are further evidence that the imperial project is not only being contested but also being transformed on a daily basis. According to Mark Engler,

> The powerful will abandon their strategies of control only when it grows too costly for them to do otherwise. It is the concerted efforts of people coming together in local communities and in movements spanning borders that will raise the costs. Empire becomes unsustainable ... when the people of the world resist.[31]

Whether in the rural villages of Brazil or India, the jungles of Mexico or Ecuador, the city squares of Cochabama or Genoa, the streets of Seattle or Soweto, there has been, and continues to be, resistance around the globe to the imperial project. If the ruling elite and many of the citizens of the United States have not yet accepted the fact that the empire is dying, the global multitudes have been busy at work, digging its future grave and planting the seeds for another possible world.[32]

Notes

Notes to Introduction

1 The world-systems approach to the rise and fall of empires can be found in the extensive writings of Giovanni Arrighi and Immanuel Wallerstein. For more focused and abbreviated analysis of the rise and fall of the American Empire from these two scholars, see Giovanni Arrighi, "Hegemony Unraveling 1 and 2," *New Left Review* 32 and 33 (March/April 2005 and May/June 2005), esp. 51–74 and 102–16; and Immanuel Wallerstein, "The Curve of American Power," *New Left Review* 40 (July–August 2006): 77–94. For an anthropological perspective on U. S. empire and imperialism and the resistance it has engendered, see Bruce M. Knauft, "Provincializing America," *Current Anthropology* 48:6 (December 2007): 781–93. For additional insights into empires and their decline in comparative perspective, see Eric Hobsbawm, *On Empire: America, War, and Global Supremacy* (New York: Pantheon Books, 2008); and Jonathan Friedman and Christopher Chase-Dunn. eds., *Hegemonic Declines: Past and Present* (Boulder, CO: Paradigm Publishers, 2005). On the "new" imperialism as a less direct expression of territorial and political control and more recent historical phenomena, see David Harvey, *The New Imperialism* (New York: Oxford University Press, 2005); and Ellen Meiksins Wood, *Empire of Capital* (New York: Verso, 2003). It will be clear throughout the book that my reference to U. S. imperialism is primarily to the "new" version.

2 Gabriel Kolko, *The Age of War: The United States Confronts the World* (Boulder, CO: Lynne Rienner Publishers, 2006), 95.

3 For a concise overview of the origins and development of Witness for Peace, see Christian Smith, *Resisting Reagan: The U. S. Central America Peace Movement* (Chicago: University of Chicago Press, 1996), 70–8 and *passim*. On the impact of U. S. imperialism in Latin America over the last few decades, see Greg Grandin, *Empire's Workshop: Latin America, the United States, and the Rise of the New Imperialism* (New York: Holt Paperbacks, 2007). For older, although still insightful analysis of U. S. policy in Central America, see Noam Chomsky, *Turning the Tide: U. S. Intervention in Central America and the Struggle for Peace* (Boston: South End Press, 1985); and Walter LaFeber, *Inevitable Revolutions: The United States in Central America* (New York: W.W. Norton & Co., 1984).

4 Chris Hedges, *War is a Force That Gives Us Meaning* (New York: Public Affairs, 2002), 35–7.

5 Carol Gould, *Globalizing Democracy and Human Rights* (New York: Cambridge University Press, 2004), 254.

6 On media manipulation and Reagan machinations during the 1984 election, see Thomas Walker, *Nicaragua: Living in the Shadow of the Eagle*, 4th ed. (Boulder,

CO: Westview Press, 2003), 52–3, 156–9, and *passim*. For a discussion of the framing by the Reagan Administration through the discourse of the Cold War, see Smith, *Resisting Reagan*, 239–42.

7 Smith, *Resisting Reagan*, 374.

8 William Appleman Williams, *Empire as a Way of Life* (New York: Oxford University Press, 1982), xi–xii.

9 Ziauddin Sardar and Merryl Wyn Davies, *Why Do People Hate America?* (New York: The Disinformation Co., 2002), 13–14. It is perhaps instructive, and depressing, that Barack Obama maintained in his inauguration address that the United States did not need to apologize for its way of life.

10 Edward Said, "The Other America," *CounterPunch*, March 21, 2003. Online. Available HTTP: <http://www.counterpunch.org/said0322203.html> (accessed October 28, 2008).

11 Naomi Klein, *The Shock Doctrine: The Rise of Disaster Capitalism* (New York: Metropolitan Books, 2007), 406–26.

12 Chalmers Johnson, *Blowback: The Costs and Consequences of American Empire* (New York: Henry Holt, 2000), 68. Even the globally adored (for now) and savvy Barack Obama endorses the inevitable reluctant sheriff role. He writes in *The Audacity of Hope* (New York: Vintage, 2006) that "there will be times when we must again play the role or the world's reluctant sheriff. This will not change – nor should it (306)."

13 Susan George, *Another World is Possible If …* (New York: Verso, 2004), 22–4.

14 Mike Davis, *Planet of Slums* (New York: Verso, 2006).

15 Eduardo Galeano, *Upside Down: A Primer for the Looking-Glass World*, trans. Mark Fried (New York: Metropolitan Books, 2000), 357.

Notes to Chapter 1

1 Ernest W. Lefever, *America's Imperial Burden: Is the Past Prologue?* (Boulder, CO: Westview Press, 1999), 158.

2 Thomas Donnelly, "The Past as Prologue: An Imperial Manual," *Foreign Affairs* 81:4 (July/August 2002):165–70. On Kipling's connections to U. S. imperialism, see John Bellamy Foster, Harry Magdoff, and Robert W. McChesney, "Kipling, the 'White Man's Burden,' and U. S. Imperialism," in John Bellamy Foster and Robert W. McChesney, eds., *Pox Americana: Exposing the American Empire* (New York: Monthly Review Press, 2004), 12–21.

3 William Appleman Williams, *Empire as a Way of Life* (New York: Oxford University Press, 1982), 62.

4 For a recent study of the role of race, gender, and other cultural constructions in the development of U. S. imperialism and its impact on national ideological hegemony, see Walter L. Hixson, *The Myth of American Diplomacy: National Identity and U. S. Foreign Policy* (New Haven, CT: Yale University Press, 2008).

5 Williams, *Empire as a Way of Life*, 26.

6 David Harvey, *The New Imperialism* (New York: Oxford University Press, 2005), 45 and 137–82.

7 Barbara Jean Fields, "Slavery, Race, and Ideology in the United States of America," *New Left Review* 181 (May–June 1990):114.

8 Michael Paul Rogin, *Fathers and Children: Andrew Jackson and the Subjugation of the American Indian* (New York: Vintage Books, 1976), 169. For a brilliant exploration of Jefferson's attitudes towards the Indians, see Richard Drinnon, *Facing West: The Metaphysics of Indian-Hating and Empire-Building* (Norman: University of Oklahoma Press, 1997), 78–116.

9 Alexis de Tocqueville, *Journey to America*, trans. George Lawrence (New York: Doubleday Anchor, 1971), 206.

10 Quoted in Eric T. L. Love, *Race Over Empire: Racism and U. S. Imperialism, 1865–1900* (Chapel Hill: The University of North Carolina Press, 2004), 21–2.
11 Quoted in Howard Zinn, *A People's History of the United States*, rev. ed. (New York: HarperPerennial, 1995), 155.
12 Richard Slotkin, *Gunfighter Nation: The Myth of the Frontier in Twentieth-Century America* (New York: HarperPerennial, 1993), 45–6. On the racial meanings of manifest destiny, see Reginald Horsman, *Race and Manifest Destiny: The Origins of American Racial Anglo-Saxonism* (Cambridge, MA: Harvard University Press, 1981).
13 On "martial manhood," see Amy S. Greenberg, *Manifest Manhood and the Antebellum American Empire* (New York: Cambridge University Press, 2005). On "manifest domesticity," see Amy Kaplan, *The Anarchy of Empire in the Making of U. S. Culture* (Cambridge, MA: Harvard University Press, 2002), 23–50.
14 Quoted in Retort, *Afflicted Powers: Capital and Spectacle in a New Age of War* (New York: Verso, 2006), 84. The authors draw a direct line from this "nineteenth-century dissimulation" to the Bush Doctrine.
15 Quoted in Ronald T. Takaki, *Iron Cages: Race and Culture in 19th-Century America* (Seattle: University of Washington Press, 1982), 278. For the most extensive discussion of the racial and gender dimensions of the U. S. intervention in Cuba and the Philippines, see Kristin L. Hoganson, *Fighting for American Manhood: How Gender Politics Provoked the Spanish American and Philippine American Wars* (New Haven, CT: Yale University Press, 1998). On the interconnected meanings of rescue, popular romance novels of the turn of the century, and imperial masculinity, see Kaplan, *The Anarchy of Empire in the Making of U. S. Culture*, 92–120.
16 Love, *Race over Empire*, 184 and 181. On the contradictory role of racism in debates over the Philippines, see ibid., 159–95. On the interconnections of immigration and empire-building during this period, see Matthew Frye Jacobson, *Barbarian Virtues: The United States Encounters Foreign Peoples at Home and Abroad, 1876–1917* (New York: Hill & Wang, 2000).
17 Neil Smith, *American Empire: Roosevelt's Geographer and the Prelude to Globalization* (Berkeley: University of California Press, 2003), 19.
18 Williams, *Empire as a Way of Life*, 131.
19 Chalmers Johnson, *The Sorrows of Empire: Militarism, Secrecy, and the End of the Republic* (New York: Owl Books, 2005), 48.
20 On the imperial brotherhood during the Cold War, see Robert D. Dean, *Imperial Brotherhood: Gender and the Making of Cold War Foreign Policy* (Amherst: University of Massachusetts Press, 2001).
21 Zillah Eisenstein, *Against Empire: Feminisms, Racism, and the West* (New York: Zed Books, 2004), 1.
22 David Harvey, *The New Imperialism*, 197. On the contradictions of empire-building and U. S. involvement in the Middle East, see Rashid Khalidi, *Resurrecting Empire: Western Footprints and America's Perilous Path in the Middle East* (Boston: Beacon Press, 2004).
23 On the emergence of the United States as global hegemon, see Michael H. Hunt, *The American Ascendancy: How the United States Gained and Wielded Global Dominance* (Chapel Hill: The University of North Carolina Press, 2007).
24 Luce quoted in Neil Smith, *The Endgame of Globalization* (New York: Routledge, 2005), 18. For an extensive analysis of the social context of the "American Century," see Olivier Zunz, *Why the American Century?* (Chicago: University of Chicago Press, 1998). On the U. S. as redeemer nation, see Ernest Tuveson, *Redeemer Nation: The Idea of America's Millennial Role* (Chicago: University of Chicago Press, 1968). On the messianic roots of America's missions in the world, see Anders Stephanson, *Manifest Destiny and the Empire of Right* (New York: Hill & Wang, 1995).

25 Smith, *American Empire*, 20. For further discussion of the origins of the "American Century," see Luce's original 1941 essay in *Diplomatic History* 23:2 (Spring 1999): 159–71. For the impact of the "American Century," see the articles in ibid., 172–370.

26 Charles Bright, "Where in the World is America? The History of the United States in the Global Age," in Thomas Bender, ed. *Rethinking American History in a Global Age* (Berkeley: University of California Press, 2002), 64.

27 Ziauddin Sardar and Merryl Wyn Davies, *Why Do People Hate America?* (New York: The Disinformation Co., 2002), 10. See also Peter J. Taylor, "Locating the American Century: A World-Systems Analysis," in David Slater and Peter J. Taylor, eds. *The American Century: Consensus and Coercion in the Projection of American Power* (Malden, MA: Blackwell Publishers, 1999), 3–16.

28 Immanuel Wallerstein, *The Decline of American Power: The U. S. in a Chaotic World* (New York: The New Press, 2003), 3.

29 Bruce M. Knauft, "Provincializing America: Imperialism, Capitalism, and Counter-hegemony in the Twenty-First Century," *Current Anthropology* 48:6 (December 2007): 787.

30 Sardar and Davies, *Why Do People Hate America?*, 68. On the history of the twentieth- and twenty-first-century regime changes promoted by the U. S., see Stephen Kinzer, *Overthrow: America's Century of Regime Change from Hawaii to Iraq* (New York: Henry Holt & Co., 2006). On "stealth imperialism," see Chalmers Johnson, *Blowback: The Costs and Consequences of American Empire* (New York: Henry Holt & Co., 2000), 65–94.

31 Tom Engelhardt, *The End of Victory Culture: Cold War America and the Disillusioning of a Generation* (New York: Basic Books, 1995).

32 Walden Bello, *Dilemmas of Domination: The Unmaking of the American Empire* (New York: Metropolitan Books, 2005), 60.

33 On the impact of Vietnam and Iraq in undermining U. S. hegemony, see Giovanni Arrighi, "Hegemony Unravelling 1," *New Left Review* 32 (March–April 2005): 23–80.

34 For the most illuminating discussion of the U. S. air war on Southeast Asia, see James William Gibson, *The Perfect War: Technowar in Vietnam* (New York: Atlantic Monthly Press, 2000).

35 John Donnelly and Robert Schlesinger, "Military Criticized for Type of Ordnance," *Boston Globe*, April 2, 2003. Online. Available HTTP: <http://www.commondreams.org/headlines03/0402–7.htm> (accessed November 5, 2008); Robert Higgs, "Military Precision versus Moral Precision," *The Independent Institute* 23 March 2003. Online. Available HTTP: <http://www.independent.org/newsroom/article.asp?id=1154> (accessed November 5, 2008). Neil Mackay, "U. S. Forces Use of Depleted Uranium is 'Illegal,'" *The Sunday Herald* 30 March 2003. Online. Available HTTP: <http://www.commondreams.org/headlines03/0330–02.htm> (accessed November 5, 2008).

36 Christian Appy, *Working Class War: American Combat Soldiers and Vietnam* (Chapel Hill: The University of North Carolina Press, 1993).

37 Ron Kovic, *Born on the Fourth of July* (New York: Pocket Books, 1977).

38 Engelhardt, *The End of Victory Culture*, 224. On the connection between My Lai and Haditha, see Tom Englehardt, "The Real Meaning of Haditha," *Tom. Dispatch.com*, June 6, 2006. Online. Available HTTP: <http://www.tomdispatch.com/month=2006–6 > (accessed November 12, 2008). On the relationship between the Vietnam War and America's violent solipsistic culture, see Slotkin, *Gunfighter Nation*, 441–623.

39 Mark Franchetti, "Slaughter at the Bridge of Death," *London Times*, March 31, 2003. Online. Available HTTP: < http;//counterpunch.org/franchetti03312003.html> (accessed November 12, 2008). Richard Norton-Taylor and Rory McCarthy, "British Military Critical of U. S. Troops' Heavy-Handed Style with Civilians,"

Guardian/UK, April 1, 2003. Online. Available HTTP: <http://www.common-dreams.org/headlines03/0401-4.htm > (accessed November 12, 2008).

40 On the ideological and personnel linkages of Reaganism, the Project for the New American Century, and the Bush Doctrine, see Gary Dorrien, *Imperial Designs: Neoconservatism and the New Pax Americana* (New York: Routledge, 2004); and Mel Gurtov, *Superpower on Crusade: The Bush Doctrine in U. S. Foreign Policy* (Boulder, CO: Lynne Rienner Publishers, 2006), 28–36.

41 Project for the New American Century, Statement of Principles, June 3, 1997. Online. Available HTTP: <http://www.newamericancentury.org/statementofprinciplies.htm> (accessed November 12, 2008).

42 Ira Chernus, *Monsters to Destroy: The Neoconservative War on Terror and Sin* (Boulder, CO: Paradigm Publishers, 2006), 167.

43 Zbigniew Brzezinski, *The Choice: Global Domination or Global Leadership* (New York: Basic Books, 2004); and Francis Fukuyama, *America at the Crossroads: Democracy, Power, and the Neoconservative Legacy* (New Haven, CT: Yale University Press, 2006).

44 Robert Kagan, *Of Paradise and Power: American and Europe in the New World Order* (New York: Alfred A. Knopf, 2003), 100 and 41. For a critique of Kagan and the Bush Doctrine, see Carl Boggs, *Imperial Delusions: American Militarism and Endless War* (Lanham, MD: Rowman & Littlefield, 2005), 41–2.

45 Wallerstein, *The Decline of American Power*, 27.

46 Harvey, *The New Imperialism*; and Smith, *The Endgame of Globalization*.

47 Chernus, *Monsters to Destroy*, 202.

48 Boggs, *Imperial Delusions*; and Johnson, *The Sorrows of Empire*.

49 Emmanuel Todd, *After the Empire: The Breakdown of the American Order*, trans. C. Jon Delogu (New York: Columbia University Press, 2003), xviii.

50 Susan George, *Another World is Possible if …* (New York: Verso, 2004), 110.

51 Ibid., 119–23. George even cites her own experience with educational and health care benefits that would have been unavailable to her in the United States.

52 Ibid., 122.

53 Ibid., 131.

54 George's overview of the "Washington Consensus" can be found in ibid., 14–28. For another concise discussion of the rise and fall of the "Washington Consensus," see Jan Nederveen Pieterse, *Globalization or Empire?* (New York: Routledge, 2004), 9–15.

55 Evo Morales, "I Believe only in the Power of the People," *Countercurrents,* December 22, 2005. Online. Available HTTP: <http://www.countercurrents.org/bolivia-morales221205.htm> (accessed November 12, 2008). On the background of Bolivian social movements and their role in the elevation of indigenous leaders like Morales, see Benjamin Dangl, *The Price of Fire: Resource Wars and Social Movements in Bolivia* (Oakland, CA: AK Press, 2007).

56 On Chávez's politics and his challenge to the U. S., see Nikolas Kozloff, *Hugo Chávez: Oil, Politics, and the Challenge to the U. S.* (New York: Palgrave Macmillan, 2006).

57 On U. S. imperial intervention in Latin America, see the relevant chapters in Kinzer, *Overthrow*. On the distinction between imperialism as a political project and its molecular political economic structures, see Harvey, *The New Imperialism*, esp. 26–36.

58 James Petras, "Is Latin America Really Turning Left?" *CounterPunch*, June 3/4, 2006. Online. Available HTTP: <http://www.counterpunch.org/petras06032006.html> (accessed November 12, 2008). For a counterview of the Latin American challenge, especially the radical thrust from Chávez and Morales, see Greg Grandin, "Latin America's New Consensus," *The Nation*, April 13, 2006. Online. Available HTTP: <http://thenation.com/doc/20060501/grandin> (accessed November 19, 2008).

59 Steve Ellner, "The Hugo Chávez Phenomenon: Anti-Imperialism from Above or Radical Democracy from Below," in Fred Rosen, ed. *Empire and Dissent: The United States and Latin America* (Durham, NC: Duke University Press, 2008), 222–3.

60 For the positive spin on Morales and the "de-colonization of the state," see Walter Mignolo, "Nationalization of Natural Gas in Bolivia," *CounterPunch*, May 9, 2006. Online. Available HTTP: <http://www.counterpunch.org/mignolo05082006.html> (accessed November 12, 2008). For the critical perspective, see Petras, "Is Latin America Really Turning Left?"

61 See Kozloff, *Hugo Chávez*. For a brief overview of Chávez's legacy in Venezuela, see Christian Parenti, "Hugo Chávez and Petro Populism," *The Nation*, March 24, 2005. Online. Available HTTP: <http://thenation.com/doc/20050411/parenti> (accessed November 12, 2008).

62 Roger Burbach, *Globalization and Postmodern Politics: From Zapatistas to High-Tech Robber Barons* (London: Pluto Press, 2001), 11. For another elaboration of postmodern politics, with a nod to the Zapatistas, see Gustavo Esteva and Madhu Suri Prakash, *Grassroots Post-Modernism: Remaking the Soil of Cultures* (New York: Zed Books, 1998); and Neil Harvey, "Beyond Hegemony: Zapatismo, Empire, and Dissent," in Rosen, ed. *Empire and Dissent*, 117–36.

63 Boaventura de Sousa Santos, *The Rise of the Global Left: The World Social Forum and Beyond* (New York: Zed Books, 2006), 128.

64 Naomi Klein, "Reclaiming the Commons," *New Left Review* 9 (May–June 2001): 89. For a more extensive elaboration of the epistemological, political, and organizational contexts of the WSF, see Santos, *The Rise of the Global Left*. For a more concise overview of the background and current situation of the WSF, see John L. Hammond, "The World Social Forum and the Emergence of Global Grassroots Politics," *New Politics* 42 (Winter 2007). Online. Available HTTP: <http://www.wpunj.edu/~newpol/issue42/Hammond42.htm> (accessed November 19, 2008).

65 For a concise overview of the Caracas World Social Forum, see Michael Blanding, "The World Social Forum: Protest or Celebration," *The Nation*, February 16, 2006. Online. Available HTTP: <http://www.thenation.com/doc/20060306/blanding> (accessed November 19, 2008).

66 Michael Hardt and Antonio Negri, *Empire* (Cambridge, MA: Harvard University Press, 2000); and *Multitude: War and Democracy in the Age of Empire* (New York: Penguin Books, 2004). For the critique of Hardt and Negri's dismissal of reterritorialized power, see Smith, *The Endgame of Globalization*, 51.

67 Boggs, *Imperial Delusions*, 190.

68 Quoted in Pieterse, *Globalization or Empire?*, 57.

69 Samir Amin, *Beyond U. S. Hegemony: Assessing the Prospects for a Multipolar World*, trans. Patrick Camiller (London: Zed Books, 2006), 12.

70 Wallerstein, *The Decline of American Power*, 215.

71 Michael Mann, *Incoherent Empire* (New York: Verso, 2003), 120. For an exploration of that militarism, see Andrew J. Bacevich, *The New American Militarism* (New York: Oxford University Press, 2005).

72 Kolko, *Another Century of War?* (New York: New Press, 2002), 150.

Notes to Chapter 2

1 William Greider, *Fortress America: The American Military and the Consequences of Peace* (New York: Public Affairs, 1999), ix.

2 Robert Fisk, "Divide and Rule – America's Plan for Baghdad," *The Independent*, April 11, 2007. Online. Available HTTP: <http://informationclearinghouse.info/article17515.htm> (accessed December 5, 2008).

3 Helene Moglen and Sheila Namir, "War and the Dis-eases of Othering," *International Journal of Applied Psychoanalytic Studies* 3:2 (June 2006): 206.
4 For incisive analyses of the ethnic/racial dimensions of Hurricane Katrina, see Michael Eric Dyson, *Come Hell or High Water: Hurricane Katrina and the Color of Disaster* (New York: Basic Civitas, 2006); and Chester Hartman and Gregory D. Squires, eds., *There is no Such Thing as a Natural Disaster: Race, Class, and Hurricane Katrina* (New York: Routledge, 2006).
5 William Appleman Williams, *Empire as a Way of Life* (New York: Oxford University Press, 1982), 221.
6 Morris Berman, *Dark Ages America: The Final Phase of Empire* (New York: W.W. Norton & Co., 2006), 265. Berman also notes the connection between gated communities and SUVs and Hummers, those vehicles "clearly tied to the militarization of American society and to our imperial foreign policy." Ibid., 256.
7 Setha Low, *Behind the Gates: Life, Security, and the Pursuit of Happiness in Fortress America* (New York: Routledge, 2003), 17 and 231.
8 Robert Dreyfuss, "Financing the Imperial Armed Forces: A Trillion Dollars and Nowhere to Go But Up," *TomDispatch.com*, June 6, 2007. Online. Available HTTP: <http://www.commondreams.org/archive/2007/06/06/1701/> (accessed December 5, 2008).
9 Quoted in Ismael Hossein-Zadeh, "Domestic Imperialism," in Jerry Harris, ed. *Contested Terrains of Globalization* (Chicago: Changemaker Press, 2007), 204.
10 David Harvey, *The New Imperialism* (New York: Oxford University Press, 2005), 75.
11 Barbara Kingsolver, *Small Wonder* (New York: HarperCollins, 2002), 262–3.
12 Gar Alperovitz, *America Beyond Capitalism: Reclaiming Our Wealth, Our Liberty, and Our Democracy* (Hoboken, NJ: John Wiley & Sons, 2005), 239.
13 Mansour Farhang, *U. S. Imperialism: From the Spanish-American War to the Iranian Revolution* (Boston: South End Press, 1981), 69.
14 For an excellent portrait of the roots and development of the national security state, see Douglas T. Stuart, *Creating the National Security State* (Princeton, NJ: Princeton University Press, 2008).
15 For a discussion of the contents of NSC-68 and its connections to the Bush Administration's Homeland Security operations, see Andrew J. Bacevich, *The Limits of Power: The End of American Exceptionalism* (New York: Metropolitan Books, 2008), 107–19. Also, on NSC-68, see Williams, *Empire as a Way of Life*, 187–91.
16 Ibid., 101.
17 Arundhati Roy, *Public Power in the Age of Empire* (New York: Seven Stories Press, 2004), 7–8.
18 Rebecca Solnit, *Hope in the Dark: Untold Histories, Wild Possibilities* (New York: Nation Books, 2004), 13–14.
19 Cornel West, *Democracy Matters: Winning the Fight Against Imperialism* (New York: Penguin Books, 2004), 5–8.
20 Carl Boggs, *Imperial Delusions: American Militarism and Endless War* (Lanham, MD: Rowman & Littlefield, 2005), 202. For a further exploration of the corrosive effects of modern U. S. militarism, see Andrew Bacevich, *The New American Militarism* (New York: Oxford University Press, 2005).
21 Cindy Sheehan, "Matriotism," *The Huffington Post*, January 22, 2006. Online. Available HTTP: <http://www.huffingtonpost.com/cindy-sheehan/matriotism/b/14283.html > (accessed December 10, 2008).
22 Ziauddin Sardar and Merryl Wyn Davies, *Why Do People Hate America?* (New York: The Disinformation Co., 2002), 140. Sardar and Davies underscore this point by their critical readings of network television programs, such as NBC's *West Wing* and ABC's *Alias*, that represent the rest of the world through jingoistic

images and simplistic discourse. See ibid., 15–38 and 63–5. A more critical examination of the perspectives of Sardar and Davies on the impact of the U. S. cultural apparatus will be found in Chapter 6.

23 Cited in Sheldon Rampton and John Stauber, *Weapons of Mass Deception: The Uses of Propaganda in Bush's War on Iraq* (New York: Penguin, 2003), 175–6.

24 Ibid. See also Danny Schechter, *When News Lies: Media Complicity and the Iraq War* (New York: SelectBooks, 2006).

25 Harris Poll, July 2006. Online. Available HTTP: <http://www.harrisinteractive.com/harris/poll/index.asp?PID=684 > (accessed December 12, 2008).

26 Sardar and Davies, *Why Do People Hate America?*, 87. Morris Berman notes that "the ability or unwillingness to look at ourselves through foreign eyes, to see those who object to being steamrolled by us as anything but knaves or ingrates, has a long history." *Dark Ages America,* 107.

27 Ibid., 12

28 Jan Nederveen Pieterse, *Globalization or Empire?* (New York: Routledge, 2004), 138.

29 Christian Smith, *Resisting Reagan: The U. S. Central American Peace Movement* (Chicago: University of Chicago Press, 1996), 186–7. Chapters 4 and 7 will explore in more depth U. S. interventions in Latin America and the response by U. S. activists to those interventions.

30 Sarder and Davies, *Why Do People Hate America?*, 79–80.

31 Retort, *Afflicted Powers: Capital and Spectacle in a New Age of War* (New York: Verso, 2006), 94.

32 Andrew Bacevich, "I Lost My Son to a War I Oppose," *Washington Post*, May 27, 2007, B01.

33 For criticism of "America's Army" and other militaristic video games and entertainment, see Nick Turse, "Bringing the War Home: The New Military-Industrial-Entertainment Complex at War and Play," *TomDispatch.com*, October 17, 2003. Online. Available HTTP: <http://www.commondreams.org/views03/1017–09.htm> (accessed December 10, 2008).

34 Quoted in West, *Democracy Matters*, 80. It is also instructive to see that Cornel West appears in parts 2 and 3 of *The Matrix* trilogy.

35 Retort, *Afflicted Powers*, 20–1.

36 Boggs, *Imperial Delusions*, 195.

37 West, *Democracy Matters*, 28–9.

38 James Bovard, *Attention Deficit Disorder* (New York: Palgrave Macmillan, 2005), 32–48.

39 Cindy Sheehan, "Good Riddance Attention Whore," *Daily Kos*, May 28, 2007. Online. Available HTTP: <http://www.dailykos.com/story/2007/5/28/12530/1525> (accessed December 10, 2008).

40 At the level of emotional labor, the hectored heart is the equivalent to what Arlie Russell Hochschild calls the "managed heart." See Hochschild, *The Managed Heart: Commercialization of Human Feeling* (Berkeley: University of California Press, 2003).

41 Robert Jensen, *Citizens of the Empire* (San Francisco: City Lights Books, 2004), 98.

42 Wendy Farley, *Eros for the Other: Retaining Truth in a Pluralistic World* (University Park: The Pennsylvania State University Press, 1996), 17–25.

43 Ibid., 30 and 69.

44 Moglen and Namir, "War and the Dis-eases of Othering," 212.

45 Kevin Phillips, *American Theocracy: The Peril and Politics of Radical Religion, Oil and Borrowed Money in the 21st Century* (New York: Viking, 2006), 328.

46 Iris Marion Young, "The Logic of Masculinist Protection: Reflections on the Current Security State," *Signs* 29:1 (Autumn 2003): 1–25.

47 Zygmunt Bauman, *Liquid Love: On the Frailty of Human Bonds* (Cambridge: Polity Press, 2003), 88–9.
48 Judith Warner, *Perfect Madness: Motherhood in the Age of Anxiety* (New York: Riverhead Books, 2006), 54.
49 Vaclav Havel, *Disturbing the Peace* (New York: Knopf, 1990), 181.
50 Wendell Berry, *Sex, Economy, Freedom* and *Community* (New York: Pantheon, 1993), 11.
51 West, *Democracy Matters*, 216.
52 James Baldwin, *The Fire Next Time* (New York: Dell, 1963), 123–4.
53 West, *Democracy Matters*, 96.
54 Baldwin, *The Fire Next Time*, 124–5.
55 Cited in Taylor Branch, *Pillar of Fire: America in the King Years, 1963–1965* (New York: Touchstone, 1999), 193. On the remarkable life of Ella Baker and the black freedom movement she inspired, see Barbara Ransby, *Ella Baker and the Black Freedom Movement* (Chapel Hill: The University of North Carolina Press, 2003). Guyot and others in the Mississippi freedom struggle went on to build the Mississippi Freedom Democratic Party and other grassroots organizations that transformed the environment of racial injustice in the South.
56 Paul Rogat Loeb, *The Impossible Will Take a Little While* (New York: Basic Books, 2004), 12.

Notes to Chapter 3

1 For insights into ethical and political responsibility and solidarity, see Zygmunt Bauman, *Liquid Love: On the Fragility of Human Bonds* (Cambridge: Polity Press, 2003); bell hooks, *Where We Stand: Class Matters* (New York: Routledge, 2000); Paul Rogat Loeb, *Soul of a Citizen* (New York: St. Martin's Press, 1999); and Iris Young, "From Guilt to Solidarity: Sweatshops and Political Responsibility," *Dissent* 59: 2 (Spring 2003): 39–44.
2 Millard Fuller, *No More Shacks: The Daring Vision of Habitat for Humanity* (Waco, TX: Word Books Publisher, 1986), 127.
3 Leslie Williams, "Baptists Pledge to Build 300 Houses in 5-Year Period," *The Times-Picayune*, June 12, 2007: B1–2.
4 Ananta Kumar Giri, *Building in the Margins of Shacks: The Vision and Projects of Habitat for Humanity* (New Delhi: Orient Longman, 2002), 254.
5 R. Allen Hays, "Habitat for Humanity: Building Social Capital through Faith-Based Service," *Journal of Urban Affairs* 24: 3 and 4 (Fall 2002): 266.
6 Giri, *Building in the Margins of Shacks*, 94.
7 Hays, "Habitat for Humanity," 267.
8 Giri, *Building in the Margins of Shacks*, 123.
9 See, for example, Meizhu Lui *et al.*, *The Color of Wealth: The Story Behind the U. S. Racial Wealth Divide* (New York: New Press, 2006). For the discussion of credit problems for New Orleans' musicians and the building of Musicians Village, see Katy Reckdahl, "Sour Note," *The Times-Picayune*, January 2, 2007. Online. Available HTTP: <http://www.soros.org/resources/multimedia/Katrina/projects/Struggling/story/SourNote.php> (accessed March 9, 2009).
10 For further analysis of the impact of immigrant labor, both documented and undocumented in post-Katrina New Orleans, see Katharine M. Donato *et al.*, "Reconstructing New Orleans after Katrina: The Emergence of An Immigrant Labor Market," in *The Sociology of Katrina: Perspectives on a Modern Catastrophe*, eds. David L. Brunsma *et al.* (Lanham: MD: Rowman & Littlefield, 2007); and Elizabeth Fussell, "Latino Immigrants in Post-Katrina New Orleans," paper presented to the Regional Seminar on Labor Rights, New Orleans, October 19–22,

2006. (Copies of both in author's possession. Thanks to Nicole Trujillo-Pagan for the former and Elizabeth Fussell for the latter.) My primary focus is not whether using immigrant labor, documented or undocumented, is wrong. My concern is that an organization such as Habitat, which ostensibly is committed to social justice, should not be facilitating any exploitation of immigrant labor.

11 Craig A. Rimmerman, *The New Citizenship: Unconventional Politics, Activism, and Service* (Boulder, CO: Westview Press, 1997), 105.

12 When Bush appeared at a house dedication in Musician's Village on August 29, 2006, he visited with the owner of the new house, Honduran native and New Orleans musician, Fredy Omar. Trying to act congenial, Bush asked Omar whether there was anything he could do to help. When Fredy told Bush he could move a piece of furniture from one end of the room to the other, Bush willingly obliged. This may have been the most constructive act Bush has done in his two-term Presidency. (Thanks to my cousin, Eric Shuman, a former saxophone player in Fredy's salsa band, for this story. The final editorial opinion is mine.)

13 Giri, *Building in the Margins of Shacks*, 246.

14 Andrei Codrescu, *New Orleans, Mon Amour* (Chapel Hill, NC: Algonquin Books, 2006), 165–6.

15 Quoted in Manuel Roig-Franzia, " A City Fears for its Soul," *The Washington Post*, February 3, 2006: A01. Thanks to my colleague, Julie Klein, for bringing this to my attention.

16 Naomi Klein, *The Shock Doctrine: The Rise of Disaster Capitalism* (New York: Metropolitan Books, 2007), 413.

17 George Lipsitz, "Learning from New Orleans: The Social Warrant of Hostile Privatism and Competitive Consumer Citizenship," *Cultural Anthropology* 21:3 (August 2006): 464 and 454.

18 For a concise overview of the modern contradictions underlying the housing bubble and home ownership, see Max Fraser, "The House Folds," *The Nation*, December 15, 2008, 29–33.

19 Valeria Fernandez, "Communities Foreclosed," *ColorLines* (Jan/Feb 2009). Online. Available HTTP: <http://colorlines.com/article.php?ID=475> (accessed March 1, 2009).

20 Bill McKibben, *Deep Economy: The Wealth of Communities and the Durable Future* (New York: Holt, 2007), 97.

21 Bauman, *Liquid Love*, 64.

22 Ethel Brooks, *Unraveling the Garment Industry: Transnational Organizing and Women's Work* (Minneapolis: University of Minnesota Press, 2007), xv.

23 Naomi Klein, *No Logo: Taking Aim at the Brand Bullies* (New York: Picador, 2000), 200.

24 Ibid., 212.

25 Ibid., 198. As anti-sweatshop activists would later note, Disney CEO Michael Eisner earned $9,783 an hour while a Haitian worker earned 28 cents an hour and it would take a Haitian worker 16.8 years to earn Eisner's hourly income. See ibid., 352.

26 Ibid., 211, 202–3, and 205.

27 Quoted in Arnie Alpert, "Bringing Globalization Home is No Sweat," in John Feffer, ed. *Living in Hope: People Challenging Globalization* (London: Zed Books, 2002), 42.

28 Ibid., 43–4.

29 Jeff Ballinger, "No Sweat: Corporate Social Responsibility and the Dilemma of Anti-Sweatshop Activism," *New Labor Forum* 17:2 (Summer 2008): 95 and 92.

30 Ibid., 98.

31 Brooks, *Unraveling the Garment Industry*, 42–3. For a complete overview of the NLC-Gap campaign, see ibid., 27–44. For a more positive assessment of the results

of the NLC campaign, see Andrew Ross, *Low Pay, High Profile: The Global Push for Fair Labor* (New York: The New Press, 2004), 34–5.

32 Liza Featherstone, *Students Against Sweatshops* (New York: Verso, 2002) 30. See ibid. for a full account of the national and local developments of USAS. See also Altha J. Cravey, "Students and the Anti-Sweatshop Movement," *Antipode* 36:2 (March 2004): 203–8; and Ross, *Low Pay, High Profile*, 43–5.

33 Ibid., 10.

34 Brooks, *Unraveling the Garment Industry*, 159.

35 Featherstone, *Students Against Sweatshops*, 72 and 54.

36 Ibid., 73. For an analysis of the similar impact that visiting Central America had on the solidarity campaigns of the 1980s, see Christian Smith, *Resisting Reagan: The U. S. Central America Peace Movement* (Chicago: University of Chicago Press, 1996), esp. 154.

37 Ibid., 44–5 and 19–27. For additional criticism of the FLA and discussion of the difficulties encountered by the WRC, see Ballinger, "No Sweat?," 93 and 96–7. On student anti-sweatshop and campus apparel campaigns, also see Klein, *No Logo*, 397–401, 405–10, and 432–7.

38 Klein, *No Logo*, 368.

39 Ibid., 372.

40 Ibid., 373–4.

41 Ibid., 412.

42 Featherstone, *Students Against Sweatshops*, 80–3.

43 Ibid., 70. On the role of women garment workers in global sweatshops, see Brooks, *Unraveling the Garment Industry*, esp. 114–37.

44 An incisive extended examination of this campaign can be found in Brooks, *Unraveling the Garment Industry*, 54–81.

45 Ibid., 61.

46 Ibid., 24.

47 Featherstone, *Students Against Sweatshops*, 85.

48 hooks, *Where We Stand*, 130.

49 Alberto Melucci, *Challenging Codes: Collective Action in the Information Age* (New York: Cambridge University Press, 1996), 167.

50 On the forms of altruistic and mutual solidarity, see Thomas Olesen, *International Zapatismo: The Construction of Solidarity in the Age of Globalization* (New York: Zed Books, 2005), 107–11.

51 Klein, *No Logo*, 429.

52 See, for example, Jeremy Brecher, Tim Costello, and Brendan Smith, *Globalization from Below: The Power of Solidarity* (Cambridge, MA: South End Press, 2000).

Notes to Chapter 4

1 Thomas L. Friedman, *The Lexus and the Olive Tree* (New York: Farrar, Straus & Giroux, 1999), 378.

2 Ibid., 373. For an extended critique of Friedman's triumphalism, see Mark Engler, *How to Rule the World: The Coming Battle Over the Global Economy* (New York: Nation Books, 2008), 170–87.

3 Carl Boggs, *Imperial Delusions: American Militarism and Endless War* (Lanham, MD: Rowman & Littlefield, 2005), x. For a particularly poignant and pointed critique of the rise and fall of U. S. imperialism and militarism, see Andrew J. Bacevich, *The Limits of Power: The End of American Exceptionalism* (New York: Metropolitan Books, 2008).

4 Walden Bello, *Dilemmas of Domination: The Unmaking of the American Empire* (New York: Metropolitan Books, 2005), 217. On the contradictions between

reliance on military force and maintenance of hegemony, see Boggs, *Imperial Delusions*, 193–212. For another perspective on the difficulties of realizing global dominance, see Engler, *How to Rule the World*, 51–74.

5 Greg Grandin, *Empire's Workshop: Latin America, the United States, and the Rise of the New Imperialism* (New York: Metropolitan Books, 2007), 5. For Grandin's discussion of the support for counterinsurgency and paramilitary policies by Presidents Kennedy and Reagan, see *ibid.*, 87–120.

6 On petro-dollars and U. S. dollar hegemony, see Vassilis K. Fouskas and Birlent Gokay, *The New American Imperialism* (Westport, CT: Praeger, 2005), esp. 24–7.

7 Quoted in Grandin, *Empire's Workshop*, 60. For a concise overview of the destabilization campaign, see William I. Robinson, *Promoting Polyarchy: Globalization, U. S. Intervention, and Hegemony* (New York: Cambridge University Press, 1996), 159–63.

8 Naomi Klein, *The Shock Doctrine: The Rise of Disaster Capitalism* (New York: Metropolitan Books, 2007), 75–87. For the most detailed documentation of the CIA campaign against Allende and the Pinochet coup, see Peter Kornbluh, *The Pinochet File: A Declassified Dossier on Atrocity and Accountability* (New York: New Press, 2004).

9 Quoted in Robinson, *Promoting Polyarchy*, 201. For an extensive discussion of the background of U. S. intervention in Nicaragua in the pre- and post-Sandinista eras, see *ibid.*, 201–55.

10 On the sponsorship by the Reagan Administration of low-intensity conflict and democracy promotion in Nicaragua, see ibid., 215–39. Robinson estimates that the result of such low-intensity warfare for Nicaragua was "50,000 casualties and $12 billion in damages in a society of barely 3.5 million people with an annual GNP of some 2 billion (220)." On the opposition role of various U. S. supporters of the Sandinista revolution, see Christian Smith, *Resisting Reagan: The U. S. Central American Peace Movement* (Chicago: University of Chicago Press, 1996).

11 Grandin, *Empire's Workshop*, 71. On the El Salvador and Guatemalan massacres, see *ibid.*, 90 and *passim*. See also Noam Chomsky, *Turning the Tide: U. S. Intervention in Central America and the Struggle for Peace* (Boston: South End Press, 1985).

12 On Kirkpatrick, see ibid., esp. 71–80.

13 John Perkins, *Confessions of an Economic Hit Man* (New York: Plume, 2006), 203–10; and Chalmers Johnson, *The Sorrows of Empire: Militarism, Secrecy, and the End of the Republic* (New York: Owl Books, 2004), 69.

14 Grandin, *Empire's Workshop*, 192.

15 For an incisive look at the background to the Gulf War and, especially, the role of the U. S. corporate media, see Douglas Kellner, *The Persian Gulf TV War* (Boulder, CO: Westview Press, 1992), 12–108.

16 Ibid., 386.

17 Ibid., 72.

18 Ibid., 404–8.

19 Quoted in John Pilger, *The New Rulers of the World* (New York: Verso, 2002), 49.

20 Ibid., 46–8; and Chalmers Johnson, *The Sorrows of Empire*, 100–2.

21 For an overview of the varying opinions about the impact of the sanctions policy, see David Rieff, "Were Sanctions Right?," *New York Times Magazine*, July 27, 2003. Online. Available HTTP: <http://www.nytimes.com/2003/07/27/magazine/were-sanctions-right.html> (accessed December 28, 2008).

22 David Harvey, *The New Imperialism* (New York: Oxford University Press, 2005), 75. On Clinton's Iraq policy and Albright's rationalization of the tragic consequences of the sanctions, see Bacevich, *The Limits of Power*, 55–8.

23 On the CIA's secret war in Afghanistan and the rise of the Taliban, see Steve Coll, *Ghost Wars* (New York: The Penguin Press, 2004); and Ahmed Rashid, *Taliban* (New Haven, CT: Yale University Press, 2001).

24 For Unocal and U. S. policy in Afghanistan during the 1990s see, Rashid, *Taliban*, 157–82.

25 Ahmed Rashid, *Descent into Chaos: The United States and the Failure of Nation Building in Pakistan, Afghanistan, and Central Asia* (New York: Viking, 2008), 61–106, 125–44, and 349–73. For a detailed overview of the killing of civilians in Kandahar and other villages in Afghanistan, see Marc Herold, "A Dossier on Civilian Victims of United States Aerial Bombing of Afghanistan." Online. Available HTTP: <http://cursor.org/stories/civilian/deaths.htm> (accessed December 28, 2008).

26 Bacevich, *The Limits of Power*, 127. Bacevich identifies this vision of "reinventing armed conflict" through technology as one of the central illusions about recent U. S. imperial warfare. For a further analysis of what is called the "revolution in military affairs" (RMA) and its contradictions, see Michael Hardt and Antonio Negri, *Multitude: War and Democracy in an Age of Empire* (New York: Penguin Books, 2005), 41–8.

27 Retort, *Afflicted Powers: Capital and Spectacle in a New Age of War* (New York: Verso, 2006), 123–5. The authors do an excellent job of exploring the changes and contradictions of the strategic alliance between the U. S. and Israel and its future implications. See ibid., 108–31.

28 Ira Chernus, *Monsters to Destroy: The Neoconservative War on Terror and Sin* (Boulder, CO: Paradigm, 2006), 202.

29 Bacevich, *The Limits of Power*, 11. On Obama's commitment to U. S. "global leadership," see ibid., 79–80. On permanent war, see Retort, *Afflicted Powers*, 78–107.

30 Arundhati Roy, *An Ordinary Person's Guide to Empire* (Cambridge, MA: South End Press, 2004), 34. On U. S. imperial militarism as a "deep strategic project," see Retort, *Afflicted Powers*, 81–2.

31 Quoted in Johnson, *The Sorrows of Empire*, 151. For Johnson's complete discussion of the impact of the "empire of bases" as the key component of military imperialism, see ibid., 151–85. For a more recent update on base figures, see Chalmers Johnson, "Mission Creep: America's Unwelcome Advances," *Mother Jones*, August 22, 2008. Online. Available HTTP: <http://www.motherjones/politics/2008/08/americas-unwelcome-advances.html> (accessed December 28, 2008). On the overall expense of such bases, see Nick Turse, "It's Time for a Trillion-Dollar Tag Sale at the Pentagon," *AlterNet*, October 29, 2008. Online. Available HTTP: <http://www.alternet.org/story/105106> (accessed December 28, 2008).

32 Johnson, *The Sorrows of Empire*, 151–2.

33 Ibid., 168–85.

34 Ibid., 155 and 187–215.

35 Arno Mayer, "The U. S. Empire will Survive Bush," *CounterPunch*, October 29, 2008. Online. Available HTTP: <http://www.counterpunch.org/mayer/10292008.html> (accessed December 15, 2008).

36 Johnson, "Mission Creep."

37 Johnson, *The Sorrows of Empire*, 167 and 155–67.

38 Ibid., 81.

39 Quoted in Noam Chomsky, *Hegemony or Survival: America's Quest for Global Dominance* (New York: Metropolitan Books, 2003), 229.

40 Quoted in Johnson, *The Sorrows of Empire,* 142. On Vinnell, DynCorp, and other military subcontractors, see ibid., 135–49. For a discussion of the recent incidents involving Blackwater, see Jeremy Scahill's 2008 listed articles on AlterNet Authors. Online. Available HTTP: <http://www.alternet.org/authors/5434> (accessed December 24, 2008).

41 Klein, *The Shock Doctrine*, 382. For Klein's discussion of privatized war and reconstruction in Iraq, see 326–82. On Afghanistan, see Ann Jones, "The Afghan

Scam," *TomDispatch.com*, January 12, 2009. Online. Available HTTP: <http://www.commondreams.org/view/2009/01/12> (accessed January 14, 2009).

42 Ibid., 380 and *passim.*

43 Jones, "The Afghan Scam."

44 William Grieder, *Fortress America: The American Military and the Consequences of Peace* (New York: Public Affairs, 1999), 106, 52, and *passim.*

45 Ishmael Hossein-Zadeh, "Escalating Military Spending: Income Redistribution in Disguise," *CounterPunch*, April 16, 2007. Online. Available HTTP: <http://www.counterpunch.org/hossein04162007.html> (accessed December 29, 2008).

46 For a precise overview of the role of foreign arms sales for the U. S. military-industrial complex, see Greider, *Fortress America*, 97–110. For up-to-date details on arms sales to Israel and other U. S. allies around the world, see William D. Hartung and Frida Berrigan, *U. S. Weapons at War 2008*, New America Policy Paper. Online. Available HTTP: <http://www.newamerica.net/publications/policy/u/s/weapons/war/2008/0 > (accessed December 28, 2008). For a penetrating discussion of IDF use of such weapons as GBU-39s and white phosphorus during the Israeli assault on Gaza in January 2009, see Amira Hass, "Is Israel Using Illegal Weapons in Its Offensive in Gaza?" *Haaretz*, January 16, 2009. Online. Available HTTP: <http://www.common dreams.org/headline/2009/0116–0> (accessed January 17, 2009).

47 Friedman, *The Lexus and the Olive Tree*, 375. Friedman might have been sobered up by what happened in the war on Iraq, a war he initially enthusiastically endorsed. Nonetheless, he still remains an ideological cheerleader for U. S. imperialism.

48 Emmanuel Todd, *After the Empire: The Breakdown of the American Order*, trans. C. Jon Delogu (New York: Columbia University Press, 2003), xviii.

49 Ibid., 134 and 202.

50 Samir Amin, *The Liberal Virus: Permanent War and the Americanization of the World* (New York: Monthly Review Press, 2004), 76.

51 Ibid., 83.

52 Samir Amin, *Beyond U. S. Hegemony: Assessing the Prospects for a Multipolar World*, trans. Patrick Camiller (London: Zed Books, 2006), 84–111.

53 Gilbert Achar, *The Clash of Barbarisms: The Making of the New World Disorder*, trans. Peter Drucker (Boulder, CO: Paradigm, 2006), 97.

54 Bacevich, *The Limits of Power*, 156.

55 Gary Dorrien, *Imperial Designs: Neoconservatism and the New Pax Americana* (New York: Routledge, 2004), 18–22, 223, and *passim.*

56 Boggs, *Imperial Delusions*, 207.

57 Giovanni Arrighi, "Hegemony Unravelling – I," *New Left Review* 32 (March/April 2005), 80. For a related analysis from another world-systems scholars, see Immanuel Wallerstein, *The Decline of American Power: The U. S. in a Chaotic World* (New York: The New Press, 2003). For another perspective on hegemony and decline, see David C. Hendrickson, "The Curious Case of American Hegemony: Imperial Aspirations and National Decline," *World Policy Journal* 22:2 (Summer 2005): 1–22.

58 Johnson, *The Sorrows of Empire,* 310; and Michael Mann, "The Fist Failed Empire of the 21st Century," *Review of International Studies* 30:4 (October 2004): 641. Another formulation of the flaws of imperial overstretch can be found in the following perspective: "While the U. S. military has enough firepower to destroy the world many times over, and while it may be bankrupting itself by continually augmenting its arsenal, it has been unable to exercise control even in limited, regional conflicts." See Engler, *How to Rule the World*, 79.

59 Boggs, *Imperial Delusions*, 198.

60 Dorrien, *Imperial Designs*, 257. On the various forms of opposition and resistance to U. S. imperial rule, see Bruce M. Knauft, "Provincializing America: Imperialism,

Capitalism, and Counterhegemony in the Twenty-First Century," *Current Anthropology* 48:6 (December 2007): 787–92.
61 Walter L. Hixson, *The Myth of American Diplomacy: National Identity and U. S. Foreign Policy* (New Haven, CT: Yale University Press, 2008), 14.
62 Ibid., 304.

Notes to Chapter 5

1 Dana Frank, *Bananeras: Women Transforming the Banana Unions of Latin America* (Cambridge, MA: South End Press, 2005), 2–3 and 9–13.
2 Greg Grandin, *Empire's Workshop: Latin America, the United States, and the Rise of New Imperialism* (New York: Holt Paperback, 2007), 42–4 and 187.
3 Kevin Gray, "The Banana War," *Portfolio.com*, October 2007. Online. Available HTTP: <http://www.portfolio.com/newsmarkets/internationalnews/portfolio/2007/09/17/ Chiquita-Death-Squads > (accessed February 25, 2009).
4 Ibid.
5 For a fuller discussion of Chiquita and the banana wars, see Gordon Myers, *Banana Wars: The Price of Free Trade* (New York: Zed Books, 2004), esp. 75–82 and 83–100.
6 David Harvey, *The New Imperialism* (New York: Oxford University Press, 2005), 26 and *passim*.
7 Ellen Meiksins Wood's perspective on this contradictory dynamic is germane. She writes: "Imperial dominance in a global capitalist economy requires a delicate balance between suppressing competition and maintaining conditions in competing economies that generate markets and profit." *Empire of Capital* (New York: Verso, 2003), 157.
8 Benjamin Dangl, *The Price of Fire: Resource Wars and Social Movements in Bolivia* (Oakland, CA: AK Press, 2007), 57–73.
9 Ibid., 60.
10 Ibid., 67.
11 Vandana Shiva, *Earth Democracy: Justice, Sustainability, and Peace* (Cambridge, MA: South End Press, 2005), 168–72; and Shivali Tukdeo, "Mapping Resistance: Coca-Cola and the Struggle in Plachimada, India," in Jerry Harris, ed. *Alternative Globalizations* (Chicago: ChangeMaker Publications, 2006), 291–305.
12 Cited in Shiva, *Earth Democracy*, 169.
13 My recounting of this incident, the aftermath, and continuing consequences relies primarily on the website, Students for Bhopal, and the entry, "No More Bhopals." Online. Available HTTP <http://www.studentsforbhopal.org/.WhatHappened.htm> (accessed March 2, 2009).
14 Cited in David Watson, "We All Live in Bhopal," in Watson *Against the Megamachine: Essays on Empire & its Enemies* (Brooklyn, NY: Autonomedia, 1998), 42.
15 William K. Tabb, *Unequal Partners: A Primer on Globalization* (New York: The New Press, 2002), 2. Other useful texts that provide insightful links between U. S. economic imperialism, empire, and corporate globalization in the recent period are as follows: Mark Engler, *How to Rule the World: The Coming Battle Over the Global Economy* (New York: Nation Books, 2008); Jeff Faux, *The Global Class War* (Hoboken, NJ: John Wiley & Sons, 2006); Vassilis K. Fouskas and Birkent Gokay, *The New American Imperialism* (Westport, CT: Praeger, 2005); James Petras and Henry Veltmeyer, *Globalization Unmasked: Imperialism in the 21st Century* (New York: Zed Books, 2001); Jan Nederveen Pieterse, *Globalization or Empire?* (New York: Routledge, 2004); Robert Pollin, *Contours of Descent: U. S. Economic Fractures and the Landscapes of Global Austerity* (New York: Verso, 2003); and Wood, *Empire of Capital*, esp. 130–42.

16 Faux, *The Global Class War*, 137.
17 SAPRIN, *Structural Adjustment: The Policy Roots of Economic Crisis, Poverty and Inequality* (New York: Zed Books, 2004).
18 Mike Davis, *Planet of Slums* (New York: Verso, 2006), 15.
19 Ibid., 25.
20 Ibid., 152.
20 Ibid., 153.
22 Ibid., 160 and 155.
23 Ibid., 173.
24 Ibid., 172.
25 Journalist Edward Luce cited in ibid., 171.
26 Shiva, *Earth Democracy*, 121.
27 *Ibid.*, 67–8 and 121–3.
28 Tony Weis, "Restructuring and Redundancy: The Impact and Illogic of Neoliberal Agricultural Reforms in Jamaica," *Journal of Agrarian Change* 4:4 (October 2004): 461–91.
29 On the Mexican economy, U. S. economic imperialism, and the resultant social and political impact, see David Harvey, *Spaces of Global Capitalism: Towards a Theory of Uneven Geographical Development* (New York: Verso, 2006), 48–9 and 63; Neil Harvey, "Beyond Hegemony: Zapatismo, Empire, and Dissent," in Fred Rosen, *Empire and Dissent: The U. S. and Latin America* (Durham, NC: Duke University Press, 2008), 124–6; and Carlos Marichal, "The Finances of Hegemony in Latin America: Debt Negotiations and the Role of the U. S. Government, 1945–2005," in ibid., 101–7. For brief overviews of the particulars of the "Washington Consensus," see Susan George, *Another World is Possible if …* (New York: Verso, 2004), 14–22; and Pieterse, *Globalization or Empire?*, 9–15.
30 William H. Marling, *How "American" is Globalization* (Baltimore: The Johns Hopkins University Press, 2006), 66–79; and Petras and Veltmeyer, *Globalization Unmasked*, 61–73.
31 Tabb, *Unequal Partners*, 162–4.
32 Retort, *Afflicted Powers: Capital and Spectacle in a New Age of War* (New York: Verso, 2006), 71. For the complete discussion on the role of oil and war, see ibid., 38–77.
33 Tabb, *Unequal Partners*, 112–13. For an extensive analysis of the political economy of AIDS, see ibid., 107–20.
34 Ibid., 120.
35 Ibid., 48–9. See also Eduardo Galeano, *Upside Down: A Primer for the Looking-Glass World*, trans. Mark Fried (New York: Metropolitan Books, 2000), 219.
36 Galeano, *Upside Down*, 219; Paul Kingsnorth, *One No, Many Yeses* (London: The Free Press, 2003), 133; and Shiva, *Earth Democracy*, 59.
37 Peter Singer, *One World: The Ethics of Globalization* (New Haven, CT: Yale University Press, 2002), 164 and 151.
38 Bill McKibben, *Deep Economy: The Wealth of Communities and the Durable Future* (New York: Holt Paperbacks, 2007), 64.
39 Shiva, *Earth Democracy*, 2.
40 Tabb, *Unequal Partners*, 31.
41 Ibid., 96.
42 Marco A. Gandasequi, Jr., "Latin America and Imperialism in the 21st Century," *Critical Sociology* 32:1 (January 2006): 51.
43 Will Hutton, *A Declaration of Interdependence: Why America Should Join the World* (New York: W. W. Norton & Co., 2003), 173. For insight into the financialization crisis from a Marxist perspective, see John Bellamy Foster and Fred Magdoff, *The Great Financial Crisis: Causes and Consequences* (New York, Monthly Review Press, 2009). For a non-Marxist approach to the crisis, see Kevin

Phillips, *Bad Money: Reckless Finance, Failed Politics, and the Global Crisis of American Capitalism* (New York: Viking, 2008).

44 Bellamy and Magdoff, *The Great Financial Crisis,* 130. For a concise overview of the present economic crisis, see Mike Whitney's interview with John Bellamy Foster, "The Great Financial Crisis," Information Clearing House, February 27, 2009. Online. Available HTTP: <http://informationclearinghouse.info/article22116.htm> (accessed March 2, 2009)

45 George, *Another World is Possible if,* 23 and 21.

46 Galeano, *Upside Down*, 25.

Notes to Chapter 6

1 For a concise and compelling overview of the historical role of the U. S. film industry as an element of an increasingly diffuse cultural imperialism, see William H. Marling, *How "American" is Globalization* (Baltimore, MD: The Johns Hopkins University Press, 2006), 18–40. A more tendentious look at Hollywood's global impact can be found in Matthew Fraser, *Weapons of Mass Distraction: Soft Power and American Empire* (New York: Thomas Dunne Books, 2005), 35–80 and 92–111. For more critical discussion of *Dancer in the Dark* and *Moulin Rouge*, see John Kenneth Muir, *Singing a New Tune: The Rebirth of the Modern Film Musical* (New York: Applause Theatre and Cinema Books, 2005), 156–82.

2 For one of the most incisive analyses of the fluidity and hybridity of popular music, see George Lipsitz, *Footsteps in the Dark: The Hidden Histories of Popular Music* (Minneapolis: University of Minnesota Press, 2007). For a brief overview of the music industry and cultural imperialism, see David Hesmondhalgh, *The Cultural Industries,* 2nd ed. (Thousand Oaks, CA: Sage Publications, 2007), 235–9. On the connections between privileged instruments of transmission, cultural imperialism, and anti-colonialism, see Frantz Fanon, "This is the Voice of Algeria," in Fanon *A Dying Colonialism*, trans. Haakon Chevalier (New York: Grove Press, 1967), 69–97. For a critical explanation of the meaning of hegemony as a contested concept, see Raymond Williams, *Marxism and Literature* (New York: Oxford University Press, 1977), 108–14. On popular music as a "site where hegemonic processes are contested," see Robin Balliger, "Sounds of Resistance," in Louise Amoore, ed. *The Global Resistance Reader* (New York: Routledge, 2005), 424 and *passim.*

3 John Tomlinson, *Cultural Imperialism: A Critical Introduction* (London: Pinter Publishers, 1991), 3.

4 Mel van Elteren, "U. S. Cultural Imperialism Today: Only a Chimera?," *SAIS Review* 23:2 (Summer–Fall 2003): 172.

5 For key dialectical and critical readings of globalization and U. S. cultural imperialism, see ibid., 169–88; Douglas Kellner, "Theorizing Globalization," *Sociological Theory* 20:3 (November 2002): 285–305; Marling, *How 'American' is Globalization*; David Morley, "Globalization and Cultural Imperialism Reconsidered: Old Questions in New Guises," in James Curran and David Morley *Media and Cultural Theory* (New York: Routledge, 2006), 30–43; Manfred B. Steger, *Globalism: Market Ideology Meets Terrorism*, 2nd ed. (Lanham, MD.: Rowman & Littlefield, 2005); and Tomlinson, *Cultural Imperialism*.

6 van Elteren, "U. S. Cultural Imperialism Today," 174.

7 Ibid., 180.

8 John Gray quoted in Jeff Faux, *The Global Class War* (Hoboken, NJ: John Wiley & Sons, 2006), 100.

9 This is Fraser's term. His discussion of the global success of Coke and its battle with Pepsi for global hegemony can be found in *Weapons of Mass Distraction*, 223–40.

10 Cited in Paul Kingsnorth, *One No, Many Yeses* (London: The Free Press, 2004), 126.

11 On the lure of advertising, the "aestheticization of reality," and cultural imperialism, see van Elteren, "U. S. Cultural Imperialism Today," 182–4. There is some similarity between the Coke ad's projection of human harmony and what Roland Barthes called "the ambiguous myth of human 'community'" which "aims to suppress the determining weight of History" in his essay, "The Great Family of Man." See Barthes, *Mythologies*, trans. Annette Lavers (New York: Hill & Wang, 1972), 100–2.

12 Fraser, *Weapons of Mass Distraction*; and Ziauddin Sardar and Merryl Wyn Davies, *Why Do People Hate America?* (New York: The Disinformation Company, 2002). All references to both books will be in the body of the chapter.

13 For a more extensive discussion of the impact of McDonald's, see the essays in Barry Smart, ed. *Resisting McDonaldization* (Thousand Oaks, CA: Sage Publications, 1999).

14 Marwan M. Kraidy, *Hybridity or the Cultural Logic of Globalization* (Philadelphia, PA: Temple University Press, 2005). Kraidy's concept of "critical transculturalism" does provide another perspective on the diminishing influences of cultural imperialism, even though he tends to neglect the dynamics of power and inequality that still require some reformulated sense of cultural imperialism.

15 Douglas Kellner, "Theorizing/Resisting McDonaldization: A Multiperspectivist Approach," in Smart *Resisting McDonaldization*, 198.

16 Ibid., 200; and van Elteren, "U. S. Cultural Imperialism Today," 183.

17 Quoted in Kellner, "Theorizing/Resisting McDonaldization," 197.

18 For wide-ranging analyses of the connections between imperialism, ideological hegemony, and domestic U. S. culture, see the essays in Amy Kaplan and Donald E. Pease, eds., *Cultures of United States Imperialism* (Durham, NC: Duke University Press, 1993).

19 For a balanced, nuanced, and empirical look at how audiences interpret American media constructions with multiple meanings, see Tomlinson, *Cultural Imperialism*, 34–67. It may be that as a consequence of more sobering assessments of the pernicious effects of anti-Arab and anti-Islamic stereotypes in the aftermath of 9/11, Hollywood has turned away from one-dimensional cinematic images, developing more nuanced understandings of Arabs, the Middle East, and Islamic culture as in films like *Syriana*.

20 Kraidy, *Hybridity or the Cultural Logic of Globalization*, vi and *passim*.

21 van Elteren, "U. S. Cultural Imperialism Today," 183. See also Tomlinson, *Cultural Imperialism*, 136.

22 Jean Baudrillard, *America*, trans. Chris Turner (New York: Verso, 1989), 77.

23 Thomas Friedman, *The Lexus and the Olive Tree* (New York: Farrar, Straus & Giroux, 1999), 235.

24 van Elteren, "U. S. Cultural Imperialism Today," 183–4.

25 Steger, *Globalism*, 41. For an extended discussion of the persistence and resistance of the local, see Marling, *How "American" is Globalization*, 81–143.

26 For the definitive biography of Bob Marley which incorporates insights into the Rastafarian movement, see Timothy White, *Catch a Fire: The Life of Bob Marley* (New York: Owl, 1998). For a discussion of the discursive connections between reggae and Rastafarianism, see Stephen King and Richard J. Jensen, "Bob Marley's 'Redemption Song': The Rhetoric of Reggae and Rastafari," *Journal of Popular Culture* 29:3 (Winter 1995): 17–36. On the influence of Marley, reggae, and Rastafarianism in Great Britain, see Paul Gilroy, *"There Ain't No Black in the*

Union Jack:" The Cultural Politics of Race and Nation (London: Hutchinson, 1987), 169–71 and 187–92. On Marley's hybrid identity and music, especially the Asian-Caribbean influences on that music, see Lipsitz, *Footsteps in the Dark*, 43–5.

27 Quoted in Robin Balliger, "Sounds of Resistance," 433.

28 *Grassroots Post-Modernism: Remaking the Soil of Cultures* (New York: Zed Books, 1998), 202.

29 White, *Catch a Fire*, 207.

30 Gilroy, *"There Ain't No Black in the Union Jack,"* 171.

Notes to Chapter 7

1 Noam Chomsky, *Turning the Tide: U. S. Intervention in Central America and the Struggle for Peace* (Boston: South End Press, 1985), 170.

2 Manuel Castells, "Grassrooting the Space of Flows," in Louise Amoore, ed. *The Global Resistance Reader* (New York: Routledge, 2005), 363–70. For further analysis of the impact of the Internet for transnational social movements, see Donatella della Porta *et al.*, *Globalization from Below: Transnational Activists and Protest Networks* (Minneapolis: University of Minnesota Press, 2006), 92–117; and Thomas Olesen, *International Zapatismo: The Construction of Solidarity in the Age of Globalization* (New York: Zed Books, 2005), 47–51.

3 Nancy Fraser, *Justice Interruptus: Critical Reflections on the 'Postsocialist' Condition* (New York: Routledge, 1997), 75. In particular, Fraser focuses on what she calls "subaltern counterpublics" that work both off and on stage to agitate for more inclusive, albeit oppositional, political space. See ibid., 81–5.

4 Victor Roudometof, "Transnationalism and Cosmopolitanism: Errors of Globalism," in Richard P. Appelbaum and William I. Robinson, eds. *Critical Globalization Studies* (New York: Routledge, 2005), 68. See also Kumai Naidoo, "Claiming Global Power: Transnational Civil Society and Global Governance," in Srilatha Batliwala and L. David Brown, eds. *Transnational Civil Society: An Introduction* (Bloomfield, CT: Kumarian Press, 2006), 54.

5 Olesen, *International Zapatismo,* 101. Olesen utilizes the concept of transnational counterpublics as part of his analysis of international Zapatismo. See ibid., 93–101.

6 Jackie Smith's elaboration on the concept of "rival transnational networks" obviously incorporates my sense of transnational counterpublics as the site of one of those rival networks. See her *Social Movements for Global Democracy* (Baltimore, MD: The Johns Hopkins University Press, 2008), 19–35.

7 Christopher Chase Dunn and Barry Gills, "Waves of Globalization and Resistance in the Capitalist World-System: Social Movements and Critical Global Studies," in *Critical Globalization Studies*, 53. For further discussion of "globalization of resistance" and "globalization from below," see Barry Gills, ed., *Globalization and the Politics of Resistance* (New York: St. Martin's Press, 2000); James H. Mittelman, *The Globalization Syndrome: Transformation and Resistance* (Princeton, NJ: Princeton University Press, 2000), 165–78; and Jeremy Brecher, Tim Costello, and Brendan Smith, *Globalization from Below* (Cambridge, MA: South End Press, 2000). Also on contesting globalization from above, see Marjorie Mayo, *Global Citizens and the Challenge of Globalization* (London: Zed Books, 2005); Ronaldo Munck, *Globalization and Contestation: The New Great Counter-Movement* (New York: Routledge, 2007); and Smith, *Social Movements for Global Democracy*.

8 Ruth Reitan, *Global Activism* (New York: Routledge, 2007), 20–1.

9 On the transnational Central American connections, see Norma Chinchilla, "Globalization, International Migration, and Transnationalism: Some Observations Based on the Central American Experience," in *Critical Globalization Studies*, 167–76. For discussion of the emergence of Central American solidarity networks

in the 1980s and the attendant U. S. government surveillance and intimidation, see Christian Smith, *Resisting Reagan: The U. S. Central America Peace Movements* (Chicago: University of Chicago, 1996); and Greg Grandin, *Empire's Workshop: Latin America, the United States, and the Rise of New Imperialism* (New York: Holt Paperbacks, 2007), 137–40. On the U. S. supported free trade zones in El Salvador, the labor repression in those areas, and labor campaigns focused on the garment industry in the free trade zones, see Ethel C. Brooks, *Unraveling the Garment Industry: Transnational Organizing and Women's Work* (Minneapolis: University of Minnesota Press, 2007), esp. 104–11.

10 David Cortright and Ron Pagnucco, "Transnational Activism in the Nuclear Weapons Freeze Campaign," in Thomas R. Rochon and David S. Meyer, eds. *Coalitions and Political Movements: The Lessons of the Nuclear Freeze* (Boulder, CO: Lynne Rienner Publishers, 1997), 91.

11 Grandin, *Empire's Workshop*, 87–158. See also Smith, *Resisting Reagan*, esp. 18–56.

12 For a quick descriptive overview of Sanctuary, Witness for Peace, and the Pledge of Resistance, see Smith, *Resisting Reagan*, 59–86.

13 On the U. S. anti-nuclear weapons movement, see David S. Meyer, *A Winter of Discontent: The Nuclear Freeze and American Politics* (New York: Praeger, 1990). On the Western European anti-nuke movements, see Thomas Rochon, *Mobilizing for Peace: The Antinuclear Movements in Western Europe* (Princeton, NJ: Princeton University Press, 1988). For a broader, but concise, discussion of transnational peace activism in the Cold War and Post-Cold War eras, see Motoko Mekata, "Waging Peace: Transnational Peace Activism," in *Transnational Civil Society*, 181–203.

14 Meyer, *A Winter of Discontent*, 75.

15 Ibid., 124–6.

16 Cortright and Pagnucco, in *Coalitions and Political Movements*, 82.

17 Meyer, *A Winter of Discontent*, 151–2.

18 Ibid., 102.

19 Ibid., 119–35.

20 Ibid., 133.

21 Quoted in ibid., 162.

22 On the dissent within the June 12 coalition around such issues, see ibid., 184–8.

23 Ibid., 196–8.

24 Mekata, in *Transnational Civil Society*, 188–9; Cortright and Pagnucco, in *Coalitions and Political Movements*, 84; and Rochon, *Mobilizing for Peace*, 3–8, 11–14, and *passim*.

25 Petra Kelly, *Fighting for Hope*, trans. Marianne Howarth (Boston: South End Press, 1984). All future references to this text are in the body of the chapter.

26 For a brief overview of the Greens, Kelly and some of the organizational contradictions during this period, such as the rotation of office holders which Kelly eventually repudiated, see Rochon, *Mobilizing for Peace*, 83–6. Kelly was a member of the German Parliament (Bundestag) from 1983–90. In 1992, at the age of 44, she was murdered in Bonn under mysterious circumstances.

27 Cited in Mary Kaldor, *Global Civil Society: An Answer to War* (Malden, MA: Polity Press, 2003), 57–8.

28 Ibid., 58.

29 Ibid., 50–77.

30 Quoted in ibid., 61.

31 Cited in ibid., 58. On the WSF as an "alternative political space," see Smith, *Social Movements for Global Democracy*, 199–225. Additional material on the WSF will be found in the next chapter.

32 Ibid., 77.

33 Ibid., 142. Other approaches to global civil society can be found in the essays in Batliwala and Brown, eds., *Transnational Civil Society.*

34 Joss Hands, "Civil Society, Cosmopolitics and the Net," *Information, Communication & Society* 9:2 (April 2006): 232.

35 W. Lance Bennett, "Social Movements beyond Borders: Understanding Two Eras of Transnational Activism," in Donatella della Porta and Sidney Tarrow, eds. *Transnational Protest and Global Activism* (Lanham, MD: Rowman & Littlefield, 2005), 206–7.

36 R. Kelly Garrett, "Protest in an Information Society," *Information, Communication & Society* 9:2 (April 2006): 202–24; and Donatella della Porta *et al.*, *Globalization From Below: Transnational Activists and Protest Networks* (Minneapolis: University of Minnesota Press, 2006), 92–117.

37 Harry Cleaver, quoted in Olesen, *International Zapatismo*, 184.

38 Cleaver, "The Zapatistas and the Electronic Fabric of Struggle," in John Holloway and Eloina Palaez, eds. *Zapatista! Reinventing Revolution in Mexico* (London: Pluto Press, 1998), 98.

39 Quoted in Olesen, *International Zapatismo*, 191.

40 Paul Kingsnorth, *One No, Many Yeses* (London: Free Press, 2003), 73. On the influence of *La Neta* on the Zapatistas, see Castells, "Grassrooting the Space of Flows," 367.

41 Ibid., 72–5 and 82–3.

42 Lesley J. Wood, "Bridging the Chasms: The Case of the Peoples Global Action," in Joe Bandy and Jackie Smith, eds. *Coalitions Across Borders: Transnational Protest and the Neoliberal Order* (Lanham, MD.: Rowman & Littlefield, 2005), 95–6.

43 Ibid., 117.

44 Ibid., 101, 106–8, and 117.

45 Ibid., 104.

46 Charlotte Bunch *et al.*, "International Networking for Women's Human Rights," in Michael Edwards and John Gaventa, eds. *Global Citizen Action* (Boulder, CO: Lynne Rienner Publishers, 2001), 217–20.

47 Ibid., 224–6.

48 Matthew J. O. Scott, "Danger-Landmines! NGO–Government Collaboration in the Ottawa Process," in ibid., 123.

49 Ibid., 125–8.

50 Doug Tuttle, "The Mine Ban Treaty's 10th Anniversary," Center for Defense Information Monitor Website, February 27, 2009. Online. Available HTTP: <http://www.cdi.org/program/document.cfm?DocumentID=4472&from/page=./index.cfm> (accessed March 2, 2009).

51 Doug Tuttle, Cluster Bomb Report, Center for Defense Information Monitor Website, February 11, 2009. Online. Available HTTP: <http://www.cdi.org/program/document.cfm?DocumentID=4458&frompage=./index.cfm> (accessed March 2, 2009).

52 Bennett, "Social Movements Beyond Borders," in Della Porta and Tarrow, eds. *Transnational Protest and Global Activism*, 214–15 and 222.

53 Ibid., 205.

Notes to Chapter 8

1 Russell Jacoby, *Picture Imperfect: Utopian Thought for an Anti-Utopian Age* (New York: Columbia University Press, 2005), 12–13. On the connection between emancipation and the overcoming of domination, see Stanley Aronowitz, *The Death and Rebirth of American Radicalism* (New York: Routledge, 1996), 169 and *passim.*

2 Peter Ruppert, *Reader in a Strange Land: The Activity of Reading Literary Utopias* (Athens: The University of Georgia Press, 1986), 56. For additional discussion about the links between social practice, the imagination, and revolutionary social dreaming, see Robin D. G. Kelley, *Freedom Dreams: The Black Radical Imagination* (Boston: Beacon Press, 2002). On the grounding of Piercy's contestatory politics and utopian imagination in *Woman on the Edge of Time*, see Tom Moylan, *Demand the Impossible: Science Fiction and the Utopian Imagination* (New York: Methuen, 1986), 121–55; and Anna M. Martinson, "Ecofeminist Perspectives on Technology in the Science Fiction of Marge Piercy," *Extrapolation* 44:1 (Spring 2003): 50–68. All page references to *Woman on the Edge of Time* are from the seventh printing of the Fawcett Crest paperback (New York, 1987).

3 Andrew J. Bacevich, *The Limits of Power: The End of American Exceptionalism* (New York: Metropolitan Books, 2008), 16.

4 Barbara Kingsolver, *Small Wonder* (New York: Harper Collins, 2002), 262.

5 Bill McKibben, *Deep Economy: The Wealth of Communities and the Durable Future* (New York: Holt Paperbacks, 2007), 67.

6 Moylan, *Demand the Impossible*, 143.

7 Cited in Kelley, *Freedom Dreams,* 147–8. For a discussion of the inspiration of the radical movements of the late 1960s on Piercy's writings, see Moylan, *Demand the Impossible*, esp. 124, 127, and 147–8.

8 Jay Winter, *Dreams of Peace and Freedom: Utopian Moments in the 20th Century* (New Haven, CT: Yale University Press, 2006), 130. For a discussion of Gutiérrez's background, see ibid., 125–30; and Robert McAfee Brown, "Preface," in Gustavo Gutiérrez *The Power of the Poor in History*, trans. Robert R. Barr (Maryknoll, NY: Orbis Books, 1984), vi–xvi. Additional references to the Gutiérrez text will be found in the body of this chapter.

9 James C. Scott, *Domination and the Arts of Resistance* (New Haven, CT: Yale University Press, 1990), 81.

10 Winter, *Dreams of Peace and Freedom*, 130.

11 For the Nicaraguan roots of liberation theology, see ibid., 132–6.

12 Cited in Enrique Rajchenberg and Catherine Heau-Lambert, "History and Symbolism in the Zapatista Movement," in John Holloway and Eloina Palaez, eds. *Zapatista! Reinventing Revolution in Mexico* (London: Pluto Press, 1998), 28. For a concise overview of the emergence and first few years of the Zapatistas, see Holloway and Pelaez, "Introduction," *Zapatista!*, 1–18; and Luis Lorenzano, "Zapatismo: Recomposition of Labour, Radical Democracy and Revolutionary Project," *Zapatista*, 126–58. For more recent assessments of the Zapatistas, see Thomas Olesen, *International Zapatismo: The Construction of Solidarity in the Age of Globalization* (New York: Zed Books, 2005); and Neil Harvey, "Beyond Hegemony: Zapatismo, Empire, and Dissent," in Fred Rosen, ed. *Empire and Dissent: The U. S. and Latin America* (Durham, NC: Duke University Press, 2008), 119–36.

13 Cited in Lorenzano, "Zapatismo," *Zapatista*, 126.

14 Cited in Holloway and Palaez, "Introduction," *Zapatista!*, 15. On the Zapatista use of the internet and global response, see Harry Cleaver, "The Zapatistas and the Electronic Fabric of Struggle," in ibid., 81–103.

15 Ernst Bloch, *The Principle of Hope*. Vol. 1, trans. Neville Plaice, Stephen Plaice, and Paul Knight (Cambridge, MA: MIT Press, 1986), 5.

16 Holloway and Palaez, "Introduction," *Zapatista!*, 15.

17 John Holloway, "Dignity's Revolt," in *Zapatista!*, 160.

18 June C. Nash, *Mayan Visions: The Quest for Autonomy in an Age of Globalization* (New York: Routledge, 2001), 133–4. For an incisive discussion of the indigenous roots of the Zapatistas, see ibid., esp. 122–58.

19 For the global implications of the Zapatista's, see Olesen, *International Zapatismo*, esp. 102–52.

20 Nash, *Mayan Visions*, 150.
21 Olesen, *International Zapatismo*, 118.
22 Quoted in Holloway and Pelaez, "Introduction," *Zapatista!*, 11–12.
23 Olesen, *International Zapatismo*, 122.
24 Quoted in Holloway, "Dignity's Revolt," *Zapatista!*, 195–6.
25 Fiona Jeffries, "Zapatismo and the Intergalactic Age," in Roger Burbach *Globalization and Postmodern Politics: From Zapatistas to High-Tech Robber Barons* (London: Pluto Press, 2001), 136. See also Olesen, *International Zapatismo*, 116.
26 Boaventura de Sousa Santos, *The Rise of the Global Left: The World Social Forum and Beyond* (New York: Zed Books, 2006), 11. Critical utopias also attempt to "achieve a breach in the ideological and cultural structures that surround us." On the critical utopia, see Moylan, *Demand the Impossible,* esp. 213. On third world utopianism, see Ashis Nandy, *Traditions, Tyranny and Utopias: Essays in the Politics of Awareness* (Delhi: Oxford University Press, 1987), 20–55. For an overview of the origins and impact of the World Social Forum, see Tom Mertes, ed., *A Movement of Movements: Is Another World Really Possible?* (New York: Verso, 2004); and Jackie Smith *et al., Global Democracy and the World Social Forums* (Boulder, CO: Paradigm Publishers, 2008).
27 Ibid., 38.
28 Ibid., 10.
29 Cited in Smith *et al.*, *Global Democracy and the World Social Forums*, 65.
30 de Sousa Santos, *The Rise of the Global Left*, 114–15 and 115–17.
31 Cited in ibid., 115.
32 Quoted in Jackie Smith, *Social Movements for Global Democracy* (Baltimore, MD: The Johns Hopkins University Press, 2008), 218.
33 On the connections between liberation theology and the indigenous communities in Mexico, see Nash, *Mayan Visions*, 112–14 and 163–9.
34 *Subcomandante* Marcos, "Globalize Hope," *ZNet*, September 12, 2003. Online. Available HTTP: <http://www.zmag.org/znet/viewArticle/9855> (accessed March 12, 2009).
35 John Holloway, *Change the World Without Taking Power: The Meaning of Revolution Today* (Ann Arbor, MI: Pluto Press, 2005), 36. For a critical left look at Holloway's perspective and the autonomists throughout Latin America, see Claudio Katz, "Problems of Autonomism," *International Socialist Review* 44 (Nov–Dec 2005). Online. Available HTTP: < http:// www.isreview.org/issues/44/autonomism.shtml> (accessed March 12, 2009).
36 Olesen, *International Zapatismo,* 10.
37 de Sousa Santos, *The Rise of the Global Left*, 129.
38 On the criticisms of the WSF, see ibid., 53–4 and 70.
39 Ibid., 12.
40 Michael Hardt and Antonio Negri, *Multitude: War and Democracy in the Age of Empire* (New York: Penguin Books, 2005), 215.
41 Francis Shor, "A Better (or, Battered) World is Possible: Utopian/Dystopian Dialectics in the American Century," in Elizabeth Russell, ed. *Trans/Forming Utopia: Looking Forward to the End*, Vol. 1 (Oxford: Peter Lang, 2009), 145–64. According to Rebecca Solnit: "We cannot eliminate all devastation for all time, but we can reduce it, outlaw it, undermine its sources and foundations: these are victories. A better world, yes; a perfect world, never." *Hope in the Dark: Untold Histories, Wild Possibilities* (New York: Nation Books, 2004), 82.
42 Noam Chomsky, *Hegemony or Survival: America's Quest for Global Dominance* (New York: Metropolitan Books, 2003), 236.
43 Solnit, *Hope in the Dark*, 106–7.
44 Vandana Shiva, *Earth Democracy: Justice, Sustainability, and Peace* (Cambridge, MA: South End Press, 2005), 63. On Lijjat Papad, see ibid., 68–70.

45 Ibid., 61.
46 Ibid., 4. For the principles of "Earth Democracy," see ibid., 9–11.
47 Bloch, *The Principle of Hope*; and Ruth Levitas, *The Concept of Utopia* (London: Phillip Allen, 1990), 89.

Conclusion

1 Alexis de Tocqueville, *Democracy in America*, ed. and abridged by Richard D. Heffner (New York: Mentor, 1956), 144.
2 Jean Baudrillard, *America*, trans. Chris Turner (New York: Verso, 1989), 38.
3 Marilyn B. Young, "The Age of Global Power," in Thomas Bender, ed. *Rethinking American History in a Global Age* (Berkeley: University of California Press, 2002), 279. On knowledgeable ignorance, see Ziuddin Sardar and Merryl Wyn Davies, *Why Do People Hate America?* (New York: The Disinformation Company, 2002), 11–12. For a discussion of the role of nationalist dogma in the development of an imperial America, see Walter L. Hixson, *The Myth of American Diplomacy: National Identity and U. S. Foreign Policy* (New Haven, CT: Yale University Press, 2008); and Anatol Lieven, *America Right or Wrong: An Anatomy of American Nationalism* (New York: Oxford University Press, 2004).
4 For an incisive overview of the emergence and decline of U. S. global hegemony after World War II until the beginning of the twenty-first century, see Michael H. Hunt, *The American Ascendancy: How the United States Gained and Wielded Global Dominance* (Chapel Hill: The University of North Carolina Press, 2007), 151–324. Hunt asserts that the "leaders of the United States have managed hegemony with a lamentably heavy hand – with scant respect for human life and scant respect for human diversity. Millions died and many societies suffered profound disruption as a result of U. S. interventions (321)."
5 William Appleman Williams, *Empire as a Way of Life* (New York: Oxford University Press, 1982), 4.
6 Ibid., 84.
7 Robert Jay Lifton, *Superpower Syndrome: America's Apocalyptic Confrontation with the World* (New York: Nation Books, 2003), 129.
8 Ibid., 178.
9 Ibid., 191–2.
10 Ibid., 199.
11 Elisabeth Kubler-Ross, *On Death and Dying* (New York: Macmillan Publishing, 1978), 13. For Lifton part of that acceptance of death is the realization of our human vulnerability and "our all too fallible and fragile humanity (199)." *Superpower Syndrome*.
12 Gabriel Kolko, *The Age of War: The United States Confronts the World* (Boulder, CO: Lynne Rienner Publishers, 2006), 95.
13 Cited in Andrew J. Bacevich, *The Limits of Power: The End of American Exceptionalism* (New York: Metropolitan Books, 2008), 79–80.
14 For a brief overview of the contradictions of Obama's policy in Iraq and Afghanistan, see Phyllis Bennis, "Contested Terrain: Obama's Iraq Withdrawal Plan and the Peace Movement," *CommonDreams.org*, March 9, 2009. Online. Available HTTP: <http://commondreams.org/view/2009/03/09–8 > (accessed March 9, 2009). For an incisive discussion of the trends in Obama's foreign and military policies, see Joanne Landy, "The Change We Really Want?," *New Politics* 46 (Winter 2009). Online. Available HTTP: <http://www.wpunj.edu/~newpol/issue46/Landy46.htm> (accessed March 17, 2009).

15 Michael Klare, "'2025' Report: A World of Resource Strife," *CommonDreams.org*, December 3, 2008. Online. Available HTTP: <http://www.commondreams.org/view/2008/12/03–08 > (accessed March 17, 2009).

16 Tom Englehardt, "The Imperial Unconscious," *CommonDreams.org*, March 3, 2009. Online. Available HTTP: <http://www.commondreams.org/view/2009/03/02–1> (accessed March 4, 2009).

17 Chalmers Johnson, "The Looming Crisis at the Pentagon," *TomDispatch.com*, February 2, 2009. Online. Available HTTP: <http://tomdispatch.com/post/175029> (accessed February 4, 2009).

18 Michael Hudson, "The Oligarchs' Escape Plan," *CounterPunch*, February 17, 2009. Online. Available HTTP: <http://www.counterpunch.org/hudson02172009.html> (accessed February 18, 2009).

19 John Foster Bellamy interviewed by Mike Whitney, *Online Journal*, February 27, 2009. Online. Available HTTP: <http://onlinejournal.com/artman/publish/article4420.shtml> (accessed March 4, 2009).

20 Immanuel Wallerstein, *Alternatives: The United States Confronts the World* (Boulder: CO: Paradigm Publishers, 2004), 108. For a more recent exchange of Wallerstein's views on the collapse of capitalism, see "Capitalism's Demise," Immanuel Wallerstein interviewed by Jae-Jung Suh, *Japan Focus*, January 8, 2009. Online. Available HTTP: <http://japanfocus.org/products/todf/3005> (accessed January 14, 2009). For the Marxist perspective on the connections between the global capitalist crisis and domestic policies, see David Harvey, "Why the U. S. Stimulus Package is Bound to Fail," David Harvey's Blog. Online. Available HTTP: <http://davidharvey.org/2009/02/why-the-stimulus-package-is-bound-to-fail> (accessed February 18, 2009); and Harry Shutt, "Redistribution and Stability: Beyond the Keynesian/Neoliberal Impasse," *MRZine*, February 27, 2009. Online. Available HTTP: <http://www.monthlyreview.org/mrzine/shutt270209.html> (accessed March 11, 2009). For a detailed study of the emergence of global capital from ancient to modern times, see Amiya Kumar Bagchi, *Perilous Passage: Mankind and the Global Ascendancy of Capital* (Lanham, MD: Rowman & Littlefield, 2005).

21 One such dire warning about the death of our planet can be found in the following pessimistic view: "There is nothing to indicate ... that the crisis of global capitalism ... will not end up in the breakdown of civilization and the destruction of our species, or indeed, of our planet." William I. Robinson, *Promoting Polyarchy: Globalization, U. S. Intervention, and Hegemony* (New York: Cambridge University Press, 1996), 381. Another such admonition was part of an address on global warming by Evo Morales, President of Bolivia, in November 2008. Morales asserted that "competition and the thirst for profit without limits of the capitalist system are destroying the planet." For a full account of his address online, see <http://links.org.au/node/769> (accessed January 5, 2009).

22 Kajsa Ekholm Friedman, "Structure, Dynamics, and the Final Collapse of Bronze Age Civilizations in the Second Millennium B.C.," in Jonathan Friedman and Christopher Chase-Dunn, eds. *Hegemonic Declines: Past and Present* (Boulder, CO: Paradigm Publishers, 2005), 63. On the long history and impact of patriarchy, see Marilyn French, *Beyond Power: Of Women, Men, and Morals* (New York: Ballantine Books, 1985). For a brilliant probing of the evolutionary contamination of power over, see Andrew Bard Schmookler, *The Parable of the Tribes: The Problem of Power in Social Evolution* (New York: Houghton Mifflin Paperback, 1986). On the role of racism and male chauvinism as components of empire-building in the West, see Zillah Eisenstein, *Against Empire: Feminisms Racism, and the West* (New York: Zed Books, 2004). For a probing exposition of the persistence of war, see Barbara Ehrenreich, *Blood Rites: Origins and History of the Passions of War* (New York: Owl Paperback, 1998).

23 Eric Hobsbawm, *On Empire: America, War, and Global Supremacy* (New York: Pantheon, 2008), 25.
24 On the history of U. S. military interventions since World War II, see William Blum, *Killing Hope: U. S. Military and CIA Interventions Since World War II* (Monroe, ME: Common Courage Press, 2004). For how and why "permanent war" has become a defining feature of the American empire today, see Retort, *Afflicted Powers: Capital and Spectacle in a New Age of War* (New York: Verso, 2006), 78–107. On the irrational nature of the American Empire's commitment to war, see Lifton, *Superpower Syndrome.*
25 Jared Diamond, *Collapse: How Societies Choose to Fail or Succeed* (New York: Viking, 2005).
26 Ibid., 486–99. His "cautious optimism" (499) about possible solutions (499–525) needs to be balanced by the kind of pessimism among environmental scientists like James Lovelock who believe we have passed the "tipping point" of planetary survival. Cited in Bill McKibben, *Deep Economy: The Wealth of Communities and the Durable Future* (New York: Holt Paperback, 2008), 230.
27 Anthony Giddens, "The Climate Crunch Heralds the End of the End of History," *Guardian/UK*, March 11, 2009. Online. Available HTTP: <http://www.common-dreams/org/view/2009/03/11–14 > (accessed March 11, 2009).
28 James Gustave Speth, "Progressive Fusion," *The Nation*, October 6, 2008, 29. The imperial logic underlying consumption, from the perspective of William Appleman Williams, is as follows: "The imperial satisfaction with riches, even its conception of riches, is defined not by how much we require to meet our human needs, but by how much more we acquire than our neighbors." *Empire as a Way of Life*, 221.
29 Eduardo Galeano, *Upside Down: A Primer for the Looking Glass World*, trans. Mark Fried (New York: Metropolitan Books, 2000), 267.
30 Vandana Shiva, *Earth Democracy: Justice, Sustainability, and Peace* (Cambridge, MA: South End Press, 2005), 62.
31 Mark Engler, *How to Rule the World: The Coming Battle Over the Global Economy* (New York: Nation Books, 2008), 303–4. On global activism, resistance, and solidarity, see Ruth Reitan, *Global Activism* (New York: Routledge, 2007).
32 For a stimulating and sprawling discussion of the global multitudes, albeit often overly schematic and lacking in enough sociological underpinning, see Michael Hardt and Antoni Negri, *Multitude: War and Democracy in the Age of Empire* (New York: Penguin Books, 2004).

Bibliography

Achar, Gilbert. *The Clash of Barbarisms: The Making of the New World Disorder*, trans. Peter Drucker. Boulder, CO: Paradigm, 2006.

Alperovitz, Gar. *America Beyond Capitalism: Reclaiming Our Wealth, Our Liberty, and Our Democracy*. Hoboken, NJ: John Wiley & Sons, 2005.

Alpert, Arnie. "Bringing Globalization Home is No Sweat." In John Feffer, ed. *Living in Hope: People Challenging Globalization*, 37–52. London: Zed Books, 2002.

Amin, Samir. *The Liberal Virus: Permanent War and the Americanization of the World*. New York: Monthly Review Press, 2004.

——. *Beyond US Hegemony: Assessing the Prospects for a Multipolar World*, trans. Patrick Camiller. London: Zed Books, 2006.

Appy, Christian. *Working Class War: American Combat Soldiers and Vietnam*. Chapel Hill: The University of North Carolina Press, 1993.

Aronowitz, Stanley. *The Death and Rebirth of American Radicalism*. New York: Routledge, 1996.

Arrighi, Giovanni. "Hegemony Unravelling – 1." *New Left Review* 32 (March/April 2005): 23–80.

——. "Hegemony Unravelling – 2." *New Left Review* 33 (May/June 2005): 83–116.

Bacevich, Andrew. *The New American Militarism*. New York: Oxford University Press, 2005.

——. "I Lost My Son to a War I Oppose." *Washington Post*, May 27, 2007. B01.

——. *The Limits of Power: The End of American Exceptionalism*. New York: Metropolitan Books, 2008.

Bagchi, Amiya Kumar. *Perilous Passage: Mankind and the Global Ascendancy of Capital*. Lanham, MD: Rowman & Littlefield, 2005.

Baldwin, James. *The Fire Next Time*. New York: Dell, 1963.

Balliger, Robin. "Sounds of Resistance." In Louise Amoore, ed. *The Global Resistance Reader*, 423–36. New York: Routledge, 2005.

Ballinger, Jeff. "No Sweat: Corporate Social Responsibility and the Dilemma of Anti-Sweatshop Activism." *New Labor Forum* 17:2 (Summer 2008): 91–8.

Barthes, Roland. *Mythologies*, trans. Annette Lavers. New York: Hill & Wang, 1972.

Batliwala, Srilatha and L. David Brown, eds. *Transnational Civil Society: An Introduction*. Bloomfield, CT: Kumarian Press, 2006.

Baudrillard, Jean. *America*, trans. Chris Turner. New York: Verso, 1989.

Bauman, Zygmunt. *Liquid Love: On the Frailty of Human Bonds*. Cambridge: Polity Press, 2003.

Bello, Walden. *Dilemmas of Domination: The Unmaking of the American Empire.* New York: Metropolitan Books, 2005.

Bennett, W. Lance. "Social Movements beyond Borders: Understanding Two Eras of Transnational Activism." In Donatella della Porta and Sidney Tarrow, eds. *Transnational Protest and Global Activism*, 203–26. Lanham, MD: Rowman & Littlefield, 2005.

Bennis, Phyllis. "Contested Terrain: Obama's Iraq Withdrawal Plan and the Peace Movement." *CommonDreams.org*, March 9, 2009. Online. Available HTTP: <http://commondreams.org/view/2009/03/09–8 > (accessed March 9, 2009).

Berman, Morris. *Dark Ages America: The Final Phase of Empire.* New York: W.W. Norton & Co., 2006.

Berry, Wendell. *Sex, Economy, Freedom & Community.* New York: Pantheon, 1993.

Blanding, Michael. "The World Social Forum: Protest or Celebration," *The Nation*, February 16, 2006. Online. Available HTTP: <http://www.thenation.com/doc/20060306/blanding> (accessed November 19, 2008).

Bloch, Ernst. *The Principle of Hope.* Vol. 1, trans. Neville Plaice, Stephen Plaice, and Paul Knight. Cambridge, MA: MIT Press, 1986.

Blum, William. *Killing Hope: U. S. Military and CIA Interventions Since World War II.* Monroe, ME: Common Courage Press, 2004.

Boggs, Carl. *Imperial Delusions: American Militarism and Endless War.* Lanham, MD: Rowman & Littlefield, 2005.

Bovard, James. *Attention Deficit Disorder.* New York: Palgrave Macmillan, 2005.

Branch, Taylor. *Pillar of Fire: America in the King Years, 1963–1965.* New York: Touchstone, 1999.

Brecher, Jeremy, Tim Costello, and Brendan Smith. *Globalization from Below: The Power of Solidarity.* Cambridge, MA: South End Press, 2000.

Bright, Charles. "Where in the World is America? The History of the United States in the Global Age." In Thomas Bender, ed. *Rethinking American History in a Global Age*, 63–99. Berkeley, CA: University of California Press, 2002.

Brooks, Ethel. *Unraveling the Garment Industry: Transnational Organizing and Women's Work.* Minneapolis, MN: University of Minnesota Press, 2007.

Brown, Robert McAfee. "Preface,". In Gustavo Gutierrez *The Power of the Poor in History.* vi–xvi. Maryknoll, NY: Orbis Books, 1984.

Brzezinski, Zbigniew. *The Choice: Global Domination or Global Leadership.* New York: Basic Books, 2004.

Bunch, Charlotte *et al.* "International Networking for Women's Human Rights." In Michael Edwards and John Gaventa, eds. *Global Citizen Action*, 217–20. Boulder, CO: Lynne Rienner Publishers, 2001.

Burbach, Roger. *Globalization and Postmodern Politics: From Zapatistas to High-Tech Robber Barons.* London: Pluto Press, 2001.

Castells, Manuel. "Grassrooting the Space of Flows." In Louise Amoore, ed. *The Global Resistance Reader*, 363–70. New York: Routledge, 2005.

Chase-Dunn, Christopher and Barry Gills. "Waves of Globalization and Resistance in the Capitalist World-System: Social Movements and Critical Global Studies." In Richard P. Appelbaum and William I. Robinson, eds. *Critical Globalization Studies*, 45–54. New York: Routledge, 2005.

Chernus, Ira. *Monsters to Destroy: The Neoconservative War on Terror and Sin.* Boulder, CO: Paradigm Publishers, 2006.

Chinchilla, Norma. "Globalization, International Migration, and Transnationalism: Some Observations Based on the Central American Experience." In Richard P.

Appelbaum and William I. Robinson, eds. *Critical Globalization Studies*, 167–76. New York: Routledge, 2005.

Chomsky, Noam. *Turning the Tide: U. S. Intervention in Central America and the Struggle for Peace*. Boston, MA: South End Press, 1985.

——. *Hegemony or Survival: America's Quest for Global Dominance*. New York: Metropolitan Books, 2003.

Cleaver, Harry. "The Zapatistas and the Electronic Fabric of Struggle." In John Holloway and Eloina Palaez, eds. *Zapatista! Reinventing Revolution in Mexico*, 81–103. London: Pluto Press, 1998.

Codrescu, Andrei. *New Orleans, Mon Amour*. Chapel Hill, NC: Algonquin Books, 2006.

Coll, Steve. *Ghost Wars*. New York: The Penguin Press, 2004.

Cortright, David and Ron Pagnucco. "Transnational Activism in the Nuclear Weapons Freeze Campaign." In Thomas R. Rochon and David S. Meyer, eds. *Coalitions and Political Movements: The Lessons of the Nuclear Freeze*, 81–94. Boulder, CO: Lynne Rienner Publishers, 1997.

Cravey, Altha J. "Students and the Anti-Sweatshop Movement." *Antipode* 36:2 (March 2004): 203–8.

Dangl, Benjamin. *The Price of Fire: Resource Wars and Social Movements in Bolivia*. Oakland, CA: AK Press, 2007.

Davis, Mike. *Planet of Slums*. New York: Verso, 2006.

Dean, Robert D. *Imperial Brotherhood: Gender and the Making of Cold War Foreign Policy*. Amherst, MA: University of Massachusetts Press, 2001.

della Porta, Donatella and Sydney Tarrow. *Globalization from Below: Transnational Activists and Protest Networks*. Minneapolis. MN: University of Minnesota Press, 2006.

Diamond, Jared. *Collapse: How Societies Choose to Fail or Succeed*. New York: Viking, 2005.

Donato, Katherine M. *et al.* "Reconstructing New Orleans after Katrina: The Emergence of an Immigrant Labor Market." In David L. Brunsma *et al. The Sociology of Katrina: Perspectives on a Modern Catastrophe* (draft copy in author's possession). Lanham: MD: Rowman & Littlefield, 2007.

Donnelly, John and Robert Schlesinger. "Military Criticized for Type of Ordnance." *Boston Globe*, April 2, 2003. Online. Available HTTP: <http://www.commondreams.org/headlines03/0402–7.htm > (accessed November 5, 2008).

Donnelly, Thomas. "The Past as Prologue: An Imperial Manual." *Foreign Affairs* 81:4 (July/August 2002): 165–70.

Dorrien, Gary. *Imperial Designs: Neoconservatism and the New Pax Americana*. New York: Routledge, 2004.

Dreyfuss, Robert. "Financing the Imperial Armed Forces: A Trillion Dollars and Nowhere to Go But Up." *TomDispatch.com*, June 6, 2007. Online. Available HTTP: <http://www.commondreams.org/archive/2007/06/06/1701/> (accessed December 5, 2008).

Drinnon, Richard. *Facing West: The Metaphysics of Indian-Hating and Empire-Building*. Norman, OK: University of Oklahoma Press, 1997.

Dyson, Michael Eric. *Come Hell or High Water: Hurricane Katrina and the Color of Disaster*. New York: Basic Civitas, 2006.

Ehrenreich, Barbara. *Blood Rites: Origins and History of the Passions of War*. New York: Owl Paperback, 1998.

Eisenstein, Zillah. *Against Empire: Feminisms, Racism, and the West*. New York: Zed Books, 2004.

Ellner, Steve. "The Hugo Chavez Phenomenon: Anti-Imperialism from Above or Radical Democracy from Below." In Fred Rosen, ed. *Empire and Dissent: The United States and Latin America*, 205–27. Durham, NC: Duke University Press, 2008.

Engelhardt, Tom. *The End of Victory Culture: Cold War America and the Disillusioning of a Generation*. New York: Basic Books, 1995.

——. "The Imperial Unconscious." *CommonDreams.org*, March 3, 2009. Online. Available HTTP: <http://www.commondreams.org/view/2009/03/02–1 > (accessed March 4, 2009).

——. "The Real Meaning of Haditha." *Tom.Dispatch.com*, June 6, 2006. Online. Available HTTP: <http://www.tomdispatch.com/month=2006–6> (accessed November 12, 2008).

Engler, Mark. *How to Rule the World: The Coming Battle Over the Global Economy*. New York: Nation Books, 2008.

Esteva, Gustavo and Madhu Suri Prakash. *Grassroots Post-Modernism: Remaking the Soil of Cultures*. New York: Zed Books, 1998.

Fanon, Frantz. "This is the Voice of Algeria." In *A Dying Colonialism*, trans Haakon Chevalier, 69–97. New York: Grove Press, 1967.

Farhang, Mansour. *U.S. Imperialism: From the Spanish-American War to the Iranian Revolution*. Boston, MA: South End Press, 1981.

Farley, Wendy. *Eros for the Other: Retaining Truth in a Pluralistic World*. University Park: The Pennsylvania State University Press, 1996.

Faux, Jeff. *The Global Class War*. Hoboken, NJ: John Wiley & Sons, 2006.

Featherstone, Liza. *Students Against Sweatshops*. New York: Verso, 2002.

Fernandez, Valeria. "Communities Foreclosed." *ColorLines* (Jan/Feb 2009). Online. Available HTTP: <http://colorlines.com/article.php?ID=475> (accessed March 1, 2009).

Fields, Barbara Jean. "Slavery, Race, and Ideology in the United States of America." *New Left Review* 181 (May–June 1990): 95–118.

Fisk, Robert. "Divide and Rule – America's Plan for Baghdad." *Independent*, April 11, 2007. Online. Available HTTP: <http://informationclearinghouse.info/article17515.htm> (accessed December 5, 2008).

Foster, John Bellamy and Fred Magdoff. *The Great Financial Crisis: Causes and Consequences*. New York: Monthly Review Press, 2009.

——, Harry Magdoff, and Robert W. McChesney. "Kipling, the 'White Man's Burden,' and US Imperialism." In John Bellamy Foster and Robert W. McChesney, eds. *Pox Americana: Exposing the American Empire*, 12–21. New York: Monthly Review Press, 2004.

——. Mike Whitney Interview. "The Great Financial Crisis." Information Clearing House, February 27, 2009. Online. Available HTTP: <http://informationclearinghouse.info/article22116.htm> (accessed March 2, 2009).

Fouskas, Vassilis K. and Birlent Gokay. *The New American Imperialism*. Westport, CT: Praeger, 2005.

Franchetti, Mark. "Slaughter at the Bridge of Death." *London Times*, March 31, 2003. Online. Available HTTP: <http://counterpunch.org/franchetti03312003.html> (accessed November 12, 2008).

Frank, Dana. *Bananeras: Women Transforming the Banana Unions of Latin America*. Cambridge, MA: South End Press, 2005.

Fraser, Matthew. *Weapons of Mass Distraction: Soft Power and American Empire*. New York: Thomas Dunne Books, 2005.

Fraser, Max. "The House Folds," *The Nation*, December 15, 2008, 29–33.

Fraser, Nancy. *Justice Interruptus: Critical Reflections on the 'Postsocialist' Condition.* New York: Routledge, 1997.

French, Marilyn. *Beyond Power: Of Women, Men, and Morals.* New York: Ballantine Books, 1985.

Friedman, Jonathan and Christopher Chase-Dunn. eds. *Hegemonic Declines: Past and Present.* Boulder, CO: Paradigm Publishers, 2005.

Friedman, Kajsa Ekholm. "Structure, Dynamics, and the Final Collapse of Bronze Age Civilizations in the Second Millennium B.C." In Jonathan Friedman and Christopher Chase-Dunn, eds. *Hegemonic Declines: Past and Present*, 51–87. Boulder, CO: Paradigm Publishers, 2005.

Friedman, Thomas L. *The Lexus and the Olive Tree.* New York: Farrar, Straus & Giroux, 1999.

Fukuyama, Francis. *America at the Crossroads: Democracy, Power, and the Neoconservative Legacy.* New Haven, CT: Yale University Press, 2006.

Fuller, Millard. *No More Shacks: The Daring Vision of Habitat for Humanity.* Waco, TX: Word Books Publisher, 1986.

Fussell, Elizabeth. "Latino Immigrants in Post-Katrina New Orleans." Paper presented at the Regional Seminar on Labor Rights, New Orleans, October 19, 2006 (copy in author's possession).

Galeano, Eduardo. *Upside Down: A Primer for the Looking-Glass World*, trans. Mark Fried. New York: Metropolitan Books, 2000.

Gandasequi, Marco A. Jr. "Latin America and Imperialism in the 21st Century." *Critical Sociology* 32:1 (January 2006): 45–66.

Garrett, R. Kelly. "Protest in an Information Society." *Information, Communication & Society* 9:2 (April 2006): 202–24.

George, Susan. *Another World is Possible If ...* New York: Verso, 2004.

Gibson, William. *The Perfect War: Technowar in Vietnam.* New York: Atlantic Monthly Press, 2000.

Giddens, Anthony. "The Climate Crunch Heralds the End of the End of History." *Guardian/UK*, March 11, 2009. Online. Available HTTP: <http://www.common-dreams/org/view/2009/03/11–14 > (accessed March 11, 2009).

Gills, Barry, ed. *Globalization and the Politics of Resistance.* New York: St. Martin's Press, 2000.

Gilroy, Paul. *"There Ain't No Black in the Union Jack:" The Cultural Politics of Race and Nation.* London: Hutchinson, 1987.

Giri, Ananta Kumar. *Building in the Margins of Shacks: The Vision and Projects of Habitat for Humanity.* New Delhi: Orient Longman, 2002.

Gould, Carol. *Globalizing Democracy and Human Rights.* New York: Cambridge University Press, 2004.

Grandin, Greg. "Latin America's New Consensus." *The Nation*, April 13, 2006. Online. Available HTTP: <http://thenation.com/doc/20060501/grandin> (accessed November 19, 2008).

——. *Empire's Workshop: Latin America, the United States, and the Rise of the New Imperialism.* New York: Holt Paperbacks, 2007.

Gray, Kevin. "The Banana War," *Portfolio.com*, October 2007. Online. Available HTTP: <http://www.portfolio.com/newsmarkets/internationalnews/portfolio/2007/09/17/Chiquita-Death-Squads > (accessed February 25, 2009).

Greenberg, Amy S. *Manifest Manhood and the Antebellum American Empire.* New York: Cambridge University Press, 2005.

Greider, William. *Fortress America: The American Military and the Consequences of Peace*. New York: Public Affairs, 1999.

Gurtov, Mel. *Superpower on Crusade: The Bush Doctrine in US Foreign Policy*. Boulder, CO: Lynne Rienner Publishers, 2006.

Gutierrez, Gustavo. *The Power of the Poor in History*, trans. Robert R. Barr. Maryknoll, NY: Orbis Books, 1984.

Hammond, John L. "The World Social Forum and the Emergence of Global Grass-roots Politics." *New Politics* 42 (Winter 2007). Online. Available HTTP: <http://www.wpunj.edu/~newpol/issue42/Hammond42.htm> (accessed November 19, 2008).

Hands, Joss. "Civil Society, Cosmopolitics and the Net." *Information, Communication & Society* 9:2 (April 2006): 225–43.

Hardt, Michael and Antonio Negri. *Empire*. Cambridge, MA: Harvard University Press, 2000.

——. *Multitude: War and Democracy in the Age of Empire*. New York: Penguin Books, 2004.

Hartman, Chester and Gregory D. Squires, eds. *There is no Such Thing as a Natural Disaster: Race, Class, and Hurricane Katrina*. New York: Routledge, 2006.

Hartung, William D. and Frida Berrigan, *U. S. Weapons at War 2008*, New America Policy Paper. Online. Available HTTP: <http://www.newamerica.net/publications/policy/u_s_weapons_war_2008_0 > (accessed December 28, 2008).

Harvey, David. *The New Imperialism*. New York: Oxford University Press, 2005.

——. *Spaces of Global Capitalism: Towards a Theory of Uneven Geographical Development*. New York: Verso, 2006.

——. "Why the U. S. Stimulus Package is Bound to Fail." David Harvey's Blog. Online. Available HTTP: <http://davidharvey.org/2009/02/why-the-stimulus-package-is-bound-to-fail> (accessed February 18, 2009).

Harvey, Neil. "Beyond Hegemony: Zapatismo, Empire, and Dissent." In Fred Rosen, ed. *Empire and Dissent: The U. S. and Latin America*, 117–36. Durham, NC: Duke University Press, 2008.

Hass, Amira. "Is Israel Using Illegal Weapons in Its Offensive in Gaza?," *Haaretz*, January 16, 2009. Online. Available HTTP: <http://www.commondreams.org/headline/2009/0116–0 > (accessed January 17, 2009).

Havel, Vaclav. *Disturbing the Peace*. New York: Knopf, 1990.

Hays, R. Allen. "Habitat for Humanity: Building Social Capital through Faith-Based Service," *Journal of Urban Affairs* 24:3 & 4 (Fall 2002): 247–69.

Hedges, Chris. *War is a Force That Gives Us Meaning*. New York: Public Affairs, 2002.

Hendrickson, David C. "The Curious Case of American Hegemony: Imperial Aspirations and National Decline." *World Policy Journal* 22:2 (Summer 2005): 1–22.

Herold, Marc. "A Dossier on Civilian Victims of United States Aerial Bombing of Afghanistan." Online. Available HTTP: <http://cursor.org/stories/civilian_deaths.htm > (accessed December 28, 2008).

Hesmondhalgh, David. *The Cultural Industries*, 2nd ed. Thousand Oaks, CA: Sage Publications, 2007.

Higgs, Robert. "Military Precision versus Moral Precision." *The Independent Institute*, March 23, 2003. Online. Available HTTP: <http://www.independent.org/newsroom/article.asp?id=1154> (accessed November 5, 2008).

Hixson, Walter L. *The Myth of American Diplomacy: National Identity and U. S. Foreign Policy*. New Haven, CT: Yale University Press, 2008.

Hobsbawm, Eric. *On Empire: America, War, and Global Supremacy.* New York: Pantheon, 2008.

Hochschild, Arlie Russell. *The Managed Heart: Commercialization of Human Feeling.* Berkeley: University of California Press, 2003.

Hoganson, Kristin L. *Fighting for American Manhood: How Gender Politics Provoked the Spanish American and Philippine American Wars.* New Haven, CT: Yale University Press, 1998.

Holloway, John. *Change the World Without Taking Power: The Meaning of Revolution Today.* Ann Arbor, MI: Pluto Press, 2005.

——. "Dignity's Revolt." In John Holloway and Eloina Palaez, eds. *Zapatista! Reinventing Revolution in Mexico,* 159–98. London: Pluto Press, 1998.

——and Eloina Palaez. "Introduction: Reinventing Revolution." In John Holloway and Eloina Palaez, eds. *Zapatista! Reinventing Revolution in Mexico,* 1–18. London: Pluto Press, 1998.

hooks, bell. *Where We Stand: Class Matters.* New York: Routledge, 2000.

Horsman, Reginald. *Race and Manifest Destiny: The Origins of American Racial Anglo-Saxonism.* Cambridge, MA: Harvard University Press, 1981.

Hossein-Zadeh, Ismael. "Domestic Imperialism." In Jerry Harris, ed. *Contested Terrains of Globalization,* 198–217. Chicago: Changemaker Press, 2007.

——. "Escalating Military Spending: Income Redistribution in Disguise," *Counter-Punch,* April 16, 2007. Online. Available HTTP: <http://www.counterpunch.org/hossein04162007.html> (accessed December 29, 2008).

Hudson, Michael. "The Oligarchs' Escape Plan," *CounterPunch,* February 17, 2009. Online. Available HTTP: <http://www.counterpunch.org/hudson02172009.html> (accessed February 18, 2009).

Hunt, Michael H. *The American Ascendancy: How the United States Gained and Wielded Global Dominance.* Chapel Hill, NC: The University of North Carolina Press, 2007.

Hutton, Will. *A Declaration of Interdependence: Why America Should Join the World.* New York: W. W. Norton & Co., 2003.

Jacobson, Matthew Frye. *Barbarian Virtues: The United States Encounters Foreign Peoples at Home and Abroad, 1876–1917.* New York: Hill & Wang, 2000.

Jacoby, Russell. *Picture Imperfect: Utopian Thought for an Anti-Utopian Age.* New York: Columbia University Press, 2005.

Jeffries, Fiona. "Zapatismo and the Intergalactic Age," In Roger Burbach *Globalization and Postmodern Politics: From Zapatistas to High-Tech Robber Barons,* 129–44. London: Pluto Press, 2001.

Jensen, Robert. *Citizens of the Empire.* San Francisco: City Lights Books, 2004.

Johnson, Chalmers. *Blowback: The Costs and Consequences of American Empire.* New York: Henry Holt, 2000.

——. "The Looming Crisis at the Pentagon." *TomDispatch.com,* February 2, 2009. Online. Available HTTP: <http://tomdispatch.com/post/175029> (accessed February 4, 2009).

——. "Mission Creep: America's Unwelcome Advances." *Mother Jones,* August 22, 2008. Online. Available HTTP: <http://www.motherjones/politics/2008/08/americas-unwelcome-advances.html> (accessed December 28, 2008).

——. *The Sorrows of Empire: Militarism, Secrecy, and the End of the Republic.* New York: Owl Books, 2005.

Jones, Ann. "The Afghan Scam." *TomDispatch.com,* January 12, 2009. Online. Available HTTP: <http://www.commondreams.org/view/2009/01/12> (accessed January 14, 2009).

Kagan, Robert. *Of Paradise and Power: America and Europe in the New World Order.* New York: Alfred A. Knopf, 2003.

Kaldor, Mary. *Global Civil Society: An Answer to War.* Malden, MA: Polity Press, 2003.

Kaplan, Amy. *The Anarchy of Empire in the Making of U. S. Culture.* Cambridge, MA: Harvard University Press, 2002.

——. and Donald E. Pease, eds. *Cultures of United States Imperialism.* Durham, NC: Duke University Press, 1993.

Katz, Claudio. "Problems of Autonomism." *International Socialist Review* 44 (Nov–Dec 2005). Online. Available HTTP: <http://www.isreview.org/issues/44/autonomism.shtml> (accessed March 12, 2009).

Kelley, Robin D. G. *Freedom Dreams: The Black Radical Imagination.* Boston, MA: Beacon Press, 2002.

Kellner, Douglas. *The Persian Gulf TV War.* Boulder, CO: Westview Press, 1992.

——. "Theorizing Globalization." *Sociological Theory* 20:3 (November 2002): 285–305.

——. "Theorizing/Resisting McDonaldization: A Multiperspectivist Approach." In Barry Smart, ed. *Resisting McDonaldization,* 186–206. Thousand Oaks, CA: Sage Publications, 1999.

Kelly, Petra. *Fighting for Hope,* trans. Marianne Howarth. Boston: South End Press, 1984.

Khalidi, Rashid. *Resurrecting Empire: Western Footprints and America's Perilous Path in the Middle East.* Boston, MA: Beacon Press, 2004.

King, Stephen and Richard J. Jensen. "Bob Marley's 'Redemption Song': The Rhetoric of Reggae and Rastafari." *Journal of Popular Culture* 29:3 (Winter 1995): 17–36.

Kingsnorth, Paul. *One No, Many Yeses.* London: The Free Press, 2003.

Kingsolver, Barbara. *Small Wonder.* New York: HarperCollins Publishers, 2002.

Kinzer, Stephen. *Overthrow: America's Century of Regime Change from Hawaii to Iraq.* New York: Henry Holt & Co., 2006.

Klare, Michael. " '2025' Report: A World of Resource Strife." *CommonDreams.org,* December 3, 2008. Online. Available HTTP: <http://www.commondreams.org/view/2008/12/03–08 > (accessed March 17, 2009).

Klein, Naomi. *No Logo: Taking Aim at the Brand Bullies.* New York: Picador, 2000.

——. "Reclaiming the Commons." *New Left Review* 9 (May–June 2001): 81–9.

——. *The Shock Doctrine: The Rise of Disaster Capitalism.* New York: Metropolitan Books, 2007.

Knauft, Bruce M. "Provincializing America." *Current Anthropology* 48:6 (December 2007): 781–93.

Kolko, Gabriel. *Another Century of War?* New York: New Press, 2002.

——. *The Age of War: The United States Confronts the World.* Boulder, CO: Lynne Rienner Publishers, 2006.

Kornbluh, Peter. *The Pinochet File: A Declassified Dossier on Atrocity and Accountability.* New York: New Press, 2004.

Kovic, Ron. *Born on the Fourth of July.* New York: Pocket Books, 1977.

Kozloff, Nikolas. *Hugo Chavez: Oil, Politics, and the Challenge to the U. S.* New York: Palgrave Macmillan, 2006.

Kraidy, Marwan M. *Hybridity or the Cultural Logic of Globalization.* Philadelphia, PA: Temple University Press, 2005.

Kubler-Ross, Elisabeth. *On Death and Dying.* New York: Macmillan Publishing, 1978.

Landy, Joanne. "The Change We Really Want?" *New Politics* 46 (Winter 2009). Online. Available HTTP: <http://www.wpunj.edu/~newpol/issue46/Landy46.htm> (accessed March 17, 2009).

LaFeber, Walter. *Inevitable Revolutions: The United States in Central America.* New York: W.W. Norton & Co., 1984.

Lefever, Ernest W. *America's Imperial Burden: Is the Past Prologue?* Boulder, CO: Westview Press, 1999.

Levitas, Ruth. *The Concept of Utopia.* London: Phillip Allen, 1990.

Lieven, Anatol. *America Right or Wrong: An Anatomy of American Nationalism.* New York: Oxford University Press, 2004.

Lifton, Robert Jay. *Superpower Syndrome: America's Apocalyptic Confrontation with the World.* New York: Nation Books, 2003.

Lipsitz, George. *Footsteps in the Dark: The Hidden Histories of Popular Music.* Minneapolis, MN: University of Minnesota Press, 2007.

——. "Learning from New Orleans: The Social Warrant of Hostile Privatism and Competitive Consumer Citizenship." *Cultural Anthropology* 21:3 (August 2006): 451–68.

Loeb, Paul Rogat. *Soul of a Citizen.* New York: St. Martin's Press, 1999.

——. *The Impossible Will Take a Little While.* New York: Basic Books, 2004.

Lorenzano, Luis. "Zapatismo: Recomposition of Labour, Radical Democracy and Revolutionary Project." In John Holloway and Eloina Palaez, eds. *Zapatista: Reinventing Revolution in Mexico*, 126–58. London: Pluto Press, 1998.

Love, Eric T. L. *Race Over Empire: Racism and U. S. Imperialism, 1865–1900.* Chapel Hill, NC: The University of North Carolina Press, 2004.

Low, Setha. *Behind the Gates: Life, Security, and the Pursuit of Happiness in Fortress America.* New York: Routledge, 2003.

Luce, Henry. "The American Century." *Diplomatic History* 23:2 (Spring 1999): 159–71.

Lui, Meizhu *et al. The Color of Wealth: The Story Behind the US Racial Wealth Divide.* New York: New Press, 2006.

Mackay, Neil. "US Forces Use of Depleted Uranium is 'Illegal.'" *The Sunday Herald*, March 30, 2003. Online. Available HTTP: <http://www.commondreams.org/headlines03/0330–02.htm > (accessed November 5, 2008).

McKibben, Bill. *Deep Economy: The Wealth of Communities and the Durable Future.* New York: Holt Paperbacks, 2007.

Mann, Michael. *Incoherent Empire.* New York: Verso, 2003.

——. "The First Failed Empire of the 21st Century." *Review of International Studies* 30:4 (October 2004): 631–53.

Marcos, *Subcomandante.* "Globalize Hope." *ZNet*, September 12, 2003. Online. Available HTTP: <http://www.zmag.org/znet/viewArticle/9855> (accessed March 12, 2009).

Marichal, Carlos."The Finances of Hegemony in Latin America: Debt Negotiations and the Role of the U. S. Government, 1945–2005." In Fred Rosen, ed. *Empire and Dissent: The U. S. and Latin America*, 90–113. Durham, NC: Duke University Press, 2008.

Marling, William H. *How "American" is Globalization.* Baltimore, MD: The Johns Hopkins University Press, 2006.

Martinson, Anna M. "Ecofeminist Perspectives on Technology in the Science Fiction of Marge Piercy." *Extrapolation* 44:1 (Spring 2003): 50–68.

Mayer, Arno. "The US Empire will Survive Bush." *CounterPunch*, October 29, 2008. Online. Available HTTP: <http://www.counterpunch.org/mayer/10292008.html> (accessed December 15, 2008).

Mayo, Marjorie. *Global Citizens and the Challenge of Globalization*. London: Zed Books, 2005.

Mekata, Motoko. "Waging Peace: Transnational Peace Activism." In Srilatha Batliwala and L. David Brown, eds. *Transnational Civil Society: An Introduction*, 181–203. Bloomfield, CT: Kumarian Press, 2006.

Melucci, Alberto. *Challenging Codes: Collective Action in the Information Age*. New York: Cambridge University Press, 1996.

Mertes, Tom. ed. *A Movement of Movements: Is Another World Really Possible?* New York: Verso, 2004.

Meyer, David S. *A Winter of Discontent: The Nuclear Freeze and American Politics*. New York: Praeger, 1990.

Mignolo, Walter. "Nationalization of Natural Gas in Bolivia." *CounterPunch*, May 9, 2006. Online. Available HTTP: <http://www.counterpunch.org/mignolo05082006.html> (accessed November 12, 2008).

Mittelman, James H. *The Globalization Syndrome: Transformation and Resistance*. Princeton, NJ: Princeton University Press, 2000.

Moglen, Helene and Sheila Namir. "War and the Dis-eases of Othering." *International Journal of Applied Psychoanalytic Studies* 3:2 (June 2006): 206–18.

Morales, Evo. "I Believe only in the Power of the People." *Countercurrents,* December 22, 2005. Online. Available HTTP: < http://www.countercurrents.org/bolivia-morales221205.htm> (accessed November 12, 2008).

——. "Save the Planet from Capitalism." Online. Available HTTP: <http://links.org.au/node/769> (accessed January 5, 2009).

Morley, David. "Globalization and Cultural Imperialism Reconsidered: Old Questions in New Guises." In James Curran and David Morley, eds. *Media and Cultural Theory,* 30–43. New York: Routledge, 2006.

Moylan, Tom. *Demand the Impossible: Science Fiction and the Utopian Imagination*. New York: Methuen, 1986.

Muir, John Kenneth. *Singing a New Tune: The Rebirth of the Modern Film Musical*. New York: Applause Theatre and Cinema Books, 2005.

Munck, Ronaldo. *Globalization and Contestation: The New Great Counter-Movement*. New York: Routledge, 2007.

Myers, Gordon. *Banana Wars: The Price of Free Trade*. New York: Zed Books, 2004.

Naidoo, Kumai. "Claiming Global Power: Transnational Civil Society and Global Governance." In Srilatha Batliwala and L. David Brown, eds. *Transnational Civil Society: An Introduction*, 51–64. Bloomfield, CT: Kumarian Press, 2006.

Nandy, Ashis. *Traditions, Tyranny and Utopias: Essays in the Politics of Awareness*. Delhi: Oxford University Press, 1987.

Nash, June C. *Mayan Visions: The Quest for Autonomy in an Age of Globalization*. New York: Routledge, 2001.

Norton-Taylor, Richard and Rory McCarthy. "British Military Critical of US Troops' Heavy-Handed Style with Civilians." *Guardian/UK*, April 1, 2003. Online. Available HTTP: <http://www.commondreams.org/headlines03/0401–4.htm   >   (accessed November 12, 2008).

Obama, Barack. *The Audacity of Hope*. New York: Vintage, 2006.

Olesen, Thomas. *International Zapatismo: The Construction of Solidarity in the Age of Globalization*. New York: Zed Books, 2005.

Parenti, Christian. "Hugo Chavez and Petro Populism." *The Nation*, March 24, 2005. Online. Available HTTP: <http://thenation.com/doc/20050411/parenti> (accessed November 12, 2008).

Perkins, John. *Confessions of an Economic Hit Man*. New York: Plume, 2006.

Petras, James and Henry Veltmeyer. *Globalization Unmasked: Imperialism in the 21st Century*. New York: Zed Books, 2001.

——. "Is Latin America Really Turning Left?" *CounterPunch*, June 3/4, 2006. Online. Available HTTP: <http://www.counterpunch.org/petras06032006.html> (accessed November 12, 2008).

Phillips, Kevin. *American Theocracy: The Peril and Politics of Radical Religion, Oil and Borrowed Money in the 21st Century*. New York: Viking, 2006.

——. *Bad Money: Reckless Finance, Failed Politics, and the Global Crisis of American Capitalism*. New York: Viking, 2008.

Piercy, Marge. *Woman on the Edge of Time*. New York: Fawcett Crest, 1987.

Pieterse, Jan Nederveen. *Globalization or Empire?* New York: Routledge, 2004.

Pilger, John. *The New Rulers of the World*. New York: Verso, 2002.

Pollin, Robert. *Contours of Descent: US Economic Fractures and the Landscapes of Global Austerity*. New York: Verso, 2003.

Project for the New American Century, Statement of Principles, June 3, 1997. Online. Available HTTP: <http://www.newamericancentury.org/statementofprinciplies.htm> (accessed November 12, 2008).

Rajchenberg, Enrique and Catherine Heau-Lambert. "History and Symbolism in the Zapatista Movement." In John Holloway and Eloina Palaez, eds. *Zapatista! Reinventing Revolution in Mexico,* 19–38. London: Pluto Press, 1998.

Rampton, Sheldon and John Stauber. *Weapons of Mass Deception: The Uses of Propaganda in Bush's War on Iraq*. New York: Penguin, 2003.

Ransby, Barbara. *Ella Baker and the Black Freedom Movement*. Chapel Hill: The University of North Carolina Press, 2003.

Rashid, Ahmed. *Descent into Chaos: The United States and the Failure of Nation Building in Pakistan, Afghanistan, and Central Asia*. New York: Viking, 2008.

——. *Taliban*. New Haven, CT: Yale University Press, 2001.

Reckdahl, Katy. "Sour Note." *The Times-Picayune*, January 2, 2007. Online. Available HTTP: <http://www.soros.org/resources/multimedia/Katrina/projects/Struggling/story_-SourNote.php > (accessed March 9, 2009).

Reitan, Ruth. *Global Activism*. New York: Routledge, 2007.

Retort. *Afflicted Powers: Capital and Spectacle in a New Age of War*. New York: Verso, 2006.

Rieff, David. "Were Sanctions Right?" *New York Times* Magazine, July 27, 2003. Online. Available HTTP: <http://www.nytimes.com/2003/07/27/magazine/were-sanctions-right.html> (accessed December, 28, 2008).

Rimmerman, Craig A. *The New Citizenship: Unconventional Politics, Activism, and Service*. Boulder, CO: Westview Press, 1997.

Robinson, William I. *Promoting Polyarchy: Globalization, US Intervention, and Hegemony*. New York: Cambridge University Press, 1996.

Rochon, Thomas. *Mobilizing for Peace: The Antinuclear Movements in Western Europe*. Princeton, NJ: Princeton University Press, 1988.

Rogin, Michael Paul. *Fathers and Children: Andrew Jackson and the Subjugation of the American Indian*. New York: Vintage Books, 1976.

Roig-Franzia, Manuel. "A City Fears for its Soul." *The Washington Post*, February 3, 2006: A01.

Ross, Andrew. *Low Pay, High Profile: The Global Push for Fair Labor*. New York: The New Press, 2004.

Roudometof, Victor. "Transnationalism and Cosmopolitanism: Errors of Globalism." In Richard P. Appelbaum and William I. Robinson, eds. *Critical Globalization Studies*, 65–74. New York: Routledge, 2005.

Roy, Arundhati. *An Ordinary Person's Guide to Empire*. Cambridge, MA: South End Press, 2004.

——. *Public Power in the Age of Empire*. New York: Seven Stories Press, 2004.

Ruppert, Peter. *Reader in a Strange Land: The Activity of Reading Literary Utopias*. Athens: The University of Georgia Press, 1986.

Said, Edward. "The Other America." *CounterPunch*, March 21, 2003. Online. Available HTTP: <http://www.counterpunch.org/said0322203.html> (accessed October 28, 2008).

Santos, Boaventura de Sousa. *The Rise of the Global Left: The World Social Forum and Beyond*. New York: Zed Books, 2006.

SAPRIN. *Structural Adjustment: The Policy Roots of Economic Crisis, Poverty and Inequality*. New York: Zed Books, 2004.

Sardar, Ziauddin and Merryl Wyn Davies. *Why Do People Hate America?* New York: The Disinformation Co., 2002.

Scahill, Jeremy. "2008 Reports on Blackwater." *AlterNet*. Online. Available HTTP: <http://www.alternet.org/authors/5434> (accessed December 24, 2008).

Schechter, Danny. *When News Lies: Media Complicity and the Iraq War*. New York: SelectBooks, 2006.

Schmookler, Andrew Bard. *The Parable of the Tribes: The Problem of Power in Social Evolution*. New York: Houghton Mifflin Paperback, 1986.

Scott, James C. *Domination and the Arts of Resistance*. New Haven, CT: Yale University Press, 1990.

Scott, Matthew J. O. "Danger-Landmines! NGO–Government Collaboration in the Ottawa Process." In Michael Edwards and John Gaventa, eds. *Global Citizen Action*, 121–33. Boulder, CO: Lynne Rienner Publishers, 2001.

Sheehan, Cindy. "Good Riddance Attention Whore." *Daily Kos*, May 28, 2007. Online. Available HTTP: <http://www.dailykos.com/story/2007/5/28/12530/1525> (accessed December, 10 2008).

——. "Matriotism." *The Huffington Post*, January 22, 2006. Online. Available HTTP: <http://www.huffingtonpost.com/cindy-sheehan/matriotism_b_14283.html> (accessed December 10, 2008).

Shiva, Vandana. *Earth Democracy: Justice, Sustainability, and Peace*. Cambridge, MA: South End Press, 2005.

Shor, Francis. "A Better (or, Battered) World is Possible: Utopian/Dystopian Dialectics in the American Century." In Elizabeth Russell, ed. *Trans/Forming Utopia: Looking Forward to the End*, Vol. 1, 145–64. Oxford: Peter Lang, 2009.

Shutt, Harry. "Redistribution and Stability: Beyond the Keynesian/Neoliberal Impasse." *MRZine*, February 27, 2009. Online. Available HTTP: <http://www.monthlyreview.org/mrzine/shutt270209.html> (accessed March 11, 2009).

Singer, Peter. *One World: The Ethics of Globalization*. New Haven, CT: Yale University Press, 2002.

Slotkin, Richard. *Gunfighter Nation: The Myth of the Frontier in Twentieth-Century America*. New York: HarperPerennial, 1993.

Smart, Barry, ed. *Resisting McDonaldization.* Thousand Oaks, CA: Sage Publications, 1999.

Smith, Christian. *Resisting Reagan: The US Central American Peace Movement.* Chicago: University of Chicago Press, 1996.

Smith, Jackie. *Social Movements for Global Democracy.* Baltimore, MD: The Johns Hopkins University Press, 2008.

———. *et al. Global Democracy and the World Social Forums.* Boulder, CO: Paradigm Publishers, 2008.

Smith, Neil. *American Empire: Roosevelt's Geographer and the Prelude to Globalization.* Berkeley: University of California Press, 2003.

———. *The Endgame of Globalization.* New York: Routledge, 2005.

Solnit, Rebecca. *Hope in the Dark: Untold Histories, Wild Possibilities.* New York: Nation Books, 2004.

Speth, James Gustave. "Progressive Fusion." *The Nation,* October 6, 2008: 27–30.

Steger, Manfred B. *Globalism: Market Ideology Meets Terrorism,* 2nd ed. Lanham, MD.: Rowman & Littlefield, 2005.

Stephanson, Anders. *Manifest Destiny and the Empire of Right.* New York: Hill & Wang, 1995.

Stuart, Douglas T. *Creating the National Security State.* Princeton, NJ: Princeton University Press, 2008.

Students for Bhopal. "No More Bhopals." Online. Available HTTP: <http://www.studentsforbhopal.org/.WhatHappened.htm> (accessed March 2, 2009).

Tabb, William K. *Unequal Partners: A Primer on Globalization.* New York: The New Press, 2002.

Takaki, Ronald T. *Iron Cages: Race and Culture in 19th-Century America.* Seattle: University of Washington Press, 1982.

Taylor, Peter J. "Locating the American Century: A World-Systems Analysis." In David Slater and Peter J. Taylor, eds. *The American Century: Consensus and Coercion in the Projection of American Power,* 3–16. Walden, MA: Blackwell Publishers, 1999.

Tocqueville, Alexis de. *Democracy in America,* Ed. and abridged by Richard D. Heffner. New York: Mentor, 1956.

———. *Journey to America,* trans. George Lawrence. New York: Doubleday Anchor, 1971.

Todd, Emmanuel. *After the Empire: The Breakdown of the American Order,* trans. C. Jon Delogu. New York: Columbia University Press, 2003.

Tomlinson, John. *Cultural Imperialism: A Critical Introduction.* London: Pinter Publishers, 1991.

Tukdeo, Shivali. "Mapping Resistance: Coca-Cola and the Struggle in Plachimada, India." In Jerry Harris, ed. *Alternative Globalizations,* 291–305. Chicago: Change-Maker Publications, 2006.

Turse, Nick. "Bringing the War Home: The New Military-Industrial-Entertainment Complex at War and Play." *TomDispatch.com,* October 17, 2003. Online. Available HTTP: <http://www.commondreams.org/views03/1017–09.htm > (accessed December 10, 2008).

———. "It's Time for a Trillion-Dollar Tag Sale at the Pentagon." *AlterNet,* October 29, 2008. Online. Available HTTP: <http://www.alternet.org/story/105106> (accessed December 28, 2008).

Tuttle, Doug. "The Mine Ban Treaty's 10th Anniversary," Center for Defense Information Monitor Website, February 27, 2009. Online. Available HTTP:

<http://www.cdi.org/program/document.cfm?DocumentID=4472&from_page=./ index.cfm > (accessed March 2, 2009).

Tuveson, Ernest. *Redeemer Nation: The Idea of America's Millennial Role*. Chicago: University of Chicago Press, 1968.

van Elteren, Mel. "U. S. Cultural Imperialism Today: Only a Chimera?" *SAIS Review* 23:2 (Summer–Fall 2003): 169–88.

Walker, Thomas. *Nicaragua: Living in the Shadow of the Eagle*, 4th ed. Boulder, CO: Westview Press, 2003.

Wallerstein, Immanuel. *Alternatives: The United States Confronts the World*. Boulder, CO: Paradigm Publishers, 2004.

——. "Capitalism's Demise," Interview by Jae-Jung Suh. *Japan Focus*, January 8, 2009. Online. Available HTTP: <http://japanfocus.org/products/todf/3005> (accessed January 14, 2009).

——. "The Curve of American Power," *New Left Review* 40 (July–August 2006): 77–94.

——. *The Decline of American Power: The U. S. in a Chaotic World*. New York: The New Press, 2003.

Warner, Judith. *Perfect Madness: Motherhood in the Age of Anxiety*. New York: Riverhead Books, 2006.

Watson, David. "We All Live in Bhopal," In *Against the Megamachine: Essays on Empire & its Enemies*, 42–7. Brooklyn, NY: Autonomedia, 1998.

Weis, Tony. "Restructuring and Redundancy: The Impact and Illogic of Neoliberal Agricultural Reforms in Jamaica." *Journal of Agrarian Change* 4:4 (October 2004): 461–91.

West, Cornel. *Democracy Matters: Winning the Fight Against Imperialism*. New York: Penguin Books, 2004.

White, Timothy. *Catch a Fire: The Life of Bob Marley*. New York: Owl, 1998.

Williams, Leslie. "Baptists Pledge to Build 300 Houses in 5-Year Period." *The Times-Picayune*, June 12, 2007: B1–2.

Williams, Raymond. *Marxism and Literature*. New York: Oxford University Press, 1977.

Williams, William Appleman. *Empire as a Way of Life*. New York: Oxford University Press, 1982.

Winter, Jay. *Dreams of Peace and Freedom: Utopian Moments in the 20th Century*. New Haven, CT: Yale University Press, 2006.

Wood, Ellen Meiksins. *Empire of Capital*. New York: Verso, 2003.

Wood, Lesley J. "Bridging the Chasms: The Case of the Peoples Global Action." In Joe Bandy and Jackie Smith, eds. *Coalitions Across Borders: Transnational Protest and the Neoliberal Order*, 95–117. Lanham, MD: Rowman & Littlefield, 2005.

Young, Iris. "From Guilt to Solidarity: Sweatshops and Political Responsibility." *Dissent* 59: 2 (Spring 2003): 39–44.

——. "The Logic of Masculinist Protection: Reflections on the Current Security State." *Signs* 29:1 (Autumn 2003): 1–25.

Young, Marilyn B. "The Age of Global Power." In Thomas Bender, ed. *Rethinking American History in a Global Age*, 274–94. Berkeley: University of California Press, 2002.

Zinn, Howard. *A People's History of the United States*, rev. ed. New York: Harper-Perennial, 1995.

Zunz, Olivier. *Why the American Century?* Chicago: University of Chicago Press, 1998.

Index